Comprehending C̶... sm

Comprehending Christian Zionism

Perspectives in Comparison

Göran Gunner and Robert O. Smith, editors

Fortress Press
Minneapolis

COMPREHENDING CHRISTIAN ZIONISM

Perspectives in Comparison

Cover image: "Israel Flag and The Wailing Wall Eldad Carin/iStock/Thinkstock"

Cover design: Tory Herman

Library of Congress Cataloging-in-Publication Data

Print ISBN: 978-1-4514-7226-4

eBook ISBN: 978-1-4514-8964-4

The paper used in this publication meets the minimum requirements of American National Standard for Information Sciences—Permanence of Paper for Printed Library Materials, ANSI Z329.48-1984.

Manufactured in the U.S.A.

This book was produced using PressBooks.com, and PDF rendering was done by PrinceXML.

Contents

Acknowledgments

We are grateful to the American Academy of Religion's director of meetings, Robert Puckett, and the chair of the program committee, Nelly Van Dorn Harder, for being part of enabling the Christian Zionism in Contemporary Perspective seminar. We also want to mention Dr. Maria Leppäkari (Åbo Akademi University, Finland), who was very active as a member of the seminar steering committee.

We also direct our thanks to all paper presenters, respondents, and participants in the discussions of the Christian Zionism seminar during the annual meetings of the American Academy of Religion. Not all of them were able to participate in this volume.

It is an honor to collaborate with Fortress Press in publishing this book. They caught the vision of the book and the vital necessity of discussing Christian Zionism.

1

Christian Zionism in Comparative Perspective

An Introduction

Göran Gunner

"Christian Zionism" has frequently been used both as a self-description of individuals and groups and as an issue in academic research. Its roots can be traced back through the centuries, even if the term as such is relatively new. This is not a concept that is easily captured by one obvious definition but one that easily creates positive and negative feelings, discussions, and activities. It is complex, with different connotations depending on the point of departure. Still, there is to a large extent a common knowledge about what Christian Zionism entails.

Individuals and organizations that proudly call themselves Christian Zionists will appear in this book, but also groups and individuals that suffer the consequences of activities supported by

Christian Zionists. Hopefully, the chapters presented here will provide a substantial contribution to the understanding of Christian Zionism in contemporary society by offering different approaches to and explanations of its historical, theological, and political complexity. We will end the book by returning to the questions of how to define and perceive Christian Zionism.

The Christian Zionism in Comparative Perspective Seminar

In 2009, a wildcard session called "International Christian Perspectives on Christian Zionism"[1] was held at the annual meeting of the American Academy of Religion (AAR) in Montréal. It showed the extensive interest in the issue of Christian Zionism, so the following year the AAR began a series of seminars under the headline "Christian Zionism in Comparative Perspective." The mission for the seminars—continuing for five years—was as follows:

> The phenomenon of Christian Zionism—in its contemporary forms, faith-based Christian political support for the State of Israel—provides opportunities for reflecting on the intersections of religion with history, popular culture, domestic political movements, foreign policy analysis, and interreligious engagement, among other topics. Specifically, the subject is becoming a locus of rich intra-Christian conversation, including matters of biblical interpretation, fundamentalism, and evangelicalism. Although Christian Zionism is largely an Anglo-American phenomenon, scholars in several contexts have turned their attention to the topic. More precise studies are needed so the phenomenon can be better comprehended.

Based on this mission, the theme for the 2010 seminar in Atlanta was "Setting the Stage for Christian Zionism Studies."[2] The following

---

1. Papers presented by Robert O. Smith (then of Baylor University), Göran Gunner (Church of Sweden Research Unit), and Paul Merkley (Carleton University). Donald E. Wagner (then with North Park University) responded and Amy Johnson Frykholm (*The Christian Century*) presided.

year, the theme of the seminar in San Francisco was "Christian Zionism, the Holy Land, and Identity Formation."[3] The call for papers asked: What political implications can be attributed to Christian Zionist perspectives on theology and biblical interpretation? What implications do these views have for relations between Muslims, Christians, and Jews in the region? and How does the movement inform political and communal relations in other contexts, especially in areas of Muslim–Christian tension? In Chicago in 2012, the seminar was cohosted with the Middle Eastern Christianity Group and was titled "Christian Zionist Implications for Palestinian Christians and Nationalist Theologies."[4] We asked for contributions that elucidated the doctrinal elements present in many Christian Zionist writings as well as the biblical hermeneutics used by both Western and Middle Eastern Christian communities. The contributions to this volume represent a selection of the presentations at these seminars.

---

2. Papers presented by William Girard (University of California, Santa Cruz), Gershon Greenberg (American University), Matt Westbrook (Drew University), Rosemary Ruether (Claremont Graduate University), Faydra Shapiro (Wilfrid Laurier University), and Andrew Crome (University of Manchester). Robert O. Smith (then of Baylor University) responded and Göran Gunner (Church of Sweden Research Unit) presided.

3. Papers presented by Elizabeth Phillips (Westcott House), Sean Durbin (Macquarie University), Mae Cannon (University of California, Davis), Curtis Hutt (University of Nebraska, Omaha and University of the Holy Land, Jerusalem), and Aron Engberg (Lund University). Göran Gunner (Church of Sweden Research Unit) responded and Robert O. Smith (Evangelical Lutheran Church in America) presided.

4. Papers presented by George Faithful (Seton Hall University), Yaakov Ariel (University of North Carolina), Timo Stewart (University of Helsinki), Robert Smith (Evangelical Lutheran Church in America), and Mitri Raheb (Diyar Consortium and Christmas Lutheran Church, Bethlehem). Maria Leppäkari (Åbo Akademi University, Finland) and Ginger Hanks Harwood (La Sierra University) responded and Göran Gunner (Church of Sweden Research Unit) presided.

Overview of the Contents

This book is thematically divided into three parts. In the first, Christian Zionism as a contemporary phenomenon is exemplified and analyzed through individuals, congregations, and groups with an outspoken Christian Zionist agenda.

In the chapter "Saying 'Peace' When There is No Peace: An American Christian Zionist Congregation on Peace, Militarism, and Settlements," Elizabeth Phillips describes how a congregation in Colorado reconciles their focus on praying for peace with their support of the Israeli military and a West Bank settlement. Through their activism, they understand themselves as participating in God's ultimate intentions for the world. While Phillips is critical of their political activism and eschatology, she suggests there may be lessons to learn from how they understand the relationship between eschatology and politics.

Aron Engberg analyzes and discusses data from a single personal story in the chapter "'A Fool for Christ': Sense-Making and Negotiation of Identity in the Life Story of a Christian Soldier." In order to protect the chosen people, a Swedish Christian Pentecostal decides to join the Israeli Defense Forces. His conviction that this is according to the master plan of God is treated as an example of *lived* Christian Zionism. As a soldier in the Golani brigade, the storyteller "is experiencing God."

In the next chapter, "Broadcasting Jesus' Return: Televangelism and the Appropriation of Israel through Israeli-Granted Broadcasting Rights," Matt Westbrook analyzes the Christian television networks Trinity Broadcasting Network and DayStar. These networks, measured by organizational assets, represent the largest Christian Zionist organizations in the world. Both have obtained licensing rights to broadcast live both from and into Israel. The chapter raises questions about Christian evangelization in Israel, fundraising by the networks using a millennialist view of Israel as the draw, and the influence of Messianic Judaism. It also explores the possible reasons that Israel granted these networks access to Israeli households.

Sean Durbin is the author of the chapter "Walking in the Mantle of Esther: 'Political' Action as 'Religious' Practice." He focuses on the American Christian Zionist lobby group Christians United for Israel (CUFI) and its relation to Iran, paying special attention to a reading of the book of Esther. Durbin examines how political activities can become reconstituted as acts of "religious" devotion through particular discursive practices. In his conclusion Durbin argues that "Christian Zionists are not 'forcing God's hand' through their political efforts" but are rather "walking in the mantle of Esther."

In William Girard's chapter, "Christian Zionism at *Jerusalén* Church in Copán Ruinas, Honduras, an 'Out-of-the-Way' Place," he analyzes Christian Zionist discourses and practices in a small-town Pentecostal church in Honduras. In the process, he describes the importance of "both a geographical imaginary of the nation as an autonomous actor and a specific history of ethnic and racial formation in Honduras" for the shape Christian Zionism takes within that country.

"Christian Zionist Pilgrimage in the Twenty-first Century: The 'Holy' in the 'Holy Land,'" written by Curtis Hutt, focuses on present-day pilgrims. He specifically examines Christian Zionist pilgrims of different varieties while reviewing their pilgrimages and plotting them on an "Iconoclasm Scale." He also compares Christian, Jewish, and Muslim pilgrims. Special attention is paid to identifying what is "Holy" in the "Holy Land" for these diverse groups.

In her chapter, "Living in the Hour of Restoration: Christian Zionism, Immigration, and *Aliyah*," Faydra L. Shapiro discusses evangelical Christian Zionist supporters of Israel through the angle of *aliyah,* Jewish immigration to Israel—an ongoing project promoted and encouraged by Christian Zionism. She finds an important theological framework that gains its power from its "ostensibly authoritative source (the Bible), its breadth (from Abraham to the second coming) and its scope of influence (the entire world, Jews and gentiles alike)."

The second part of the book includes chapters dealing with historical approaches to Christian Zionism but also chapters describing how others perceive Christian Zionism. Rosemary Radford Ruether is the author of "Christian Zionism and Mainline Western Christian Churches." She broadens the concept of Christian Zionism from a narrow interpretation to discuss its influence in mainline churches. Based on British and American identification of themselves as elect nations through the years and examples from Jewish-Christian dialogue, she argues for strong affiliations with Christian Zionism.

In the chapter "Palestinian Christian Reflections on Christian Zionism," Mitri Raheb analyzes the consequences of Christian Zionism as experienced by Palestinian Christians. He makes five arguments: that Christian Zionism is part of European colonial history, is politically to be placed to the right of the Likud ideology, is economically a booming business, is theologically searching for a "Deus Revelatos," and finally that Christian Zionists "might be the last allies that Israel has."

Yaakov Ariel is the author of "From the *Institutum Judaicum* to the International Christian Embassy: Christian Zionism with a European Accent." He focuses on European Pietist Protestant attempts to support Jewish restoration to Palestine, beginning with thinkers in the sixteenth century and proceeding to the present-day International Christian Embassy in Jerusalem (ICEJ). Ariel finds contradictory feelings as well as frustrations over the Jewish refusal to recognize Christian claims, and draws attention to the unusual phenomenon that one religious group can consider "members of another religious and ethnic community to be the chosen people."

In the chapter "Mischief Making in Palestine: American Protestant Christian Attitudes toward the Holy Land, 1917–1949," Mae Elise Cannon discusses American Christian involvement in Palestine during this time and its relation to the Jewish Zionist agenda. She examines liberal Protestant support for Zionism and the creation of a Jewish state. She also describes the shift in opinions after the 1948 Arab-Israeli War in favor of justice on behalf of the displaced Arab community.

In his chapter, "Israelis, Israelites, and God's Hand in History: Finnish Christian Attitudes toward the Creation of the State of Israel," Timo R. Stewart goes back in history to the establishment of the State of Israel. Analyzing Finnish newspapers of the time, especially the Christian press, he finds interpretations that range from indifference to concluding that prophecies were being fulfilled. He states that Christian Zionist interpretations of events went unchallenged, and "believers interpreted Israel as a clear and very tangible sign of God's existence through his work in history."

"The Rise of Hitler, Zion, and the Tribulation: Between Christian Zionism and Orthodox Judaism" is written by Gershon Greenberg. He analyzes Zionist Christian thinkers vis-à-vis Orthodox Jewish religious thinkers beginning with Kristallnacht (1938). While they shared themes of dispersion as a result of sin, the people of Israel as unique, and apocalyptic tensions, the respective ramifications were opposed. He concludes that in the end, Christian Zionists saw the land of Israel as a station in the final destruction of Judaism, for Orthodox Jews it was the location of Israel's redemption.

George Faithful, in the chapter "Inverting the Eagle to Embrace the Star of David: The Nationalist Roots of German Christian

Zionism," discusses how German nationalism provided a foundation for Christian Zionism in Germany in the mid-twentieth century. In particular, the Ecumenical Sisterhood of Mary exemplified an ideology in which "Christians promoted the welfare of the Jewish people as a means for advancing God's purposes on earth." He presents and analyzes the writings of the sisterhood's founding theologian, Klara Schlink—Mother Basilea.

In Robert O. Smith's concluding chapter, "The Quest to Comprehend Christian Zionism," he discusses the difficulty in precisely defining Christian Zionism and offers his own historical research as one means of interpreting the movement in its present forms in the United States and around the world. He suggests that Christian Zionism is a meme that carries forth cultural information; therefore it is an essential topic for continued academic investigation.

Contributors

The contributors to this book have all presented papers at the American Academy of Religion. They represent a variety in academic experience, from well-known professors emeriti to PhD candidates, as well as different religious affiliations. They also represent a geographical coverage that includes Australia, Finland, Israel, Palestine, Sweden, the United Kingdom, and the United States, with Honduras, Israel, Palestine, Finland, Sweden, Germany, the Netherlands, the United Kingdom, and the United States in focus. They are presented here according to the order in which their chapters appear:

Dr. **Elizabeth Phillips** is Tutor in Theology and Ethics at Westcott House, Cambridge, United Kingdom. In her doctoral thesis she examined the relationship between eschatology and politics in an

American Christian Zionist congregation. She is the author of the book *Political Theology: A Guide for the Perplexed* and several articles.[5]

PhD candidate **Aron Engberg** is doing his research at the Centre for Theology and Religious Studies, Lund University, Sweden. His specific area of research relates to Christian Zionism and identity construction in Israel, examining how Israel is understood and filled with meaning from a Christian Zionist horizon. He has also published an article in *Swedish Missiological Themes*.[6]

Dr. **Matt Westbrook** received his PhD in 2014 from the Graduate Division of Religion at Drew University, with a focus in the sociology of religion. He has presented in professional societies on Christian Zionism for a number of years, and did his dissertation field research in Israel with a Christian Zionist organization.

Dr. **Sean Durbin** received his PhD in 2014 from the Department of Modern History, Politics and International Relations at Macquarie University in Sydney, Australia. He has published articles on various aspects of contemporary Christian Zionism in *The Journal of Contemporary Religion, Culture and Religion, Relegere: Studies in Religion and Reception*, and *Political Theology*.[7]

---

5. *Political Theology: A Guide for the Perplexed* (London: T&T Clark, 2012); "Charting the 'Ethnographic Turn': Theologians and the Study of Christian Congregations," in *Perspectives on Ecclesiology and Ethnography*, ed. Pete Ward (Grand Rapids: Eerdmans, 2012); "Adopt a Settlement: Christian Zionists and the West Bank," *The Christian Century* (December 26, 2011); and "'We've Read the End of the Book': An Engagement with Contemporary Christian Zionism through the Eschatology of John Howard Yoder," *Studies in Christian Ethics* 21:3 (2008): 342–61.

6. "Evangelicalism in the Interspaces: The Construction of Judeo-Christian Identity in a Messianic Community in Jerusalem," *Swedish Missiological Themes* 100:3 (2012): 263–81.

7. "'For Such a Time as This': Reading (and Becoming) Esther with Christians United for Israel," *Relegere: Studies in Religion and Reception* 2:1 (2012): 65–90; "'I Will Bless Those Who Bless You': Christian Zionism, Fetishism, and Unleashing the Blessings of God," *Journal of Contemporary Religion* 28:3 (2013): 507–21; and "Mediating the Past Through the Present and the Present Through Past: The Symbiotic Relationship of Christian Zionism's Alien Enemies and Internal Heretics," *Political Theology* (forthcoming).

Dr. **William M. Girard** received his PhD in Anthropology at the University of California, Santa Cruz. His dissertation, *Enacting Pentecostalism: Spirit-Filled Modernity and the Honduran Coup d'État*, considers how Honduran Pentecostals work to modernize Honduras by fusing secular and religious practices.

Dr. **Curtis Hutt** is Assistant Professor of Religious Studies at the University of Nebraska Omaha. He splits his time between Nebraska and Jerusalem, teaching in both places as well as doing field research in Jerusalem. He wrote his dissertation on religion and the ethics of historical belief, and in 2012 he published a related article on comparative pilgrimage to the Holy Land.[8]

Dr. **Faydra L. Shapiro** is the Director of the Galilee Center for Studies in Jewish-Christian Relations at Yezreel Valley College, Israel. In her research she has a special interest in Jewish-evangelical relations and Christian Zionism. She has recently published several articles.[9]

Professor **Rosemary Radford Ruether** is the Carpenter Professor Emerita of Feminist Theology at Pacific School of Religion and the GTU, as well as the Georgia Harkness Professor Emerita of Applied Theology at Garrett Evangelical Theological Seminary. She currently is teaching feminist theology at the Claremont Graduate University and School of Theology in Claremont, California. She

---

8. *John Dewey and the Ethics of Historical Belief: Religion and the Representation of the Past* (Albany, NY: State University of New York Press, 2013); and "Pilgrimage in Turbulent Contexts: One Hundred Years of Pilgrimage to the Holy Land," *ID: International Dialogue* 2 (2012): 23–50.

9. "Jews Without Judaism: The Ambivalent Love of Christian Zionism," *Journal for the Study of Antisemitism* 4 (2013): 401–419; "Thank you Israel, for Supporting America: The Transnational Flow of Christian Zionist Resources," *Identities: Global Studies in Culture and Power* 5 (2012): 616–31; "Jesus for Jews: The Unique Problem of Messianic Judaism," *Journal of Religion and Society* 14 (2012): 1–17; and "The Messiah and Rabbi Jesus: Policing the Jewish–Christian Border in Christian Zionism," *Culture and Religion: An Interdisciplinary Journal* 4 (2011): 463–77.

has published several books such as *Faith and Fratricide, The Wrath of Jonah*, and *America, Amerikkka*, as well as numerous articles.[10]

Dr. **Mitri Raheb** is President of the Diyar Consortium and Pastor of Christmas Lutheran Church in Bethlehem, Palestine. His work has explored a hermeneutic of liberation in the context of the Israeli occupation of Palestinian land. Among his publications are *I Am a Palestinian Christian, Bethlehem Besieged*, and *The Biblical Text in the Context of Occupation*.[11]

Professor **Yaakov Ariel** is affiliated with the Department of Religious Studies at the University of North Carolina at Chapel Hill. One of the focuses in his research is on evangelical Christianity and its attitudes toward the Jewish people and the Holy Land. He has published several books, including *On Behalf of Israel* and *Evangelizing the Chosen People*, as well as numerous articles.[12]

Rev. Dr. **Mae Elise Cannon** holds her PhD in American history with a minor in Middle Eastern studies from the University of California, Davis. She is also Senior Director of Advocacy and

10. *Faith and Fratricide: The Theological Roots of Anti-Semitism* (New York: Seabury, 1974); *The Wrath of Jonah: The Crisis of Religious Nationalism in the Israeli-Palestinian Conflict* (San Francisco: Harper & Row, 1989); and *America, Amerikkka: Elect Nation & Imperial Violence* (Sheffield: Equinox, 2007).
11. *I Am a Palestinian Christian* (Minneapolis: Fortress Press, 1995); *Bethlehem Besieged: Stories of Hope in Times of Trouble* (Minneapolis: Fortress Press, 2004); *The Invention of History: A Century of Interplay Between Theology and Politics in Palestine*, ed. Mitri Raheb (Bethlehem: Diyar, 2011); and *The Biblical Text in the Context of Occupation: Towards a New Hermeneutics of Liberation*, ed. Mitri Raheb (CreateSpace, 2012).
12. *On Behalf of Israel: American Fundamentalist Attitudes Towards the Jewish People and Zionism* (Brooklyn: Carlson, 1991); "A Neglected Chapter in the History of Christian Zionism in America: William E. Blackstone and the Petition of 1916," in *Jews and Messianism in the Modern Era: Metaphor and Meaning*, ed. Jonathan Frankel, Studies in Contemporary Jewry 7 (New York: Oxford University Press, 1991); *Evangelizing the Chosen People: Missions to the Jews in America 1880–2000* (Chapel Hill: University of North Carolina Press, 2000); and *Philosemites or Antisemites? Evangelical Christian Attitudes toward Jews, Judaism, and the State of Israel* (Jerusalem: Hebrew University of Jerusalem, Vidal Sassoon International Center for the Study of Antisemitism, 2002).

Outreach—Middle East for World Vision USA. She is the author of *Social Justice Handbook* and *Just Spirituality*.[13]

PhD candidate **Timo R. Stewart** is doing his dissertation in Political History at the University of Helsinki, Finland. He has been working with The Ecumenical Accompaniment Programme in Palestine and Israel (EAPPI) and with the Ministry for Foreign Affairs of Finland. He has published several articles.[14]

Professor **Gershon Greenberg,** who is based in the Department of Philosophy and Religion at American University, Washington, DC, is Dorsett Fellow in Orthodox Jewish Theology at Oxford University's Centre for Hebrew and Jewish Studies. He is the author of *The Holy Land in American Religious Thought; Modern Jewish Thinkers from Mendelssohn to Rosenzweig; Wrestling with God: Jewish Theological Responses During and After the Holocaust,* and of numerous studies on Jewish and Christian responses during the Holocaust.[15]

Dr. **George Faithful** is Post-Doctoral Teaching Fellow at Seton Hall University, South Orange, NJ. At present, he teaches undergraduates. In his recent research, he has studied the Ecumenical Sisterhood of Mary in Germany.

Dr. **Robert O. Smith** is Area Program Director for the Middle East and North Africa in the Global Mission unit of the Evangelical

13. *Social Justice Handbook: Small Steps for a Better World* (Downers Grove, IL: InterVarsity, 2009); and *Just Spirituality: How Faith Practices Fuel Social Action* (Downers Grove, IL: InterVarsity, 2013).
14. "Kristillinen sionismi ja Suomen Kristillinen Liitto" [Christian Zionism and the Finnish Christian League] in *Ajankohta: poliittisen historian vuosikirja,* 2007; "Israelin siirtokuntien syntyminen Länsirannalle" [The Establishment of Israeli Settlements in the West Bank] in *Lähde: Historiatieteellinen aikakauskirja,* 2010; and "Siirtokuntien uhka Israelille" [Settlements as a Threat to Israel] in *Ulkopolitiikka* 4 (2012).
15. *The Holy Land in American Religious Thought, 1620–1948: The Symbiosis of American Religious Approaches to Scripture's Sacred Territory* (Lanham, MD: University Press of America, 1994); *Modern Jewish Thinkers from Mendelssohn to Rosenzweig* (Brighton, MA: Academic Studies, 2011); and with Steven T. Katz, *Wrestling With God: Jewish Theological Responses During and After the Holocaust: A Source Reader* (New York: Oxford University Press, 2006).

Lutheran Church in America, Chicago, IL. He serves as co-moderator of the Palestine-Israel Ecumenical Forum of the World Council of Churches and is the author of *More Desired than Our Owne Salvation: The Roots of Christian Zionism*. He is also the author of several Lutheran responses to Christian Zionism.[16]

Dr. **Göran Gunner** is Researcher at Church of Sweden Research Unit and Associate Professor at Uppsala University. His interest in research has been divided between Christian Zionism, Christianity in the Middle East, and human rights. He is the author of *När tiden tar slut* [When Time is Ending] and *Genocide of Armenians through Swedish Eyes,* as well as numerous articles.[17]

Dr. **Robert O. Smith** and Dr. **Göran Gunner** are coeditors of this book as well as cochairs of the "Christian Zionism in Comparative Perspective" seminar in the American Academy of Religion.

16. *Christians and a Land Called Holy: How We Can Foster Justice, Peace, and Hope,* with Charles P. Lutz (Minneapolis: Fortress Press, 2006);"Toward a Lutheran Response to Christian Zionism," *dialog: A Journal of Theology* 48:3 (Fall 2009): 281–93; and *More Desired than Our Owne Salvation: The Roots of Christian Zionism* (New York: Oxford University Press 2013).
17. *När tiden tar slut* [When Time is Ending: Changing Emphases in Swedish Evangelical Apocalyptic Thinking Concerning the Jewish People and the State of Israel] (Uppsala: Uppsala Universitet 1996); *Genocide of Armenians Through Swedish Eyes* (Yerevan: The Armenian Genocide Museum-Institute, 2013); and "Apocalyptic Speculations and the War of Armageddon," in *Gods and Arms: On Religion and Armed Conflict,* ed. Kjell-Åke Nordquist (Eugene, OR: Pickwick, 2013).

2

———

Saying "Peace" When There Is No Peace

*An American Christian Zionist Congregation on
Peace, Militarism, and Settlements*

Elizabeth Phillips

In a typical Colorado suburb, a skywalk stretches over a major thoroughfare connecting a 1970s church building with the congregation's larger and newer facilities (the Family Worship Center) on the other side of the road. At a corner facing a busy intersection, letters five feet tall spell the church's name (which the members shorten to FBC) and water cascades over them into a fountain below. Large electronic signs face both directions, flashing service times and upcoming events to motorists waiting at the traffic signal.

On Sunday mornings, nearly four thousand people congregate at FBC, and there are at least four police officers directing traffic around the church building. After being directed to a parking space, members walk to the Family Worship Center along paths lined with speakers amplifying praise music. Just outside the main entrance is a large, golden sculpture of a globe, which appears to be lifted up by the water of the fountain below it. At every door members greet those arriving. Inside the main entrance is a cavernous lobby with floor-to-ceiling windows and flags of the countries of the world suspended from white metal support beams that span the ceiling high above the entering worshipers. Some move straight through toward the sanctuary, others stop to peruse the various stalls of merchandise, and others buy a cup of espresso at the café.

Praying for the Peace of Jerusalem

On one wall there is a large depiction of a Jewish man blowing a shofar between two mountains and two tablets with Hebrew writing. The image is surrounded by the inscription: "Let the sound of the shofar bind the majestic mountains of Colorado with the holy mountains of Judea and bring unity of Christian and Jew." Next to another wall composed of large, white stones, a plaque reads, "This wall is made of Jerusalem stone and stands as a reminder of God's covenant promises to Israel." Across the Jerusalem stones are the words "Pray for the Peace of Jerusalem" written in large black metal letters. Many members take these words very seriously.

Members of FBC are encouraged to pray regularly for Israel, and many corporate gatherings include such prayers. Adjacent to the Family Worship Center is the freestanding Prayer Chapel. Inside, about forty seats face a small dais, flanked by American and Israeli flags. The walls of the small chapel are lined with prayer stations with large bulletin boards that have requests and guidance for prayer, each with a heading: "Our Church," "Missions," "Nations," "Urgent Needs," "Personal Requests," and "Israel." The Israel station encourages prayers for the safety and blessing of Israelis, increased immigration of Jews into Israel, a stronger Israeli economy, the rounding up and punishment of "anti-Israel world leaders and terrorists," the establishment of "biblical and secure" borders, and wisdom for Israel's leaders. Below these prayer requests and the accompanying Scriptures, photographs, and documents displayed with them, there sits a box of tissues for the use of those weeping in prayer.

One night each month, about twenty members of FBC meet in the Prayer Chapel to intercede on Israel's behalf. They are led in prayer by Cheryl, Pastor George's wife, who is on staff full time in charge of the Israel Outreach Ministry and the Women's Ministry. I happened to come to FBC on the day of the monthly Israel prayer meeting, and this was my first introduction to the congregation.[1] When Cheryl arrived in the prayer chapel, she moved the chairs into a large circle. She prayed under her breath as she arranged the room, saying, "Yes, Jesus. Thank you, Jesus." The chairs in the circle were soon filled and Cheryl led the group in prayer. She told them that she had seen an article on the *Jerusalem Post* website reporting a military buildup on Israel's border with Syria. She explained that this was significant because there was a prophecy among "the believers"[2] in Israel that there would be a war with Syria soon, and she had personally received a word from God while in the Golan Heights several years earlier regarding coming war with Syria.

The group received this news as their marching orders for the prayer meeting, but to my surprise no one prayed for an easing of tensions between Israel and Syria; no one prayed for the military buildup to end; no one prayed that there would not be war. One man prayed, "We hope there does not have to be a war. But we know

---

1. I first arrived at FBC in May, 2007.
2. A phrase used by some Christian Zionists to describe Jews who have been converted to Christianity.

that your word says that wars are coming." They prayed that the war would happen in God's good time, and that the Israeli military would be prepared and not fail as they had in Lebanon in 2006. They prayed that Jewish casualties would be minimal. They prayed that the US government would support Israel and not stand in the way of whatever Israel needed to do, and that God would turn the president's heart against the "Road Map" to peace. One man prayed, "We don't want a road map to peace." They prayed that no one would seek to restrain Israel's military, and that America would supply whatever weapons Israel needed. They prayed for Israel to be empowered to wipe out their enemies, "because they are your enemies, God." Cheryl prayed fervently for fatality among Israel's enemies. She said, "Let Syria make a fatal mistake, Lord. Let Hezbollah make a fatal mistake. Let Hamas make a fatal mistake. Let Iran make a fatal mistake." At the end of the hour everyone in the circle stood, joined hands, and sang together, "Lord we bless, Lord we love Thy people. Lord we bless, Lord we love Thy land. We weep for, we pray for, intercede for Israel. Lord, now move Thy hand."

I walked away from this prayer meeting stunned by the force with which people had prayed for violence and death. I realized that I had a lot to learn about how these average middle-class American evangelicals could reconcile what they were praying with the idea of praying for peace.

Studying Christian Zionism

I spent six weeks at FBC observing their congregational life and conducting interviews.[3] I read the books they read, listened to the prophecy teachers they trust, and explored the organizations they

3. May–June, 2007.

support. When I told friends that I was doing this research, many replied, "Oh, those are the people who think they can make Jesus return sooner by supporting Israel!" Before this project began, I had shared this assumption; I was sure one outcome of my research would be a critique of the belief that political activism can hasten the second coming.[4] I found instead what we always find when we attend to the convictions and lives of real people: that it is much more complicated. In fact, though my experiences with Christian Zionists and their Israeli partners were no less disturbing than I expected, they were far more compelling than I could have imagined.

Much of the literature on Christian Zionism is written as exposé, to convince us that Christian Zionism is politically dangerous or biblically unsound. Descriptions of the battle of Armageddon figure prominently in these portrayals, and "Armageddon" often finds its way into their titles.[5] While I share these authors' concerns, I also wanted to move beyond exposé and get to know particular Zionist Christians—to take their complexity seriously. I did not find that the people at FBC have a fanatical thirst for the bloodshed of Armageddon; instead they have an utter certitude that they are cooperating with God in the fruition of God's ultimate intentions for human history. Pastor George summarized this well in a sermon on Ezekiel's vision of the dry bones,[6] which he and many Christian Zionists interpret as a prophecy of the modern State of Israel. Pastor

---

4. It has long been of interest to me that differing forms of this conviction have been central to both conservative and liberal activist movements within American Christianity. While both historical and theological literature tend to view postmillennial and premillennial movements as opposites, it is also the case that certain forms of these eschatologies have been two sides of the same coin of confidence in the relationship between human activism and the millennium.

5. See, for example, Victoria Clark, *Allies for Armageddon: The Rise of Christian Zionism* (New Haven, CT: Yale University Press, 2007); Dan Cohn-Sherbok, *The Politics of Apocalypse: The History and Influence of Christian Zionism* (London: Oneworld, 2006); Stephen Sizer, *Christian Zionism: Road-Map to Armageddon?* (Leicester: Inter-Varsity, 2004); Donald E. Wagner, *Anxious for Armageddon: A Call to Partnership for Middle Eastern and Western Churches* (Scottdale, PA: Herald, 1995).

6. May 20, 2007.

George drew the congregation's attention to the verse in which God tells Ezekiel to prophesy to the bones (Ezek 37:3). When Ezekiel did this, the bones took on flesh and became living bodies, which is interpreted as a prediction of the return of Jews to Palestine and Israeli statehood. Pastor George related this passage to FBC's support of Israel today. He said, "God called Ezekiel into partnership to prophesy to the bones. God wants us to cooperate with his purposes. That's what we're doing . . . we're cooperating with God and we're speaking life into this situation."

This conviction about cooperating with God's purposes, and the activism through which the people of FBC believe they are enacting such cooperation, are complex realities. Through the following portraits of FBC's support for Israel, I hope to offer a glimpse into the complexity involved in both their theology and their activism and demonstrate that there are serious problems to confront but also interesting lessons to learn.

Israel as Blessing

FBC began as a small group of families meeting in homes in the mid-1960s. Most of these families had moved to Colorado from California for the purpose of planting a new church. Their efforts began with Bible studies in one another's homes, and much of their Bible study was focused on prophecies concerning Israel—a central concern of the congregation from its inception. According to members, a leader of the congregation in California received a prophetic word that God wanted the new church to "bless his people." This word was not understood until the pastor began studying his Bible in order to decipher the message and determined that Gen. 12:3 was the key.

As with many Christian Zionists, Gen. 12:3 became central for the fledgling FBC. It is part of the narrative of God's promise to Abram, in which God says to Abram, "I will bless those who bless you, and the one who curses you I will curse; and in you all the families of the earth shall be blessed."

In 1973, members of the church began touring Israel together. On their first tour, the group visited the Golan Heights (the land at the northern tip of Israel that was seized from Syria in the 1967 war). As they stood on top of a former Syrian bunker overlooking the surrounding hills and a kibbutz in the valley below, their Israeli tour guide described the 1967 conflict to them. He told them that when the question arose whether or not to take the Golan, they felt like they had to do it "for the children." He explained that before the Golan was taken, the children in this kibbutz did not know the difference between the sound of thunder and the sound of mortar fire.

The group was deeply moved by his version of the events of 1967. One of the men said, "I just feel we need to do what Gen. 12:3 says, that we need to stand here and bless Israel from this place that it's been cursed from for so many years," and they began to pray and to bless Israel. There was a young newlywed couple with that 1973 tour group who are both full-time members of the church's ministerial staff today. She often tells the story of what happened next on that day in the Golan—and she cries every time: "As we turned to leave, it was just like heaven opened, and I just heard this simple song, 'I will bless those who bless my people. I will curse those who curse them too. For this I have promised to my servant Abraham. I will keep my word.'" She sang the song for the group there on the Golan Heights and they were overcome. The song is still sung at nearly every Israel-related event at the church, and this is the song they sang at the end of the prayer meeting I attended when I first arrived at FBC.

This narrative is at the very heart of the congregation's self-understanding, and their interpretation of the Genesis passage is at the very heart of their understanding of God's purposes in the world. They believe that God created a people—Israel—to bless and to make a blessing to the rest of the world. They believe that throughout history, when an empire has cursed Jews, God has cursed that empire. Every anti-Jewish, anti-Israel empire has fallen, from ancient Rome to medieval Spain to modern Germany and Britain. They believe this will be the fate of America as well if the people do not bless Israel in every way possible. However, if America cooperates with God in blessing Israel, America will not only be blessed but will also see Israel become a blessing to all nations. Along with many Christian Zionists, the members of FBC have an eschatological vision influenced by dispensational premillennialism. They believe that after the chaos, violence, and suffering of the great tribulation at the end of this present age, the Messiah will return, all surviving Jews will accept him as Lord and King, and he will set up the millennial kingdom, ruling the earth from its capital in Jerusalem. Out of Israel there will radiate a one-thousand-year era of uninterrupted and incorruptible peace and prosperity over all the earth.

This is the congregation's vision of God's intentions for humanity; these are the purposes of God with which they believe they are cooperating. In this sense, they believe that a prayer for Israel is always a prayer for peace. However, they also believe that there will be a lot of conflict and violence between now and that coming age of peace, and as far as they are concerned, cooperating with God's purposes means cooperating in the militarism and occupation that will precede the millennium. They believe in helping God's chosen people execute violence instead of suffering violence at the hands of others. For this reason, one of the primary ways they seek to participate in the realities of the coming of the millennium is through support for the Israeli military.

Blessing the Israeli Defense Forces

Over three decades ago, FBC began sending a performance group on summer tours of Israeli military bases. While the style and content of their performances has changed over the years, the message has remained the same: they want Israeli soldiers to know that there are Christians who bless and support them, and who believe they are acting as God's chosen people. Today, the group is called The Internationals, and being a member of this group requires nearly year-round study and rehearsals. Often FBC members become interested in joining The Internationals because their parents or friends have been members. Some begin dancing with the children's group, The Little Internationals, and grow up wanting to become Internationals. Others join the group to make friends, for the opportunity to perform, or because they have been recruited, and only after joining do they come to understand the group's mission. Internationals are not only trained in singing and dancing—including coaching from Israeli consultants on choreography and pronunciation of Hebrew lyrics—they are also given lectures and assignments on Israel including readings such as "Why Christians Should Support Israel" by John Hagee.[7]

When I met The Internationals, they were five singers in their thirties and forties, and twelve dancers ranging in age from sixteen to twenty-two. On their approximately eighteen-day tour, The Internationals perform at about thirteen locations, most of which are

---

7. This brief essay has been published many places and is available online: John Hagee, "Why Christians Should Support Israel," John Hagee Ministries, http://www.jhm.org/Home/About/WhySupportIsrael (accessed May 31, 2013).

military bases. Each performance includes about a dozen numbers, and there is a costume change between every one. These range from black satin *Haredi* Jewish costumes, which the male dancers wear for a folk dance, to Orthodox Jewish wedding clothes for a dance to "*L'Haim*," to fluorescent T-shirts and Capri pants for a modern Israeli pop number, to Israeli military uniforms for a tribute number.

One dancer reflected on the significance of performing for the military. She said the military was "the core of Israel's being." Another remarked how moved she was by the differing life situations of teens in American and Israel: "We're about to go off to college, and they're about to go fight for their country." Cheryl leads the tour each year, and she warns the group in advance that their schedule will be grueling. "And I'll be yelling at you, telling you to do this and that, and if that offends you, you need to get over it. If you need to be treated like a little kid, get plenty of that from your momma before we leave!"

The people of FBC think of Israel as a fundamentally dangerous place, and the performers go on tour with a sense that it may cost them their lives. One young teenager told me he thought they would be safe due to God's protection; "But if we're not," he said, "I'm ready to go." A staff member who had participated in multiple tours and was preparing to tour again along with her daughter and son-in-law (who prepared for the tour by drafting a new will naming the legal guardian of their two-year-old twins) told me without hesitation, "If we don't come home, we don't come home, and it will have been worth it."

Another woman who had gone on tour as a chaperone along with her teenage son became emotional when she described why FBC considers the tour to be worth this level of risk:

> The thing that really was amazing to me was watching these average kids, you know, these kids that I know . . . and they go there and they

bless these soldiers who are defending this land . . . just these average, middle class, Christian kids blessing the apple of God's eye, you know? Defending the land that God gave them.

The members of FBC believe that the Israeli military is acting in accordance with God's will—even more than that, they are the foretaste and herald of the ultimate military victory of all time, which they believe will occur at Jesus' second coming. When he returns, it will be to vanquish Israel's enemies and bring Israel into her rightful place: the center of history, politics, religion, and culture. These Christian Zionists do not believe their support of Israel will persuade Jesus to come back any sooner or make him any more successful when he arrives. They do believe they are cooperating with and participating in the future military victory that they believe is sure.

Blessing the Settlements

Along with this vision of Israeli soldiers as forerunners of the coming divine military victory, FBC sees Israeli settlers in the occupied territories as pioneers on the divine frontier. Thus, FBC not only supports the Israeli military, they also have an "adopted settlement" in the West Bank. The settlement of Ariel had its humble beginning in 1978, when a young Israeli named Ron Nachman led a small group of settlers who flew in by helicopter to a West Bank hilltop and slept in tents until buildings were erected. The settlement grew quickly, and seventeen years ago it was adopted by the congregation at FBC. Today Ariel is no longer a humble outpost; it is a city with over 19,000 residents. Nachman was elected as the first mayor when the outpost became a city, and he was repeatedly reelected, serving as mayor until his death in January 2013.

The youth of Ariel can receive their entire education inside the settlement. There are multiple preschools, elementary schools, and junior high schools, one high school, and a college.[8] There is a shopping center, three medical clinics, a large public swimming pool, an extensive central park, a cultural center, a sports complex, and over one hundred small plants and factories.

Ariel is a city surrounded by a bloc of smaller settlements, all of which are known as "consensus communities"—settlements inside the Palestinian territories that Israel has determined, with the support of American leaders, will remain Israeli in any future agreement with a Palestinian state. This "consensus" status makes Ariel a particularly strategic partner for Christian Zionists, and also makes their partnership especially controversial. Ariel is situated east of the strip of Israel that would be extremely thin—just nine miles wide at some points—if the Green Line[9] became the Israel-Palestine border. Inclusion of the Ariel bloc would more than double the width of this strip of land, as Ariel is located twelve miles to the east of the Green Line. Prime Ministers Ariel Sharon, Ehud Olmert, and Benjamin Netanyahu have all committed publicly to annex the Ariel bloc into Israel proper. Netanyahu visited Ariel in 2010, proclaiming it the "capital of Samaria" and an "integral part of Israel."[10] The likelihood of annexation seems confirmed by the path of the Israeli "security fence" (which Palestinians call "the wall"); it dips deep inside the West Bank to surround Ariel. During his time as mayor, Nachman often quipped, "I don't call it a wall or a fence. I call it a gated community."[11]

8. Controversially, the college was renamed "Ariel University Center of Samaria" in 2005 in an attempt to claim for itself the status of university, which most government officials were unwilling to grant to a college in a settlement. University status was officially granted in 2012. See Joanna Paraszczuk, "Ariel Gets University Status Despite Opposition," *The Jerusalem Post* (July 17, 2012).

9. The Green Line is the border between Israel and the Palestinian territories drawn in the 1949 Armistice Agreement.

10. Tovah Lazaroff, "PM: Ariel is the 'Capital of Samaria,'" *The Jerusalem Post* (January 29, 2010).

11. All quotations from Nachman and other residents of Ariel, unless otherwise noted, are from interviews by the author conducted in Israel/Palestine, September 2007.

For most of its history, Ariel has maintained close connections with and benefited from the financial assistance of evangelical Christians. Ron Nachman and Dina Shalit, director of the Ariel Development Fund, have cultivated friendships with many Christian Zionist groups, from whom Ariel receives an average of fifteen visits per year. Nachman and Shalit were often guests at Nights to Honor Israel at American churches. Another of Nachman's characteristic quips was his statement of preference for speaking in churches rather than synagogues when visiting America. "When I visit synagogues, I get a lot of questions," he said, "but when I visit churches I get big checks."

When I visited Ariel, I was often told that the main impact of Christian support for the settlement was the improvement of the settlers' quality of life. The funds and services provided by groups such as FBC have made Ariel feel like a genuine city instead of an outpost. In fact, Ariel now feels much more like a suburb of Tel Aviv than a radical base of occupation. FBC's role in this transformation includes donations of an ark for Torah scrolls, medical and educational supplies and equipment, college scholarships, and financial support for development projects ranging from a Holocaust museum to improved soldiers' quarters. They are particularly proud of their endowment of Ariel's Child Development Center, a facility for speech, occupational, psychological, and physical therapies, as well as tutoring for children with learning disabilities. Cheryl remembers:

> When we adopted Ariel, we asked the Lord, "What do you want us to do there?" And the Scripture came to me when Jesus said, "When you've done it to the least of these my brethren, you've done it to me." So we said, "Who would be the least in Ariel?" And it would be the children who have emotional, physical, and learning disabilities.

Mearsheimer and Walt, in their controversial book on the "Israel lobby," argue that the efforts of Christian Zionist groups to support

Israeli settlements have made a significant difference in Middle East politics. They cite FBC as a "celebrated example" of this impact. "Absent their support, settlers would be less numerous in Israel, and the U. S. and Israeli government would be less constrained by their presence in the Occupied Territories as well as their political activities."[12] One of the deeply problematic aspects of this sort of support for settlements has been highlighted in *The New York Times,* which reported, "As the American government seeks to end the four-decade Jewish settlement enterprise and foster a Palestinian state in the West Bank, the American Treasury helps sustain the settlements through tax breaks on donations to support them." Even though the United States will not allow American aid money to be spent on settlements, at least forty groups in America, like FBC, currently raise funds for settlements through tax-deductible donations.[13]

Ariel's partnership with FBC has also resulted in a performance group called For Zion's Sake. Inspired by The Internationals, these Israeli teenagers tour America, performing mainly for Christian Zionists, thanking them for their support and soliciting further donations. At one performance, the teens went offstage to change into cowboy and cowgirl costumes, and Dina Shalit introduced their "Western Dance" number by drawing an analogy between the American West and the Israeli West Bank: "In the US it was settlers who built the country, spreading the borders past the original thirteen colonies. Your history, however, only reflects admiration for the settlers." By contrast, according to Shalit and many of the settlers I interviewed, Israeli settlers are scorned by international critics and fellow Israelis alike, who consider them to be dangerous extremists.

12. John J. Mearsheimer and Stephen M. Walt, *The Israel Lobby and U. S. Foreign Policy* (New York: Farrar, Straus and Giroux, 2007), 138.
13. Jim Rutenberg, Mike McIntire, and Ethan Bronner, "Tax Exempt Funds Aid Settlements in West Bank," *The New York Times* (July 5, 2010).

Youth workers in the settlement told me that this treatment leaves the Israeli teens of the West Bank feeling isolated and rejected, which often results in their rejection of Judaism and the settlement project. However, for some of these teens, a sort of conversion occurs when Christian Zionists reach out to them with stirring messages of God's purposes for Israel and the Israeli right to the occupied territories. This has led some teens to recommit to Jewish faith, to their role in the Israeli military, and to the importance of the settlements. These relationships between young Christians and young settlers are cultivating both future American supporters of Israel's claims to land in the West Bank and future Israeli defenders and expanders of the settlements.

An important chapter of Ariel's story was missing from all these conversations. Neither the members of FBC nor the people I interviewed in Ariel cared to acknowledge the darkest side of Ariel: the impact of the settlement on Palestinians in surrounding villages. According to Robert Friedman, a journalist who researched extremism among Israeli settlers, during the first intifada settlers in Ariel formed a covert, armed militia under the leadership of Ron Nachman, with weapons provided by the Israeli military. Friedman chronicled attacks carried out by Ariel's militia, including invasions of Palestinian homes, beatings, fatal shootings of both militants and innocent children, and burning of agricultural fields and olive groves.[14] Friedman also reported that as a member of the Knesset, Ron Nachman proposed that Arabs working in settlements should be required to wear yellow "alien worker" tags.

14. Robert I. Friedman, "The Settlers," *The New York Review of Books* 36:10 (June 15, 1989); and "West Bank Story," *The New York Review of Books* 36:18 (November 23, 1989), in which Dina Shalit of Ariel's mayor's office refutes Friedman's claims and Friedman responds.

Conclusion

How, then, do the members of FBC reconcile praying for peace with supporting militarism and a settlement that hinders the peace process and condones violence against its Palestinian neighbors? In the theopolitical imagination of this Christian Zionist congregation, the Israeli military functions as a forerunner of the ultimate Israeli military victory to come, and Israeli settlers function as pioneers on the frontiers of prophetic fulfillment. They believe that through their support of the military and the settlers, they are cooperating with God in the fulfillment of God's purposes and the coming of God's peace.

Many critics of Christian Zionism, both journalistic and scholarly, insist that this is the sort of misguided politics that results from the influence of eschatology. They argue that politics arising from convictions about the "end times" are inevitably dangerous. Other scholars suggest that eschatology has little or nothing to do with the core of Christian Zionist convictions and politics. We have been needlessly distracted by apocalyptic rhetoric, they argue.

I found among the particular Christian Zionist community at FBC that eschatology was in fact at the core of their theopolitics. I would argue that problems do not arise because of the interrelation between their eschatology and their politics per se, nor because they do not understand how best to relate eschatology to politics. Although the particular eschatology at the root of their Zionism is deeply problematic, and their politics are equally problematic, I found that the people of FBC do have an understanding of the relationship between eschatology and politics, and an amazing will to act on the implications of that relationship, which is surprisingly persuasive.

Christian Zionists are well known for their affinity for the end-time scenarios predicted by dispensational premillennialism. Their critics often portray them as people obsessed with this chronology, whether portrayed in the detailed charts of the dispensations from the *Scofield Reference Bible* or the more recent, action-packed novels and films from the *Left Behind* series. My findings at FBC—where, to be sure, these charts and novels have figured prominently in the past—were surprisingly different. These particular Christians have rightly discerned that eschatology is not only a chronology of end-times events; it is also a doctrine of God's intentions for humanity and all creation, and of the status of those intentions in the time between the two advents of Jesus Christ.

Even though they would not articulate it this way, I think they have rightly concluded that politics should be formed by eschatology through discernment of God's ultimate intentions for creation, of God's ways of enacting these intentions in the world, and of how Christians can cooperate with God through participation in those purposes and those ways. Their vision of a coming age of peace is a particular version of a conviction all Christians share; it is the hope of the redemption of all creation, which is central to Christian eschatology.

Yet their discernment of God's ways of inaugurating this age—through militaristic and nationalist violence and domination—are considerably more problematic, and allow them to find ethical normativity in present-day militarism and occupation. Tragically, interpretation of biblical texts as literal predictions and descriptions of the unfolding of God's nationalist and militaristic intentions obscures Scripture's own critiques of militarism, nationalism, violence, and injustice—even though these critiques are often strongest in the apocalyptic and prophetic texts that are given so much attention by Christian Zionists.

3

———

"A Fool for Christ"

Sense-Making and Negotiation of Identity in the Life Story of a Christian Soldier

Aron Engberg

More often than not, studies of Christian Zionism approach evangelical affection and support for Israel through the hermeneutical lens of premillenial dispensationalism. From this perspective, Christian Zionism is characterized by its dispensationalist view of history and individual Christian Zionists motivated by this religio-political worldview in their political, economic, and moral support of the modern-day State of Israel. Historically, especially in the Anglo-American world, dispensationalist eschatology has been at the heart of Christian Zionist efforts to facilitate the restoration of a Jewish nation in the Middle East and to comfort and support the State of Israel.

Yet other aspects of Christian Zionism, perhaps aspects of equal analytic value, have been left largely unexplored. Contemporary Christian Zionism is held together by much more—and sometimes, I believe, much less—than a common view of history and the future. More specifically, I believe that the *present* is equally important as the past and the future to understanding the motivation of individual Christian Zionists and the attraction that millions of Christians around the world feel toward Israel and the Jewish people.

Emphasizing these themes, this chapter views Christian Zionism as a global *religious movement* in its own right. This implies a view of Christian Zionism as a religious and cultural milieu with shared (but contested) values, agendas for political and social activism, and ample possibilities for individual identity construction. It furthermore means that I understand Christian Zionism dynamically: as a religious movement, it is on the move.

This chapter is based on life story data of a Swedish Christian Pentecostal who decided to join the Israeli Defense Forces out of his conviction that God wanted him to protect the chosen people. In his life narrative, love of the people and the land rather than end-times theology occupies the central position. The analysis of Jacob's life story will be performed in three steps: First, I will analyze the formal aspects of the narrative as a whole, emphasizing the thoroughgoing pattern of calling, test of faith, confirmation. Second, I will analyze how Jacob makes sense of his pro-Israeli activism—that is, what he understands as his primary motivation. Finally, I will discuss Jacob's relationship to the grand narrative of Christian Zionism, especially with regard to biblical prophecy. As an ethnographic account, it attempts to offer a "thick description"[1] of his narrative identity and his understanding of the world.

---

1. Clifford Geertz, *The Interpretation of Cultures: Selected Essays,* (New York: Basic Books, 1973), 6-7.

The Narrative Study of Life

The ethnographic study of life narratives as a means to understanding identity formation processes arose from the belief that identity, as such, remains out of grasp in a postmodern environment. The notion of human agency was severely damaged by the structuralist assault, and once the smoke cleared it was difficult to find analytic space for human subjectivity. A decade or so later, the concept of narrative traveled from literature studies into sociological, anthropological, and ethnographic areas of research. In these new realms of narrative research, life stories were—and still are—understood as a possibility to study identity formation—that is, identity as a process that occurs within language rather than as a fixed entity beyond it. When we talk about lived experience, we adopt the form of narrative. In those descriptions of "lived time," as psychologist Jerome Bruner calls it, we present our narrative identities.[2] Through the use of plots, characters, scenes, and settings—the primary categories for narrative analysis of life stories—we construct our narrative selves. Narrative identities—"the stories that we live by"[3]—are not identical to previous notions of identity; the way I employ the term in this chapter refers to the linguistic expression of personal identity as it is expressed in the life story. The extent to which this narrative identity reflects an actual identity "out there" is still covered in the smoke from the structuralist onslaught. What is "out there," however, is the linguistic and cultural context of the story. Hence every life story provides a window into the specific context of its telling.

2. Jerome Bruner, "Life as Narrative," *Social Research* 71:3 (2004): 691–711, esp. 692.
3. Dan P. McAdams, Ruthellen Josselson, and Amia Lieblich, "Introduction," in *Identity and Story: Creating Self in Narrative*, ed. Dan P. McAdams, Ruthellen Josselson and Amia Lieblich (Washington, DC: American Psychological Association, 2006), 3–11, esp. 4.

Christian Zionism as a Religious Culture

One methodological advantage of doing ethnographic research (as compared with historical studies) is the opportunity to study *reception*:[4] how participants in a religious (or secular) community interpret—and negotiate with—narratives, rituals, theologies, and artifacts intrinsic to their group. "This study of reception," writes Thomas A. Tweed, "emerges from several related convictions—that meaning is constructed (not given), multiple (not univocal), contested (not shared), and fluid (not static). And, most important meaning is inscribed by readers, listeners, participants or viewers."[5] A religious master narrative of identity is a story that tells insiders who they are as a group and how they are to locate themselves in the world. As such, master stories are social identities in the form of narrative. As Tweed argues, devotees in a religious setting are not passive receivers of religious socialization but are instead involved in the continuous practice of interpreting theologies, rituals, and stories. Meaning is never entirely immanent in the ritual practice or religious story in itself but is constructed and reconstructed in the meeting between culture and individuals. Also, no master narrative, however powerful, has a monopoly on the identity formation of religious practitioners; other cultural narratives as well as biographical particulars also influence the process. This process can be investigated through ethnographic practice. The interpretative subject always constructs the self locally, in a specific language game, but various discourses (cultural, ethnic, political, gendered, theological, and so on) are used as resources in this self-construction. As such, these

4. Thomas A. Tweed, "Between the Living and the Dead: Fieldwork, History and the Interpreter's Position," in *Personal Knowledge and Beyond: Reshaping the Ehtnography of Religion*, ed. James V. Spickard, J. Shawn Landres, and Meredith B. McGuire (New York/London: New York University Press, 2002), 63–74, esp. 63.
5. Ibid., 65.

discourses condition but never completely determine the outcome of self-construction. The relationship between the culturally available discourses and life story construction is captured in two terms coined by the two American sociologists James A. Holstein and Jaber F. Gubrium: "discursive practice" is the self-interpreting *practice* of the subject, and "discourses-in-practice" are the *resources* that the subject employs when it stories itself.[6]

Evangelical pro-Zionist culture in Israel constitutes such a religious culture, with a "canon" of possible stories, ritual practices, theological and political beliefs, and, as in any other religious setting, people on the ground enmeshed in the practice of interpreting these "signs from above." The grand narrative of Christian Zionism in Jerusalem prescribes certain ways to understand yourself and the world around you. Through Christian Zionism, devotees learn that they are the "Watchmen on the Walls," modern-day "Esthers" or "Cyruses," the protectors of God's chosen people, and sometimes that their practice of "blessing Israel" helps to facilitate the second coming of Christ. They come to understand that the State of Israel occupies a central place in God's plan of universal redemption. This master narrative and the prescribed roles for different characters in the drama can be expected to influence identity formation processes for individuals exposed to this culture. I am concerned with the *reception* and *interpretation* of this master narrative of identity as it appears in individual life stories. This practice of identity negotiation probably varies widely from individual to individual; different cultural backgrounds, individual life experiences, amounts of exposure, etc., condition the amount and content of the internalized elements of the master narrative. How individual Christian Zionists understand

---

6. James A. Holstein and Jaber F. Gubrium, *The Self We Live By: Narrative Identity in a Postmodern World* (New York: Oxford University Press, 2000), 92.

themselves in the practice of "blessing Israel" can be investigated through the analysis of life stories.

Methodological Perspectives on Life Story Interviewing

This chapter is based on a life story interview that I conducted during a pilot study in Jerusalem in October 2011. My approach is based on the premise that we cannot understand Christian Zionism purely as a theology of the end times separated from the practice and self-understanding of individual Christians who subscribe in whole or in part to Christian Zionist beliefs.

In an attempt not to control the performance of the life story, a very limited amount of structure was employed during the interview process. In the interview with Jacob,[7] only one question was asked: "Can you tell me your life story up until the situation you find yourself in today?" I also asked Jacob not only to tell me a chronology of his past but also his thoughts and emotions relating to the events told. Once the story was finished, I asked him some follow-up questions that arose from the interview.

Before I retell Jacob's story, two preliminary cautions are necessary: 1) Just as it would be pointless to argue that truth in Shakespeare's Hamlet is solely dependent on its correspondence with extra-linguistic reality "out there," the life story of Jacob is primarily not evaluated by correspondence criteria. His chronology of events might or might not be historically accurate; either way, his interpretation of the events today certainly differs from his understanding of them the moment they occurred. Also, I don't doubt that his story would be different, perhaps crucially so, if we did the interview again one year later, if the interview had been carried

---

7. The interviewee's real name has been changed and certain biographical details have been omitted.

out in Sweden instead of in Israel, or if the interviewer would have been someone else. The aim is rather to analyze how Jacob presents his identity to me, at this specific moment, what he chooses to highlight, and what he understands as important moments (turning points) in his life. The telling of his life story is a performance, a continuing construction of his narrative self; as such, there is no final version. 2) As this chapter relies solely on one interview, and as I don't employ any criteria to relate it to a larger population, the point here is not to generalize in the traditional sense of the term. I do not claim that Jacob is representative of Swedish Christian Zionism in Israel, or even less, of Christian Zionism as a whole. Instead, the analysis is best viewed as one example of how a Christian pro-Zionist individual understands himself and his love for Israel. "Ethnographic methods," writes Amy Johnson Frykholm, "should disconfirm our assumptions and discomfort us with the complexity with which human beings construct their social worlds. They should detotalize, rather than sum up."[8] This chapter is an attempt at such a detotalization; its nature, therefore, is deconstructive rather than constructive. Yet since no life story is told in a vacuum, I also hope that this example will raise some questions about how the diversity of lived Christian Zionism can and should be interpreted. This chapter presents a *reception* of the grand narrative of Christian Zionism in one life story of a Christian soldier.

Jacob's Life Story

I meet Jacob for the first time at the small bus station in a town somewhere in northern Israel. It is a warm day, so we decide to carry out the interview in a café by the Mediterranean where we can sit outside in the shade, enjoying the gentle breeze and a nice

---

8. Amy Johnson Frykholm, *Rapture Culture: Left Behind in Evangelical America* (New York: Oxford University Press, 2004), 9.

cup of freshly brewed espresso. He is a tall man, well trained and with a full beard covering his cheeks. He is dressed in a laid-back fashion in long, brown trousers, a black tank top, and a cap. He seems very confident and displays no signs of the usual nervousness that prospective interviewees often show when they meet an interviewer for the first time. Once he starts telling his story, I begin to understand why. His achievement in Israeli society is remarkable, but his story depicts a person who is confident that this achievement was not only his own. His narrative is framed as a continuous dialogue with God, where the protagonist relies on divine guidance and at every juncture makes sure that his will is in line with the will of the Lord.

Jacob begins his story by recounting his family's longstanding tradition of a strong relationship with Israel. He tells me about ancestors, uncles, aunts, and grandparents who all "had a special relationship with Israel."[9] Jacob's religious upbringing in this setting and as a son of a Pentecostal pastor is important, he says, for understanding his current relationship with Israel. At twenty, Jacob traveled to Israel for the first time along with his parents; this was a life-changing experience for him. It was *"love at first sight,"* he says; "I just knew that this is the place where I am supposed to be and that this is the place where I am supposed to help." He identifies this as a turning point in his story: "My life really changed, in one split second."[10] For the rest of his family's two-week trip to Israel, he stayed in silence and just marveled. When the trip was over, he decided that he wanted to return. He quit his job as a youth leader

9. J2011, 2. The interview carried out with Jacob on the October 3, 2011 will hereafter be referred to as J2011. All translations from the original Swedish are mine. For purposes of readability, oral language features such as non-lexical sounds, iterations, and syntactical peculiarities have been excised except when they are deemed to carry importance for the analysis. When English terms, words, or sentences occur in the Swedish transcription of the interview they will be written in italics.

10. Ibid.

in a church in Sweden and found a place in Israel to do volunteer work among Jewish messianic believers. This second stay in Israel coincided with the second intifada, so Jacob experienced the turmoil and violence of that period. He identifies one experience in particular as a second turning point in his life:

> There were many attacks. One especially I remember: I wasn't there myself but I heard about the attack against the Dolphinarium in Tel Aviv.[11] At that point died, I think, 25 youngsters. I remember that this was one of those *changer, life changer* [experiences], because I felt, alright, people are dying, and that is not good. I will have to do something about it, I mean, simply try to prevent that people are dying.[12]

The "Dolphinarium experience" made Jacob decide that he wanted to join the army, but the way he narrates it the decision was not his alone; it was a calling from above: "I also felt that God, God said: join the army!"[13] However, when the recruitment bureaucrats realized that Jacob was not Israeli, had never made *aliyah*,[14] and that he wasn't even Jewish, he was refused enrollment in spite of his dedication to the army. This caused a minor crisis and made him question God: "God, now what? You wanted me to join the army, *what else?*" The response, however, was reassuring: "I felt go on, keep on trying."[15]

Unable to join the army, Jacob searched for other possibilities to help the army defend the country and found Sar-El (an acronym for Service for Israel), an Israeli organization that organizes volunteer work, amongst other things, in the Israeli Defense Forces. Jacob was accepted into Sar-El, but even though he was happy to contribute to the defense of Israel, repairing tanks and gas masks was not enough.

11. The attack against the Dolphinarium in Tel Aviv occurred June 1, 2001. The official death toll was 21.
12. J2011, 3.
13. J2011, 4.
14. Hebrew for "ascent," the term commonly used for Jewish immigration to Israel.
15. J2011, 4.

Jacob felt that, as he said, "My child is still sick," and described what he thought at the time: "I do what I can but I still feel that it's not enough. . . . I wanted to join the army as a soldier."[16] Jacob wanted to be on the front lines.

He had decided already in 2001 that he wanted to join the Golani Brigade, an Israeli infantry brigade associated with the northern command. However, as he was refused enrollment he went back and forth between Sweden and Israel for several years. In Sweden, he worked to earn money just to be able return to Israel for more volunteer work. After some five years, "People within the Ministry of Interior began to . . . hear my *story*"[17] and contacted Jacob to find a way to help him. As a result of this contact, Jacob was granted a temporary residence permit that lasted for two years. However, enrollment was still impossible because a permanent residence permit is required to join the army.

After two years of work, Jacob decided to gather his credentials from his time as a volunteer and write to the Israeli supreme commander. When he told his plan to a friend, she urged him to also send a letter to the prime minister, Ehud Olmert.[18] For Jacob, this high point of his story was more than a bureaucratic affair. The way he tells it, the letters to the supreme commander and the prime minister were a way for him to "*reconfirm*"[19] that he had understood God's will properly:

> I told God: God, I am ready to wait, I have been waiting, but I am ready to wait more and do whatever I can but only if you want me to. I have been here for six or seven years and I haven't earned any money, I haven't studied, I haven't done anything, except worked as a volunteer and for minimal wages. I want to serve you. So . . . if you want me to

16. J2011, 5.
17. Ibid.
18. This occurred in 2007.
19. J2011, 6.

be anywhere else in this world, I can go to Africa tomorrow! I mean, I love Israel and I still want to stay here, but if YOU [oral emphasis] want me to be somewhere else entirely, *let me know*, and I'll go. I just want to serve you; I am not the one to stubbornly cling to the country.[20]

Jacob's retelling of his struggle for permanent residency in Israel is embedded in a dialogue between Jacob and God where Jacob asked God to "*reconfirm*"[21] that this was the place where God wanted him to be.

Ultimately, his wish was granted; as a result of the letter to Ehud Olmert, Jacob was given a residence permit for reasons that he does not know. Immediately he went to the recruitment office to sign up for service in the Golani Brigade. He was accepted, entered basic training, and finally passed the tests to join the Golani. In the Golani, he was assigned to a reconnaissance unit where he served as a machine gunner. His telling of his time in the military centers on meetings with his fellow soldiers, most of them Jews who were very surprised to learn that a Christian Swede wanted—and was allowed—to do military service in Israel. His narrative then develops into a more theological discourse, where his Christian faith is contrasted and compared with that of his Jewish peers.

Finally, Jacob completed his military service, and once again after a "*reality check*"[22] with God decided not to continue his military career even though he had offers to enter training for command. After his military service, Jacob once again reconsidered his life and evaluated his options:

What am I really? I am a Swedish guy, a Christian Swedish guy that understands a whole lot about Israel, Judaism, and what happens down here. . . . There are not many Swedish Golani soldiers. I still love the country; how can I continue to help? And then I felt that I could explain

20. Ibid.
21. Ibid.
22. Ibid.

to the world what is happening in Israel. I can try to be a *bridge-builder*, either between Israel and Europe, or between the Christian world and Jewish society.[23]

Jacob decided to continue to work for Israel but in another capacity: he would no longer be a soldier but a "bridge-builder."[24] Today, Jacob, now an Israeli citizen, is enrolled in a university program studying politics and diplomacy. He considers himself a bridge-builder, if one with an unusual story.

Calling and Confirmation

The protagonist in Jacob's life story is an admirable character. He stays true to his convictions in the face of severe disappointment because he believes that he follows the will of God. This belief is eventually "reconfirmed" on several occasions.

The story begins with a depiction of the pro-Jewish/pro-Israeli environment in which he grew up. The way this background is employed to create a convincing beginning for the narrative seems to suggest that the succeeding story should be understood in light of this origin. The protagonist's identity is marked from the beginning by this atmosphere, almost as if his future were somehow meant to be.

The story then gains momentum at Jacob's first meeting with the land that he had presumably heard so much about. Even if he was already intellectually convinced of Israel's theological centrality, his arrival in Israel creates an *emotional attachment* to the country that was not salient before. At this point, his relationship to Israel becomes highly personal. In fact, he falls in love. This scene is a central turning point in the story; suddenly "he knew" this was the place where God

23. J2011, 12.
24. Jacob is still in the military reserve, however, so in case of war he will be called up.

wanted him to be. The meaning of this scene is not related only to the protagonist's newfound love for Israel; it is also a spiritual awakening, a divine calling. Israel becomes intimately connected to Jacob's individual spiritual purpose. From now on, a central theme in Jacob's narrative is an ongoing dialogue with God (the impression that it is a dialogue and not only an inner monologue is reinforced by Jacob's rhetorical usage of a dialogical linguistic form) in which the protagonist iterates his submission to the divine will, and where God "*reconfirms*"[25] that the protagonist has understood his calling correctly.

At a second scene of election, the Dolphinarium scene, the hitherto primarily spatial calling ("I just knew that this is the place where I am supposed to be") is concretized and filled with content. The protagonist, until now a self-labeled "pacifist,"[26] suddenly decides that he has to join the army, and is convinced that God wants him to do so. More specifically, he decides that he wants to join the Golani Brigade.

Even in the face of several disappointments (the enrollment refusal, the difficulties in gaining a residence permit) and economic hardship (seven years of unpaid or poorly paid work), the protagonist continues to follow his calling. It is as if Jacob, in a way similar to the biblical patriarchs, is put to the test. The moment where he finally gains the permit that allows him to join the army is marked by its embeddedness in theological language. This scene, too, is highly biblical: if the protagonist were the one being tested during the seven years of work, he now confronts God and puts him to the test by offering him an ultimatum. Having done everything possible in his human power, he now asks God to confirm that he has understood his calling correctly: "If you want me to stay in the country [and] join the army, make them give me a permanent residence permit."[27] This

25. J2011, 6.
26. J2011, 3.

is one of several scenes where the protagonist's calling is evaluated and reconfirmed.

A similar, and highly cinematic, scene occurs early in basic training when the surprised recruit is asked by his hardened company commander to tell his story in front of the whole company during a morning flag-raising ritual. He accepts and tells how he, a Christian Swede, became enrolled in the Israel Defense Forces (IDF) in front of the gathered soldiers, commanders, and the Israeli flag. When he reaches the conclusion of his story, "Suddenly . . . especially one *sergeant* who is the tough, hard-nosed, commander, he starts to clap his hands. And everybody else joins in so suddenly I find myself standing there and everybody is just clapping their hands. And I [just said] well okay, thank you! [laughter]."[28]

These scenes are thematically connected through the central narrative pattern of calling, test of faith, confirmation. Understood in the light of this theme, the meaning of the scenes can be interpreted as confirmations of the morality and righteousness of the protagonist's quest. If the first "confirmation scene" was a highly *spiritual* event—plotted prefiguratively on familiar biblical narratives and with God as the character granting the confirmation—the second scene depicts a *social* confirmation where the protagonist is embraced by Israeli society, represented by his fellow soldiers in the Golani.

Both scenes confirm that the protagonist is on the right path, but at different levels. There can be no more doubt for him that the quest has received approval, both from Israeli society and, maybe even more importantly, from God. The honorary awards that he receives during his military service also contribute to this theme of confirmation: one for his dedication in the *Kurs nativ*—a preconversion course offered to "lonely soldiers" to strengthen their

27. J2011, 6.
28. J2011, 9.

Jewish identity—and another one as the "best role model" in his unit. A final confirmation scene also occurs when he has finished his military service and is granted a large scholarship to study in Israel, thereby ensuring his continued involvement with Israeli society. This scene also is discursively embedded in a dialogue with God, where the protagonist asks for God's will to be done, and as an answer receives a scholarship large enough to let him enter the university program.

It is not unusual that evangelical life stories follow biblical patterns and that storytellers employ tropes and metaphors found in the Bible to explain religious life journeys.[29] In a religious culture where the Bible occupies the most central role as a reservoir for stories, it is hardly surprising that the Bible is employed in individual life story narration. What is notable in Jacob's story is how the voice of God is thematically connected to the land of Israel. It is in Israel that God speaks to Jacob, and it is here that God calls Jacob to embark on a spiritual journey. Moreover, God's response to Jacob's insistent questions is mediated through Israeli people (politicians, bureaucrats, soldiers) or Israeli society. In Genesis 32, Jacob the patriarch-to-be wrestles with God/an angel/a man and receives a blessing and his new name, Israel. In the modern Jacob's narrative, it is not the protagonist who becomes identified with Israel so much as God. The voice of God speaks modern Hebrew and is incarnated in Israeli society. It is here that Jacob wrestles with God and prevails.

The central role in Jacob's progressive narrative is played by love. In both of Jacob's "calling scenes"—the "love at first sight" scene and the "Dolphinarium" scene—the protagonist experiences strong affection toward the country and its inhabitants. In the first scene,

---

29. A very well-written analysis of American fundamentalist language emphasizing this theme can be found in Susan F. Harding, *The Book of Jerry Falwell: Fundamentalist Language and Politics* (Princeton, NJ: Princeton University Press, 2001).

it is the love of someone who has unexpectedly—almost miraculously—fallen in love, and in the second it is the protective love that a parent feels for a child. In other words, "love" has a sense-making function in the narrative; it is employed to explain the protagonist's motivation.

Motivation and Sense-Making

From the theoretical perspective employed in this chapter, it is neither possible nor necessary to determine whether Jacob *actually* feels love towards Israel, only that love plays a crucial role within his narrative. Within the story, love is the term that Jacob employs to make sense of his life journey, without which Jacob would not be able to explain his narrative identity or the choices he has made. For example, already from the beginning of the narrative, "love" is identified as the central element motivating his personal engagement with Israel. His passionate "love at first sight" scene is identified as the reason for his decision to quit his job in Sweden, his return to Israel, and his subsequent determination to join the IDF.

Consequently, it is crucial to point out that in Jacob's story *emotion* rather than theological *reason* (in the form of covenant theology, biblical prophecy, or fidelity to Scripture) is the explicit point of departure for his pro-Israeli engagement. This theme recurs throughout the narrative. Even the (theo-)logical *rationale* of Jacob's life story is explained in terms of love: "I love God and God loves Israel, and that is the way I see it. Consequently, I say, okay, if I love God, then I ought to also love Israel."[30] Love of Israel and the Jewish people is not a unique theme for Jacob; Christian Zionists often explicitly identify with the philo-Semitic tradition and claim

30. J2011, 2.

that their political and social action on behalf of Israeli society is the concrete expression of this love.[31] Love is, however, a vague term that can signify much, and "love" is applied differently in different areas in Jacob's narrative. So how shall we understand the protagonist's love of Israel?

One hermeneutical key occurs in a passage where Jacob tries to make sense of his "conversion" from pacifist to prospective soldier. Here, Jacob compares Israel to a "sick child"—not in the sense that there is something infantile or pathological in the Israeli national character (the source of the sickness in the metaphor is clearly external: Palestinian violence), but in the sense that he felt that being in the Sar-El was not enough to bring lasting "healing" to Israel. Being involved in the Sar-El was like treating the symptoms "to give your [sick] child a glass of cold water." What he really felt called to do was stop the violence from occurring in the first place, and this meant joining the military and serving at the front.

The metaphor of Israel as a "child" is useful also for understanding his love discourse. Whenever Jacob discusses Israeli military violence (often in sharp contrast to Palestinian violence), it is interpreted as *imperfection* (while Palestinian violence is depicted as evil, or described as carried out by "people who only want to kill").[32] However imperfect the Israeli military is ("they are not totally perfect, they make mistakes")[33] and the Jewish people are ("they are just as corrupt as we non-Jews"),[34] his love and dedication to Israel are unshakable. This gives the impression that Israel is not evaluated according to its deeds or its national character; his love for Israel is not a *consequence* of its nature, at least not solely. Rather, Israel is loved regardless of its

31. The same point is argued by Stephen Spector in *Evangelicals and Israel: The Story of American Christian Zionism* (New York: Oxford University Press, 2009), 29–31.

32. J2011, 5.

33. J2011, 4.

34. J2011, 17. From the context it is clear that the corruption that Jacob refers to is theological.

character. In other words, his love for Israel is *unconditional*, like the love for a child.

In a sense, Jacob's love for Israel is also an expression of his Christian discipleship. The central narrative pattern of calling, test of faith, confirmation is bound together by the notions of love and duty: "I felt that I *ought to* be here, and I also felt a *love* for the country; these are the two things I felt by then."[35] The protagonist in the story is a servant, a caretaker, a "helper" of the Jewish people. But through his activity of "blessing" Israel, he also expresses his love for—and his devotion to—God. For Jacob, love for Israel and love of God are not only logically consistent; they seem to mutually reinforce each other. He loves Israel *because* God "put Israel on his heart," and his love for God is concretized and expressed through his life journey in Israeli society. In Jacob's story, Israel is the very place to experience God, as a locus for evangelical self-expression.

The theme of love and the virtue of simple faith are summarized in Jacob's self-description. Asked to identify a unifying theme for his life story, Jacob immediately answers, "*a fool for Christ*."[36] This Pauline allusion[37] seems almost unbelievably apt to describe Jacob's story, and it is well in line with the general narrative pattern of calling, test of faith, confirmation. In his subsequent explication of this theme, it becomes clear that, for him, it means to expect the impossible from God, to "allow God to be God."[38] This is an implicit reference to the argument Karl Barth had with liberal theology, a theology that Barth believed divinized human thinking and morals. Later on, conservative theologians picked up this theological approach from Barth in an attempt to counter liberal theological forces. For Jacob,

35. J2011, 2.
36. J2011, 18.
37. 1 Cor. 1:18, 23; 4:10. Jacob does not explicitly refer to the Bible or to the apostle Paul.
38. J2011, 19.

similarly, the "fool for Christ" is a metaphor of love and simple faith. By applying the term to his narrative self, he points to the centrality of those virtues in the interpretation of his narrative identity.

So far, there has been a harmonious relationship between Jacob's narrative identity and common Christian Zionist themes. Jacob's story about a Christian who decides to join the IDF out of his love for Israel captures core Christian Zionist ideals and values. Furthermore, he has clearly internalized large parts of the Zionist narrative and identifies his Christian identity as crucial to understand his pro-Israeli activism. This harmony, however, is disrupted as Jacob starts to discuss concrete politics and biblical prophecy. In the final part of the analysis, I will examine these tensions between Jacob's narrative identity and the grand narrative of Christian Zionism. I propose that this disruption can be understood as an identity negotiation between Jacob's narrative identity as a lover of Israel,[39] on the one hand, and his identity as a bridge-builder on the other.

Negotiating with the Master Story of Christian Zionism

Themes of biblical prophecy commonly identified with Christian Zionism have not yet surfaced in the analysis. This is because in Jacob's narrative he only confesses a belief in biblical prophecy at one point, and even then it is in passing. Except for this reference, biblical prophecy, dispensationalist philosophy of history, and end-time scenarios seem altogether peripheral to Jacob's narrative identity. Even if biblical prophecy was a prominent theme in his religious socialization before he came to Israel, he doesn't mention

39. Even when asked explicitly after the interview, Jacob refused to label himself a "Zionist" because he believes it can be misunderstood and because he dislikes labels in general. However, I have chosen to use this term, as many of Jacob's beliefs are clearly related to Christian Zionism.

this in his story; his version of Christian Zionism, as it appears in his life story, is much more down-to-earth.

Surprised by this apparent absence of apocalypticism, I ask him, once he has finished his narrative, what he believes about biblical prophecy with regard to Israel. His answer is consistent with his down-to-earth approach to theology and faith: "[To] theorize [about biblical prophecy], oh, that is fun ... to sit down with a beer ... [with] your friends and, you know, talk ... God has given us the prophecies, there is a cause for that, but people go a lot into detail."[40] Some things, he claims, we know to be true—for example, that the creation of the modern-day State of Israel was an eschatological event—but it is problematic to speculate too much about the end times. He definitely believes that God has a plan for the end times that is related to the modern-day State of Israel, a plan that includes the rebuilding of a third temple. He also mentions the parable of the fig tree in Matthew 24[41]—which has been applied by Hal Lindsey, among others, to the creation of the State of Israel—as an argument for the validity of biblical prophecy. All these beliefs should qualify him as a Christian Zionist in the traditional sense of the term, even if he seems to consider apocalyptic speculation as a theme better dealt with in the bar than in the pulpit.

The master narrative of Christian Zionism, which clearly constitutes one of the building blocks in Jacob's narrative identity, prescribes the role of the Christian as a facilitator of the Jewish return to, and the continued well-being of Jews in, Israel. Generally, in the Christian Zionist narrative there is not much space for a Palestinian

---

40. J2011, 16.
41. "From the fig tree learn its lesson: as soon as its branch becomes tender and puts forth its leaves, you know that summer is near. So also, when you see all these things, you know that he is near, at the very gates. Truly I tell you, this generation will not pass away until all these things have taken place. Heaven and earth will pass away, but my words will not pass away" (Matt. 24:32-35).

people (or state) other than as an obstacle to the return of the Messiah. Jacob, however, claims to support a two-state solution and to carry no animosity toward Palestinians. Furthermore, he is involved in Israeli-Palestinian reconciliation programs and considers himself a "bridge-builder."[42] These two aspects of Jacob's narrative identity seem hard to combine. How does Jacob negotiate his identity to encompass a Christian Zionist approach that seems to make little room for peace with the Palestinians and his professed dedication to peace-building and reconciliation?

To address this question, we need to take a closer look at one passage where this negotiation occurs. The narrative context of this passage is Jacob's current attempt to understand more about the Middle East conflict, particularly, he claims, the Palestinian perspective. Interestingly, Jacob cites Thomas Aquinas in an attempt to reconcile his identity:

He [Aquinas] had a theory of two swords. And I very much believe, in line with that theory, that we are Christian soldiers, I mean *spiritually*, but we live in the world also. So, I am a soldier in the Israeli army, and now I [try to become] more and more involved in diplomacy. But I am still a Christian. So, I pray for the salvation of people and things like that. But both things are important to me. I am a Christian soldier—I mean a *spiritual soldier*—and faith is very important to me. But I also believe that you just can't, like some Christians and many Jews do, say that, "Ahh, God has given us this country!" And [that] "the West Bank is also given to us from God." I try to see, okay, I believe that God has prophecies, if he prophesies that Israel will be restored again, I definitely believe [so], because we are here. . . . I believe that Israel is, modern-day Israel is from God. It is not perfect; it is still being led by corrupt people. God's plan is that Israel shall exist, but where the final borders are to be drawn, if it will be with or without the West Bank [I don't know]. My focus, why I joined the army was to protect Israel and to protect the Israelis, Arabs

42. In the paragraph quoted above, this term only refers to the improvement of Jewish-Christian and Israeli-Western relations, quite similar to "Bridges for Peace" understanding of bridge-building. In other passages, however, Jacob applies this term to Israeli-Palestinian relations.

and Jews alike, [to] protect the Israeli population. But if you ask me personally, I believe in a two-state solution, because you can't just say, "Well, it is [in] the Bible that there will be an Israel." But the borders are not stated there. Some people say, "Like Solomon's [kingdom]." Okay, does that imply that we should start a war with Lebanon? And invade Lebanon because God has [told us so]? I am not a person that wants to start wars to fulfill something I believe is a divine prophecy. If it is a [true] prophecy from God, it will happen anyway. But I don't believe that God says, "Go to war! In the name of God! Go to war to occupy the land!" Sure, he said that to Joshua, okay, but ehh, I can't see that right now at least. It's the same thing with Syria; it was also a part of Solomon's [kingdom]. I view the West Bank in the same way . . . the Palestinians live there! So my hope is: two countries, with Arabs living in Israel and Jews living in Pal—future Palestine,[43] and we live in peace."[44]

Jacob's discourse on the separation of the spiritual from the worldly sphere in this quotation does not really reflect the medieval doctrine of the two swords, which predates Thomas Aquinas. Jacob's discourse is in fact more in line with the Protestant doctrine of two governments (the spiritual and the worldly) than medieval theories of the separation of political power. However, the point here is to investigate how Jacob employs this "theory" to make sense of his dual identities.

Jacob confesses on the one hand his belief in biblical prophecies, that God is the cause behind the modern-day restoration of the State of Israel, and (once again) his dedication to protect Israeli citizens. On the other hand, he affirms his hope for a two-state solution and his disagreement with warmongering Christians and Jews who claim that God's biblical promise also includes Lebanon, Syria, and the West Bank. Furthermore, he moves back and forth between these two beliefs—sometimes within the same sentence—most particularly with his references to Solomon's ancient kingdom and Joshua. At

43. It is interesting to note that every time Jacob mentions Palestine referring to the contemporary situation, he corrects himself by adding, "future Palestine."
44. J2011, 14.

the end of the discourse, it is not entirely clear what Jacob believes about the future of the West Bank, or more exactly, *why* he claims to support a two-state solution. By framing the discourse within the "theory of the two swords," however, Jacob connects his different, conflicting identities to different realms of governance. His religious identity is connected to the spiritual realm ("We are Christian soldiers, I mean, spiritually") and his identity as a bridge-builder to the worldly sphere ("But we live in the world also").

It is clear that within the grand narrative of Christian Zionism, he finds no support for his dedication to peace building and his will to "surrender" the West Bank to Palestinian rule. Time and again in the passage, Jacob tries to break free from what he seems to experience as a nonconstructive, arrogant approach to the conflict, a move that he legitimizes theologically: "I don't believe that God says, 'Go to war! In the name of God! Go to war to occupy the land!'" Yet this move is difficult for him to integrate with his religious identity as Christian Zionist discourses continue to execute influence on his narrative identity construction: "Sure, he said that to Joshua, okay, but I can't see that right now at least."

The Christian Zionist discourse-in-practice seems to *condition* but never entirely *determine* Jacob's discourse. The influence of the grand narrative, furthermore, seems to operate both constructively and restrictively on Jacob's attempt to form an integrated narrative identity. It suggests possible interpretations (constructive) but also limits his attempt to express his dedication to a two-state solution (restrictive). Nevertheless, ultimately it allows enough freedom of movement for Jacob to reflect on different ways forward. In the end, the tension is never entirely resolved, and Jacob's attempt to reconcile his narrative identities[45] ends up in what could be called

---

45. For a discussion on unity vs. multiplicity in life stories, see McAdams, Josselson, and Lieblich, chapters 1–4.

a *compartmentalization* of identity. By understanding his identity in light of "Thomas Aquinas's theory of two swords," Jacob partly disconnects his bridge-building identity from the spiritual sphere. As such, bridge-building for him primarily represents a pragmatic, secular activity, and yet one that is central in his identity construction.

Conclusion

The life narrative of Jacob illustrates the extraordinary length to which an individual who identifies with the Christian Zionist narrative is prepared to go to protect the chosen people. Yet Jacob's story also shows a great amount of negotiation with the Christian Zionist narrative. The Christian story of the Jewish return serves as an anchor of identity for him, yet the chain is long enough to provide plenty of room for discursive movement in the particularities. It also shows the distance between the normative form of a master story and its reception. Rather than simply internalizing and retelling the Christian Zionist narrative that Jacob had presumably heard since childhood, he is involved in an intense process of *narrative engagement*[46] with this story. Some themes of the story seem nonnegotiable (particularly the belief in the divine hand behind the Zionist movement, the identification between the scriptural Israelites and modern-day Israelis, and the uniqueness of this people), while others are open to negotiation (the specific plan of the end times, the borders of the promised land). This is an example of the contested meaning of Christian Zionism. As a religious movement, it encompasses a multiplicity of individuals with different theological beliefs, moral values, political agendas, and interpretations of their

46. Philip L. Hammack, *Narrative and the Politics of Identity: The Cultural Psychology of Israeli and Palestinian Youth* (New York: Oxford University Press, 2011), 22.

religious tradition. At the very least, Jacob's example should caution us about generalizing too broadly about Christian Zionism and the beliefs held by members of this movement.

In accordance with the theoretical perspective employed here, I will not offer any generalized conclusion to this analysis. Instead, I would like to point to three areas where the study of *lived* Christian Zionism could enrich the study of Christian Zionism as a whole. First, many writings on Christian Zionism have emphasized the theological distance between this worldview and Christian tradition—how Christian Zionism as an "ideology" has departed from Christianity by emphasizing the continued validity of the Jewish covenant, a dispensationalist reading of the Bible, and by supporting the State of Israel on Christian theological grounds.[47] Partly this is due, I believe, to these writers' own normative views about what Christianity is and what it should be. In my reading of Jacob, I have instead emphasized how his "Zionism" seems to be an integral part of his Christian identity. For him, being a soldier in the Golani Brigade is to follow his Christian calling. Being a soldier in the IDF is for him a righteous, moral, transformative, emotional, and highly spiritual experience; as a soldier in the Golani Brigade he is experiencing God. Without recognizing this rather obvious point and what it means for the study of Christian Zionism, there is a risk of oversimplifying the phenomenon. Jacob is first and foremost a Pentecostal Christian and

---

47. For example, Stephen Sizer, *Christian Zionism: Roadmap to Armageddon?* (Leicester: Inter-Varsity, 2004); Gary M. Burge, *Whose Land? Whose Promise? What Christians Are Not Being Told About Israel and the Palestinians* (Cleveland: Pilgrim, 2003); Donald Wagner, *Anxious for Armageddon: A Call to Partnership for Middle Eastern and Western Christians* (Scottdale, PA: Herald, 1995); Grace Halsell, *Forcing God's Hand: Why Millions Pray for a Quick Rapture and Destruction of Planet Earth* (Beltsville: Amana, 2003); Colin Chapman, *Whose Promised Land? The Continuing Crisis over Israel and Palestine* (Grand Rapids: Baker, 2002); Naim Ateek, "Introduction to Challenging Christian Zionism," in *Challenging Christian Zionism: Theology, Politics and the Israel-Palestine Conflict*, ed. Naim Ateek, Cedar Duaybis, and Maurine Tobin (London: Sabeel Liberation Theology Center Jerusalem, 2005), 13–19.

only secondly a Zionist. His Zionism is understood, experienced, and expressed through his Christian identity.

Second, as was pointed out in my reading of Jacob's life story, the Rapture, various end-time scenarios, and apocalypticism in general played a peripheral and indirect role in his narrative identity formation. One possible interpretation of this might be his Swedish cultural background and the generally disenchanted atmosphere in Sweden; even within Pentecostal churches in Sweden apocalyptic theologies and elaborate end-times scenarios are not very common. Yet the self-evident character of his understanding of the role of Israel in God's master plan suggests the importance of biblical prophecy as a framework for interpretation. To explore this theme further, and to determine whether Jacob is an isolated case or he represents a changing emphasis in Christian Zionism in Israel and globally from the future to the here and now, we need to examine the precise social and psychological role of apocalypticism in contemporary Christian Zionism in its various contexts and expressions.

Finally, until now much research related to the consequences of Christian Zionist belief and practice has focused on the ideological level.[48] Perhaps this is because so much of the literature is produced in the United States, where the political influence of Christian Zionism has been the strongest. On a more individual level, however, academic research has been sparse. Christian Zionism constitutes a unique social world—a hermeneutical lens through which events

48. For example, Dan Cohn-Sherbok, *The Politics of Apocalypse: The History and Influence of Christian Zionism* (Oxford: Oneworld, 2006); Rammy M. Haija, "The Armageddon Lobby: Dispensationalist Christian Zionism and the Shaping of US Policy Towards Israel-Palestine," *Holy Land Studies* 5:1 (2006): 75–95; Clifford A. Kiracofe, *Dark Crusade: Christian Zionism and US Foreign Policy* (New York: Palgrave Macmillan, 2009); Timothy Weber, *On the Road to Armageddon: How Evangelicals Became Israel's Best Friend* (Grand Rapids: Baker Academic, 2005); Stephen Zunes, "The Influence of the Christian Right in US Middle East Policy," in *Challenging Christian Zionism: Theology, Politics and the Israel-Palestine Conflict*, ed. Naim Ateek, Cedar Duaybis, and Maurine Tobin (London: Sabeel Liberation Theology Center Jerusalem, 2005), 108–120.

in the world makes sense. From this perspective, Christian Zionist devotees are *literally* living in the end times. The confessional, emotional, psychological, and intellectual consequences of inhabiting this world can be examined through ethnographic practice. Conducting research in that direction would, I believe, greatly enhance our understanding of the attraction of contemporary Christian Zionism.

4

Broadcasting Jesus' Return

Televangelism and the Appropriation of Israel through Israeli-Granted Broadcasting Rights

Matt Westbrook

In 1977, Paul and Jan Crouch, founders of Trinity Broadcasting Network (TBN), broadcast TBN's flagship show *Praise the Lord* from the Mount of Olives in "the capital city of the world, Jerusalem" using a rudimentary satellite uplink. They were the first Christian television media to broadcast live from Israel, and they continued to broadcast the show live once a year for the next three years.[1] On the 1978 broadcast, the Crouches presented Michael Gidron, representative of the Israeli Tourism Ministry, with a gift of $1,000 "for the beautification of the holy sites in Israel," and a plaque shaped

---

1. The second of three live broadcasts, from April 30, 1978, can be seen on the TBN website in their archives: http://www.itbn.org/index/detail/lib/Praise the Lord/ec/ tkNWtwMzqDVJDT2JoHm15o10nP527NtK (accessed April 17, 2013).

like the Star of David commemorating their first broadcast from Israel in 1977. They also presented a financial gift to Rabbi Nathan Ginsbury, a representative of the Jewish National Fund and head of the "reforestation program of Israel," for the planting of trees so that "the land might be beautiful for the Lord's return." The broadcast was strongly dispensational premillennialist in theology, emphasizing the "rapture" of the church when resurrected saints would walk into the city from the Mount of Olives down to the eastern gate of the city walls. A guest pastor spoke directly to the Jews of Israel (who weren't watching, given that TBN could only be seen in the United States at the time), saying that once the rapture occurred and Christians were removed from the world, that Israelis should listen to the "two witnesses, Elijah and possibly Enoch," who would "speak the truth of the Lord" to them.[2] The one small but significant exception to the classic dispensationalist message came at the end of the broadcast when Jan Crouch dug a hole in ground and buried three stones—one for each representative of the Christian Trinity—that she had retrieved from the TBN studios in California and carried across the world as a symbol, in Paul Crouch's words, "that joins this little land of Israel and the land of America as one—we are one in the Lord!"

Christian Zionism, Inc., Media Division

American Christian television networks have been and remain economic juggernauts, and not just through their broadcasts in the United States. For the two largest Christian television networks, TBN and DayStar, global coverage is a reality, and both networks

2. This is an allusion to Rev. 11:1-14, in which, during the great tribulation schema of classic dispensational premillennialism, the witnesses were to appear after the rapture of the church and center their ministry on the land of Israel.

use their influence to aggressively position themselves as shapers of Christian Zionist ideology.

Nearly all of the programs on both networks share the following characteristics: they have high degrees of social conservatism, are almost completely charismatic in theology and worship, are evangelistic in conviction, are overwhelmingly influenced by the prosperity gospel (which drives their own revenues and is the basis of their business strategy),[3] are deeply Christian Zionist in message, and are competitive and expansionist in regard to their empires.

In 1973, Paul and Jan Crouch officially began TBN—its legal name is Trinity Christian Center of Santa Ana, Inc., according to its IRS 990 filings—with the purchase of a television station in Southern California.[4] Its goal was and is to "spread the gospel of Jesus Christ to the world."[5] Nine years later, in 1982, Marcus and Joni Lamb founded DayStar in Alabama. They moved their ministry in 1990 to Dallas, where they are now located.[6] Both organizations are registered as churches with the IRS,[7] providing them with protection

3. Generally, the prosperity gospel or "word of faith" movement advocates material and spiritual blessings for believers who "sow seeds" of material gifts to Bible teachers or, in the case of Christian Zionism, either into Israel itself or the ministries of those who advocate for Israel. There seems to be an emerging consensus that charismatics and Pentecostals who advocate "word of faith" or "prosperity gospel" teachings can be termed neo-Pentecostal. In this chapter, I leave the terms separate because of the difficulty of classifying any single teacher appearing on the networks. Kathleen Hladky, *Chasing the American Dream: Trinity Broadcasting Network and the Faith Movement* (Tallahassee: Florida State University Press, 2011), discusses the difficulties with classifying the theology of word of faith proponents. She notes that the movement is more pragmatic and less concerned with differences in theology.

4. From TBN's "History of Christian TV," http://tbnnewswire.com/tbn/history-of-christian-tv/ (accessed April 12, 2013).

5. This is the stated mission of the organization on their IRS 990 filings. For 2011's filing, see http://www.guidestar.org/FinDocuments/2011/952/844/2011-952844062-08dc34c9-9.pdf (accessed April 12, 2013). According to the 2011 filing, TBN has close to 0 million US in organizational assets and reported 6 million in revenue for the same year. TBN provided .6 million to "foreign divisions" in the form of grants; the largest single region receiving grants was the "Middle East and North Africa" at over $490,000. It should be noted that the 2011 filing was prior to the purchase of their Jerusalem studio.

6. From "About DayStar Television Network," http://www.daystar.com/about-daystar-television-network/ (accessed April 12, 2013).

not afforded to other nonprofits against more intrusive government intervention by the IRS. Now, TBN has "two dozen international networks and affiliates broadcasting the good news of Jesus Christ to every inhabited continent twenty-four hours per day—billions of souls"[8] via acquired local television stations, cable channels, high-definition web streaming of its programming, or satellite.[9] Namibian TV carries the network. Over sixty local television stations in Romania carry TBN programming. TBN's Arab-language "The Healing Channel" boasts transmission to 100 million Arabs twenty-four hours per day. TBN studios in Mexico produce Spanish-language programming on their channel Enlace, and 70 percent of this programming originates from fourteen Latin American countries.[10] TBN has thirty-five domestic market areas (DMAs) in the United States, each of which produces local programming. On their website, DayStar claims their broadcasts cover "the entire footprint of the world reaching over 200 countries and 680 million households globally."

However, there is one local market that was nearly impenetrable for either network—until recently. In May of 2006, on Israeli Independence Day, Israeli cable company HOT agreed to allow DayStar into its basic cable lineup.[11] This decision was made in

7. For TBN, see their 2011 990 filing. Though TBN does voluntarily file 990s, as "churches," neither organization is required to do so. DayStar does not file a 990 and is doing business as Word of God Fellowship, Inc. based in Georgia, according to their website.

8. For the sensitivity of government intervention in the financial situation of churches and other religious nonprofits, see Kent Garber, "Investigating Televangelist Finances," *US News & World Report,* February 15, 2008. Further, the Crouches have said that they have turned over most of their assets and estate to TBN, thereby receiving various nontaxable benefits. See Paul Crouch's letter to Charisma Magazine publisher Stephen Strang, http://www.charismamag.com/blogs/the-strang-report/17264-tbn-responds-to-steve-strang (accessed April 12, 2013). See also Erik Eckholm, "Family Battle Offers Look Inside Lavish TV Ministry," *The New York Times,* May 5, 2012. None of the donations received by the ministry are taxed.

9. TBN details the ways in which viewers around the globe can access their programming here: http://www.tbn.org/watch-us/how-to-watch-tbn (accessed April 12, 2013).

10. Trinity Broadcasting Network, "TBN Networks: Faith Channels for Everyone," http://www.tbn.org/about/images/TBN_Networks_info.pdf (accessed April 12, 2013).

consultation with Jewish leaders and after a six-month trial run of broadcasting DayStar's two flagship shows—*Celebration* and *The Joni Show*. It was a landmark decision for the State of Israel; to that point, no other Christian network had been given access to one million Israeli households. How did DayStar receive permission to broadcast in Israel?

In his recounting, DayStar founder Marcus Lamb said that "in 2005 leaders from Israel came to the DayStar headquarters [in Dallas, Texas] and presented us with a license to broadcast in Israel." Which leaders from Israel approached DayStar with the license and for what reason? The answer may lie with the Christian Allies Caucus (CAC). The CAC was formed in 2004 by the Israeli Knesset and has as its mission to "strengthen the cooperation between Christian leaders and the State of Israel."[12] It has been quite active in partnering with Christian Zionist organizations in particular.[13] The CAC is the brainchild of its former chairman Yuri Shtern (now deceased), a Russian-born Israeli economist, protégé of Avigdor Lieberman, and Knesset member (his last affiliation was with the right-wing party Yisrael Beitenu).[14] Shtern, a self-proclaimed nonbeliever who nevertheless observed Jewish religious traditions, was significantly connected to the Christian and Jewish communities in Russia and

---

11. Ilan Chaim, "24/7 Broadcast Gives New Twist to Airwaves," *The Jewish Exponent*, May 18, 2006.

12. "About us," Christian Allies Caucus website, http://cac.org.il/site/about/ (accessed April 13, 2013). The page further states, "At the inaugural meeting, the Caucus members *pledged to assist Christian organizations with their local* operations and to acquaint fellow MK's with the pro-Israel work of Christians around the world" (emphasis added).

13. On the CAC website, a statement on the "Roots of Judaism and Christianity in Israel" is quite explicit about CAC values. It reads as follows: "Israel is the birthplace of Christianity and Judaism and within this land lies the testament and the truth of our shared past. As history is displayed throughout Israel's archeological landmarks, so is the story of our common Judeo-Christian values. The values of ethical monotheism, on which our precious systems of morality are based, can be found in our shared roots and history in the Land of Israel."

14. Judy Lash Balint, "Arrivals: From Dallas to Jerusalem," *The Jerusalem Post Magazine*, November 29, 2006.

for a time considered conversion to Christianity.[15] Shtern was also passionate about the plight of his fellow Russian Jews and active in assisting Russian immigration to Israel, citing the presence of Russian anti-Semitism (to which he was subjected as a child) and anti-communist sentiments.[16] He was assisted in establishing the CAC by a young Canadian-born Israeli, Joshua Reinstein, who grew up in Dallas and whose father "was the president of the local Zionist Organization of America chapter and was the first to institute a Night to Honor Israel with Pastor John Hagee when Josh was four years old."[17] (Hagee has regular programming on DayStar and routinely makes appearances during their fundraising drives as an honored guest.)

In 2005, Reinstein, along with Shtern and former Israeli Tourism Minister Benny Elon, convinced John Hagee to start and lead Christians United for Israel (CUFI).[18] In addition to his ongoing activities with the CAC, Reinstein hosts a recurring segment on the popular DayStar show *Israel Now News* called "Ask the Source." Reinstein, with Moshe Bar Zvi (former president of *The Jerusalem Post*),[19] is cocreator and coproducer of *Israel Now News*.[20] Reinstein

15. Dimitry Pospielovsky, "Russian Nationalism and the Orthodox Revival," *Religion in Communist Lands* 15:3 (1987): 306.
16. See also Joel Greenberg, "New Israelis with Ideas as Big as the Russian Sky," *The New York Times,* July 26, 1996.
17. Balint, "Arrivals."
18. Victoria Clark, *Allies for Armageddon: The Rise of Christian Zionism* (New Haven, CT: Yale University Press, 2007), 219–23, 257.
19. See Bar Zvi's interview with charismatic prophecy guru and New Apostolic Reformation minister John Paul Jackson, on Jackson's web channel on February 14, 2013, at http://www.streamsministries.com/video/john-paul-presents/episode-1-moshe-bar-zvi (accessed April 14, 2013). Bar Zvi was president of *The Jerusalem Post* global group from 2004 until 2007, headquartered in New York City. In 2006 he started *The Jerusalem Post*, Christian Edition. He was forced out for unspecified reasons in June of 2007, though Bar Zvi alluded to his joint media efforts with Christians as a precursor to this firing. Bar Zvi still does much work for DayStar in Jerusalem, promoting DayStar and their efforts in Israel to Christians.
20. Bar Zvi mentions the role of DayStar in funding the program in the interview with John Paul Jackson. Marcus Lamb mentions that DayStar chose to fund *Israel Now News* in order to

was recently named one of the fifty most influential Jews in the world by *The Jerusalem Post*, which called him "the father of faith-based diplomacy."[21] Reinstein and Bar Zvi also provide regular airtime to overtly Christian Zionist organizations such as the International Christian Embassy Jerusalem (ICEJ), an evangelical organization with a strong presence in Israel that hosts a regular segment on *Israel Now News* and whose staff writes much of the content of the Christian edition of *The Jerusalem Post*. Reinstein, Elon, and Shtern were in Orlando in 2005, hosting the annual CAC conference and convening with Christian Zionist leaders.[22] Though likely impossible to confirm, given all of these connections it is not unreasonable to suggest that Shtern and/or Reinstein—"leaders from Israel," according to Lamb—may have flown to Dallas shortly after the formation of the CAC to meet with Lamb and offer him a license to broadcast from Jerusalem—a mutually beneficial arrangement that would allow the CAC to provide an asset to an ally (in the form of a Jerusalem studio overlooking Mount Moriah) in return for their continued and adamant support for the State of Israel and an opportunity to continue to—personally, in the case of Reinstein—build support for

---

counter the messaging of Al Jazeera globally. See video of the award presented by Lamb to Zvi published by loveisrael.com on August 27, 2012, "Marcus Lamb presents Moshe Bar Zvi Programming Award," http://www.youtube.com/watch?v=ws8xBOE8_rA (accessed April 14, 2013).

21. See Reinstein's bio, http://cac.org.il/site/staff_bio/josh-reinstein (accessed April 13, 2013). *The Jerusalem Post*'s full statement on Reinstein, ranked forty-ninth in the 2012 list, reads as follows: "Josh Reinstein, 34, is the father of 'faith-based diplomacy,' connecting Christians to Israel as the director of the Knesset Christian Allies Caucus since its inception in 2004. The KCAC, which builds direct lines of communication and cooperation with Christian leaders around the world, has established 20 sister caucuses across the globe, including the 50-member Congressional Israel Allies Caucus. Reinstein, who also serves as an external adviser to the Public Diplomacy and Diaspora Affairs Ministry, believes that Christian support for Israel is vital to its interests. As the producer and founder of *Israel Now News*, a half-hour TV weekly broadcast to 35 million Christians in 191 countries, Reinstein transforms Christian grassroots support into legislation," http://www.jpost.com/Jewish-World/Jewish-Features/50-most-influential-Jews-41-50 (accessed April 13, 2013).

22. Clark, 223.

Israel throughout the world, filtered through friendly Christian Zionist eyes.

After initial success, DayStar's contract was renewed the following year, but a month after the renewal the cable company HOT abruptly canceled the contract and returned the broadcasting fee. The reversal, according to *The Christian Post*, was due to complaints HOT received from viewers and because of "editorial content issues." The major content issue seems to have stemmed from complaints HOT received regarding programming produced by certain Jewish Christians known as Messianic Jews, whose message tends to target Jews for evangelization.[23] Reinstein's ongoing partnership with DayStar is made all the more curious because he has publicly stated that partnerships between the CAC and Messianic Jewish groups are forbidden. The CAC website also makes this explicit: "The Caucus refuses alliances with any group that actively pursues the conversion of Jews to Christianity."[24]

In Israel, laws restricting evangelization are quite weak. Coercive evangelization involving payment or exchange of goods for conversion and the evangelization of minors without parental consent have been illegal since 1977. Getting around the laws that remain is not difficult. Overcoming political obstacles has also proved easy for Christian organizations; usually a promise to not evangelize is good enough to assuage reticent Israeli public officials.[25] The Church of Jesus Christ of Latter-day Saints promised to refrain from evangelization on their way to receiving permission from the Israeli

23. Joshua Kimball, "Ousted Christian TV Network Takes Case to Israeli High Court," *The Christian Post,* September 19, 2007.

24. Daphna Berman, "Aliyah with a cat, a dog and Jesus," *Ha'aretz,* June 9, 2006. See also Spector, *Evangelicals and Israel.*

25. See Stephen Spector, *Evangelicals and Israel: The Story of Christian Zionism* (New York: Oxford University Press, 2008), 113–24, for an excellent discussion on contemporary missionary efforts by evangelicals in Israel more generally, including Messianic Judaism and the ICEJ episodes mentioned below.

government to build their Jerusalem Center in 1986.[26] The ICEJ has also taken this route to gain access to the Israeli Knesset and to curry the favor of the Israeli government.

An attempt to strengthen anti-evangelization laws in 1998 after an Orthodox rabbi complained about Messianic Jewish evangelization efforts was thwarted through pressure from evangelicals. It is telling that the ICEJ, who had renounced evangelization of Jews, vigorously denounced the proposed law in newspaper editorials and interviews.[27] Evangelicals, with the help of allies in the US Congress, spearheaded the passage of the "International Religious Freedom Act of 1998," which was seen as a shot across the bow to then-Prime Minister Benjamin Netanyahu in regard to what would constitute acceptable policy on religious freedom for a modern nation.[28] In 2007, the Chief Rabbinate in Israel called for a boycott of the ICEJ's annual Feast of Tabernacles celebration, which reserves one night of its programming for Israelis to experience, free of charge, an elaborate program of Jewish dance and singing produced and funded by the

26. Elliot Yager, "Jewish Ideas Daily: Do Jews have a Mormon Problem?" *The Jerusalem Post*, February 26, 2012.

27. At the time, the ICEJ vociferously and explicitly denied missionary activity. When asked by Michelle Chabin of the National Catholic Register why he would be concerned about an anti-missionary law being passed if the organization prohibits evangelization, David Parsons of the ICEJ responded that his organization was "first and foremost" concerned about Israel's international reputation on religious freedom, echoing concerns expressed in the United States. However, my primary research on the ICEJ (forthcoming) reveals that they practice a collective form of what is called in American evangelical circles "friendship evangelism." In other words, they want to befriend Israel in part to gain its trust. It is important to interpret this fact in light of another phenomenon within Christian Zionism: Jewish-Christian ethnonationalism, in which (certain) Jewish Israelis and American Christians come to believe themselves to be one people. This is beginning to be expressed in even institutionalized ways (e.g., the formation of the Christian Allies Caucus in 2004). Thus the ICEJ wants to win over their "sibling in denial," or, in some cases, to "gain their father's affection." The sibling and father metaphors are used in the movement to describe the relationship of Christians and Jews.

28. "International Religious Freedom Report 2010: Israel and the Occupied Territories," Bureau of Democracy, Human Rights, and Labor, US State Department (November 17, 2010), http://www.state.gov/j/drl/rls/irf/2010/148825.htm (accessed November 2, 2012). In addition to this report, an overview of anti-missionary legislation was published by *Jewish Israel*, http://jewishisrael.ning.com/page/legislative-issues (accessed April 17, 2013).

ICEJ. The rabbis complained that participants in the event proselytized Jews and promoted such proselytization.[29] Complaints by Orthodox Jewish Israelis usually cannot accomplish much, given the global pressures expected of democracies to protect religious freedom. Mass-evangelization efforts like those conducted by Christian television have—until DayStar—been easy for the Israeli government to hold at bay simply by denying broadcasting rights and permits for organized rallies involving open and direct public evangelization.

In light of this laxity of evangelization laws in Israel, it was perhaps inevitable that after a lawsuit filed by DayStar was heard before the Israeli Supreme Court, HOT caved and reinstated DayStar to their cable lineup. A second Israeli national satellite company, YES, subsequently picked up the network, making DayStar the first Christian broadcasting company to broadcast twenty-four hours per day into Israel, into 100 percent of its cable-subscribing households.[30]

DayStar's accomplishments in Israel opened new ground for Christian media and set high the competitive bar. Trinity Broadcasting Network countered in May of 2011 with the SHALOM channel, a Russian-language channel targeting Jewish immigrants from Russia now living in Israel. DayStar purchased a Jerusalem studio later in 2011. In September 2012, TBN purchased its own studio in Jerusalem but have yet to get their programming on YES.[31] Nevertheless, the two largest Christian television networks

29. Associated Press, "Evangelicals Disturbed by Rabbis' Call to Jews to Shun Joint Sukkot Event," September 23, 2007; online at http://www.haaretz.com/news/evangelicals-disturbed-by-rabbis-call-to-jews-to-shun-joint-sukkot-event-1.229885 (accessed April 13, 2013).

30. The British-based God.tv had been broadcasting regular programming from Jerusalem since 1995, according to their website, but not into Israel itself (http://www.god.tv/node/4). God.tv has had a studio in Jerusalem since 2006. Steve Linde, "Live from Jerusalem, its GOD TV!," www.jpost.com, May 26, 2007. The percentage comes from Jackson's interview with Moshe Bar Zvi.

31. Edmund Sanders, "Daystar, TBN ready for Messiah in Jerusalem," *Los Angeles Times,* October 1, 2012.

in the world were broadcasting both from and into Israel. Their programming continues to be unabashedly evangelistic, including efforts aimed at Jews.

The Influence of Messianic Judaism on Christian Television

The Messianic Jewish movement as we now know it congealed shortly after the Six-Day War (1967) as evangelical attitudes toward Jews improved.[32] According to Yaakov Ariel, the movement is composed of Jewish converts to Christianity who believe that they have "amalgamated Jewish identity and customs with the Christian faith"[33] and put to bed millennia-old animosities between Jews and Christians. Referring to themselves as "*maaminim* (believers), not converts, *Yehudim* (Jews), not *Notzrim* (Christians),"[34] Messianic Jews captured the *zeitgeist* of the 1970s, which emphasized cultural roots and ethnic expression. The movement freely uses Jewish symbols, rituals, calendars, and other cultural materials—though, as Shapiro notes,[35] to sometimes widely varying degrees—combined with an evangelical biblicism and commitment to conservative values, theology, and strong support for the State of Israel.[36] As of 2000, the movement was larger than Reconstructionist Judaism,[37] and, in observing current patterns within Christian Zionism, there is little reason to doubt that the movement's growth continues today. Shapiro's description of Messianic Judaism is informative: "Messianic

32. Yaakov Ariel, *Evangelizing the Chosen People: Missions to the Jews in America, 1880–2000* (Chapel Hill: University of North Carolina Press, 2000), 206; and Faydra Shapiro, "Jesus for Jews: The Unique Problem of Messianic Judaism," *Journal of Religion and Society* 14 (2012): 1–17.
33. Ariel, *Evangelizing the Chosen People*, 191.
34. Spector, *Evangelicals and Israel*, 116.
35. Faydra Shapiro, "Jews without Judaism: The Ambivalent Love of Christian Zionism," *Journal for the Study of Antisemitism* 4:2 (2012): 652.
36. Ariel, *Evangelizing the Chosen People*, 198; and Shapiro, "Jesus for Jews," 4.
37. Ariel, *Evangelizing the Chosen People*, 191.

Judaism differs from mainstream Christianity in its use of Hebrew terminology, attention to biblical feasts and holy days, prominent displays of Jewish symbols, and the use of Jewish liturgical forms and practices."[38] For Messianic Jews and the evangelicals who support them, belief in *Yeshua* (Heb: Jesus) is the apex of what it means to be a Jew.[39]

All of these characteristics appear in abundance on both the DayStar and TBN networks, whether a program is hosted by a Messianic Jew or not.[40] Messianic Judaism is now the "central arm of the movement to evangelize Jews in America," according to Ariel.[41] However, with the arrival of evangelical broadcasting efforts in Israel in the last few years and the deep influence of Messianic Judaism on much of the programming of these media empires, an argument can be made that Messianic Judaism is now the central arm of the *global* movement to evangelize Jews. TBN founder Paul Crouch explains the role of his media empire in promoting Messianic Judaism in this way:

> The main thing we want to do is help sponsor what we call Messianic Jews, or Jews that have received Jesus Christ as their Messiah. . . . We

38. Shapiro, "Jesus for Jews," 5.
39. Shapiro, "Jews without Judaism," 657; and Ariel *Evangelizing the Chosen People*, 205ff.
40. Some examples of programming by Messianic Jews and Gentiles influenced by Messianic Judaism on either network would include regular programming by Perry Stone, John Hagee, Larry and Tiz Huch, Sid Roth, Michael Youssef, Jonathan Bernis, Zola Levitt Ministries, the ICEJ, Jentezen Franklin, Mike Murdoch, Benny Hinn, Jesse Duplantis, Reinhard Bonnke, and both sets of founders of the networks. This partial list does not include special programming influenced by Messianic Judaism or, for that matter, more dispensationalist-minded Christian Zionists such as Charles Stanley, Jack Van Impe, and others. The segment most influenced by Messianic Judaism is probably the semi-annual, two-week fundraising telethons—a telling finding as to the place of Messianic Judaism within contemporary Christian televangelism. DayStar actively promotes the Messianic Jewish angle. A thirty-second promo on their network for Messianic Jewish programming was as follows: "*Christians and Jews, together in a single faith,* joining people, culture and ideas. Explore, examine and learn with the best teachers of our time. . . . A messianic message for today's generation, only on DayStar!" [emphasis added]. Spot captured by Jewish Israel, http://jewishisrael.ning.com/video/daystar-messianic-judaism (accessed April 17, 2013).
41. Ariel, *Evangelizing the Chosen People*, 230.

want to do some Hebrew language programs to reach out to Jews and entice them to read the word of God and become what we call a completed Jew.[42]

It is therefore not surprising that in the very first broadcast from Jerusalem in TBN's new studios, Paul Crouch would note "growth of Messianic congregations [in Israel] like you can't believe" before exclaiming: "We are living out bible prophecy! Does that soak in to you? I'm a part!" Crouch would provide chapter and verse to justify his claim, citing Amos 9:

> On that day I will raise up
> The tabernacle of David,
> which has fallen down,
> And repair its damages;
> I will raise up its ruins,
> And rebuild it as in the days of old.
> (9:11 NKJV)

"That's happening right now. The Tabernacle of David, they found it, it's right over there," he gestures over his shoulder from their balcony overlooking Mount Zion. "This is happening as we speak!" The next day's broadcast featured Crouch visiting an archaeological site, thereby making himself an active participant in his interpretation of this prophecy. He quoted again from Amos:

> "Behold, the days are coming," says the Lord,
> "When the plowman shall overtake the reaper,
> And the treader of grapes him who sows seed;
>
> The mountains shall drip with sweet wine,
> And all the hills shall flow with it."
> (9:13 NKJV)

---

42. Edmund Sanders, "Daystar, TBN ready for Messiah in Jerusalem," *Los Angeles Times*, October 1, 2012.

Crouch believed himself to be part of this verse, applying it metaphorically to his ministry's evangelization efforts, rather than literally to the Jewish people. "The harvest is coming in so fast"—he again gestures over Jerusalem—"that we are catching up to the people planting seed and we are coming up right behind them with the harvest and are overtaking them!"

The Strategic Importance of Television Studios

The parallel goals of the two networks are mirrored by the placement of their Jerusalem studios. DayStar and TBN are in adjacent buildings to the southeast of Mount Zion, with balconies facing north (see Figure 1). This is important because those balconies offer views of Mount Moriah, known in Christian circles as the Temple Mount, in Jewish circles as the Kotel, and to Muslims as the *Haram al-Sharif*. To the east is the Mount of Olives—also visible from the balconies and particularly important to Christians and Jews as the site of the appearance (or reappearance, if you are Christian) of the Messiah. Competition for the best views is fierce. The *Los Angeles Times* has documented one episode in which DayStar attempted to obstruct the view of Mount Zion from the TBN balcony by hanging—apparently permanently—a DayStar banner in the TBN camera line.[43]

The buildings themselves are located on the 1949 Armistice lines, which divided Jerusalem between East and West, between Arab and Jewish populations.[44] That line became largely symbolic and political

43. Edmund Sanders, "Live from the Holy Land . . . our rival's logo!" LA Times Blog, October 2, 2012, http://latimesblogs.latimes.com/world_now/2012/10/live-from-the-holy-landour-rivals-logo.html (accessed April 12, 2013).

44. This was mentioned in a positive manner by Matthew and Paul Crouch during their first broadcast from the studio on September 17, 2012 on their "Behind the Scenes" show. (Only the rebroadcast of October 15, 2012 is currently available on the TBN website.) Though the addresses for the studios for both TBN and DayStar are not available, through use of Google Earth® and Google Street View® I was able to positively identify their location just south of

after the Six-Day War in 1967 and the Jerusalem Law, passed in 1980 by the Knesset, which united the city under Israeli jurisdiction. The Crouches strongly emphasize the location of their Jerusalem station, saying that TBN now "owns rock, physical dirt," on the line drawn by Moshe Dayan, the Israeli general who marched on the city in the 1967 war. Instead of the usual practice of leasing Israeli soil to outside organizations, Israel, according to TBN, chose to sell them the land outright. Sam Smadja, owner of *Sar El Tours,* the influential touring company in Israel catering to evangelicals, and himself a Messianic Jew who teaches Christians how to witness to Jews,[45] played a significant role in helping TBN to purchase the property, according to the Crouches.[46] As Paul Crouch's son, Matthew, said on the first day of broadcasting from the studio: "The symbolic, prophetic gesture of having this [studio] be the line of demarcation—not figuratively, but literally—between the Arab and the Jew . . . what is Christ? What is grace? What is the message of the gospel if it isn't for the Jew first and then the Gentile?" Conservative evangelicals are often excited by the repetition of a golden past, and Paul Crouch was no exception when he exclaimed, "The gospel is going out again from Jerusalem to the world!"

The networks' presence in Jerusalem has given them versatility on several fronts, but particularly in the area of fundraising. During its semi-annual fundraising drives, DayStar strategically cuts to live shots from its balcony in Jerusalem as a means to stir emotion in—and prompt giving from—their viewers. Direct financial appeals sandwich

Mount Moriah, 3800 ft from the southwest corner of the *Kotel* (The Wailing Wall), the base of the Temple Mount. They are, indeed, located on the 1949 Armistice lines.

45. See Smadja's teaching, "Obstacles Of the Jewish Mind in Accepting Jesus As Messiah," Calvary Chapel of Ft. Lauderdale, http://media.calvaryftl.org/player/?fn=G5578 (accessed April 14, 2013).

46. Smadja was a guest on TBN's "Behind the Scenes" program on September 18, 2012, to celebrate the achievement, and his involvement was mentioned on the broadcast. Only the rebroadcast of October 16, 2012, is currently available.

the visual, and Paul and Matthew Crouch's comments provide clues to why the visual has emotional appeal. The networks know their viewers eagerly anticipate the imminent end of the age; that is, they are apocalyptic. For viewers awaiting the Messiah, there is comfort and an intuited correctness in having live shots of the Temple Mount on demand *with a home for those shots on Christian television*, taken through Christian eyes and refined through Christian producers. If Protestants, by the fault of history, do not have control of many holy sites within the land, they nevertheless have improvised by controlling the construction and distribution of *a message about* those sites to the masses.

The Jerusalem studios are a victory on several other fronts. They give the networks access to potential Jewish converts—or, using their own logic and terms, to potential Jewish believers in Yeshua. This access is significant because of the centrality of mass Jewish conversion in some schemata of evangelical eschatology, and especially within the various forms of global Christian Zionism in existence today. Signs of Jewish conversions or openness to Christianity create a rush of expectancy among Christian Zionists.[47] This expectancy generates a certainty about apocalyptic and eschatological expectations, which leads to a mountain of intransigence for policymakers that potentially jeopardizes prospects for peace in the region even further.

Contact with Israelis and the Word of Faith Movement

DayStar and TBN's theology is shaped dramatically by their encounter with modern Israelis, who, unsurprisingly, have some

---

47. Ariel, *Evangelizing the Chosen People*. This message has been explicit in large Christian Zionist organizations such as the ICEJ who have regular programming on DayStar, despite the former's public disavowal of Jewish evangelism and the latter's open embrace of it.

concerns with classic forms of dispensationalism that prophesy their slaughter in the very land in which they now reside. A further problem is that classic dispensationalists don't—indeed cannot—"fulfill" prophecy, and the theological system had never made room for Messianic Jewish beliefs and practices prior to the millennium. DayStar and TBN's theology, belief, and practice are, therefore, shaped by the growing influence of Messianic Jews and the Hebrew Roots movement, which seeks to "recapture" the Jewishness of Christianity. A powerful driver of the Messianic Jewish movement is the One New Man theology, which sees a coming together of Jews and Christians in the last days, an echo that we heard in Crouch's statement at the beginning of this chapter in his 1978 broadcast from Jerusalem. This coming together can be found (in the mind of adherents) in Jewish conversion (or belief in Yeshua), but also in Christian partnership with Israeli Jews on other fronts: in the struggle against radical Islam; in the prevention of anti-Semitism; in business dealings such as oil drilling, Christian tourism, joint chambers of commerce, and media production benefitting both parties; and, as is more commonly known, partnership in political advocacy, as for the continued expansion of the Israeli state. Each of these partnerships is interpreted as a coming together that fulfills end-times prophecies. It is a theology powered by its own self-fulfilling prophecies, which, in the context of our present subject—the DayStar and TBN networks—produces a fount of legitimation for political advocacy and substantial network revenues.

One Israeli entrepreneur in particular has formed a strategic partnership with DayStar and Christian Zionists on the ground in Israel: Moshe Bar Zvi, who was mentioned briefly above. Bar Zvi is a former executive with Motorola and Levi Strauss, and until June of 2007 was the President and CEO of *The Jerusalem Post*. His first investment in a Christian and Jewish partnership was the launch of *The Jerusalem Post*, Christian Edition, in 2006, in collaboration with the ICEJ. After leaving *The Jerusalem Post*, Bar Zvi launched *Israel Now News*, a broadcast designed to provide "objective news from Israel" regarding events important to Israel and, presumably, the Christian audience to which it is tailored. *Israel Now News* airs on the DayStar network and Bar Zvi makes regular appearances on both the news show and DayStar's telethons.

The theology of TBN and DayStar is also massively influenced by the so-called prosperity gospel, or Word of Faith movement.[48] For viewers, participating in the work of God to bring Jews and Christians together is most easily accomplished through giving, and giving unlocks the doors of the heavenly storehouse in proportion to the sacrifice made by the giver. These are not subtle appeals; they are direct and unambiguous. Also, as a kind of theological marketing strategy, the appeals target those viewers most likely to give: those with the highest social and personal needs.

The coming together of these two theological influences can be demonstrated by the following example. In September 2012, Bar Zvi, an observant Jew, appeared during the DayStar fundraising drive. He presented a prayer book from a Polish rabbi to the president of DayStar, Marcus Lamb. The rabbi was killed in the Shoah, we are told, and the book, dated April 1939, along with the rabbi's prayer shawl (Heb. *tallit*), is presented to pastor Larry Tuch, who uses it to cover his head while laying hands on and praying for blessing over the day's pledges. DayStar and Zvi appear to be leveraging the memory of the suffering of the Jewish people during the Shoah, and the newfound Christian guilt regarding anti-Semitism, to accumulate symbolic capital for the network, which can be converted into material and spiritual blessings for both the network and the viewers.

48. Although the work is quite dated, see Quentin J. Schultze, *Televangelism and American Culture: The Business of Popular Religion* (Grand Rapids: Baker, 1991).

After Pastor Tuch's prayer, the producers cut to a shot of the sun rising over Jerusalem, and the song "The Holy City" plays in the background as Marcus Lamb speaks, asking for pledges. Israel is a cash cow for Christian Zionist media.

On "Dispensationalism"

The networks themselves now have both an inroad to changing "facts on the ground" in regard to Jewish conversion in Israel, and the means by which to promote gains—real, exaggerated, or perceived. Eschatological anticipation is carefully cultivated and shaped by a theology that invites the viewers to participate in the events that immediately precede the second coming, as we saw in only one of many examples from Paul Crouch above. This theology is often referred to as "dispensationalism," a term freely associated with Christian Zionism by scholars who often identify it as the fountainhead of support for Israel. However, more careful scholars have noted that dispensationalism is difficult to define, and those considered major exponents of dispensationalism in the last forty years may not be dispensationalists at all.[49] What can be said is that major Christian Zionist organizations such as the ICEJ reject dispensationalism outright[50] and do not use key dispensationalist terms, such as "rapture," anywhere in their literature.[51] The ICEJ also claims to reject prophecy as a basis for supporting Israel.[52] More

---

49. Mark S. Sweetnam, "Defining Dispensationalism: A Cultural Studies Perspective," *Journal of Religious History* 34:2 (2010): 191–212; Sweetnam, "Tensions in Dispensational Eschatology," in *Expecting the End: Millennialism in Social and Historical Context*, ed. Kenneth G. C. Newport and Crawford Gribben (Waco, TX: Baylor University Press, 2006), 173–92.
50. Spector, *Evangelicals and Israel*, 174.
51. A review of nine years of the ICEJ flagship publication, *Word from Jerusalem*, does not reveal a single instance of the use of the term "rapture."
52. There are reasons to question this claim, but a move away from prophecy and toward more memory-driven support (emphasizing the historic and spiritual ties between the faiths) is real, though it may never be complete.

American-grown groups, such as the charismatic New Apostolic Reformation (NAR), also reject dispensationalism, advocating a more victorious, hands-on theology. "What we believe about the end times greatly influences how we approach the work of the kingdom," NAR teacher Mike Bickle states. He advocates for an "apostolic premillennialism" and a victorious church that strongly supports Israel, adding, "We should be wild-eyed realists . . . our labors matter, because there's continuity between this age and the age to come."[53]

Pentecostalism—a theology that emphasizes immediate access to the divine and victorious living through supernatural empowerment and experiences—combined with the influence of Messianic Judaism and closer contact between Christians and Jews in the last 30 years, has reshaped classic dispensational premillennialism into a swashbuckling Christian Zionism that offers a more immanent eschatology and invites political, economic, religious and social participation from adherents. When combined with the theology of the Word of Faith movement, which emphasizes mystical blessings to adherents in return for sowing blessings into Israel, neo-Pentecostal Christian Zionism is a potent force, particularly economically, and TBN and DayStar have capitalized on and helped to construct this message.

Therefore, it should no longer be in question that Christian Zionism is moving beyond dispensationalism. It is no longer adequate for scholars to simply classify Christian Zionism as a subcomponent of dispensationalism, however accurate such a

---

53. See Terri Gross's interview with C. Peter Wagner, founder of the NAR, http://www.npr.org/templates/transcript/transcript.php?storyId=140946482 (accessed April 17, 2013). Bickle teaches against dispensationalist theology explicitly. See his teaching "Historic Premillennialism and the Victorious Church," http://mikebickle.org/resources/resource/3070 (accessed April 17, 2013). The Kingdom of Christ was a concept related to the onset of the millennium in classic dispensationalism. Its acceptance as a present reality by the NAR, combined with their eschatological convictions and victorious outlook (called "dominionism"), make for probably the most politically potent form of Christian Zionism today.

classification may have been 30 years ago. Even on TBN, classic dispensationalism has taken a beating: in 2009, in a broadcast segment conspicuously removed from the TBN website (there was some online backlash), Matthew Crouch confronted his father, Paul, about the traditional dispensational teaching of TBN, specifically targeting the embarrassing date setting typical of post-1948 dispensationalism.

Christian support for Jewish return to Palestine precedes the birth of premillennial dispensationalism in the 1830s,[54] and it should not be surprising that support for the State of Israel has undergone significant mutations from the classic dispensationalist view—in fact, it would be shocking if such theology and advocacy had remained static after so many years and after such significant social changes (globalization, advances in technology, interreligious dialogue and contact, etc.) and historical events (the Shoah, the Six-Day War, the collapse of the Soviet Union, the rise of global terrorism, etc.).

It is also clear that the ethos of classic dispensationalism, dominated as it was by a largely passive approach to prophecy fulfillment, which generally held that it was enough to merely watch what was happening in the world in order to understand what *God* was doing, has been jettisoned in favor of a more hands-on approach to prophecy fulfillment. Direct appeals to participate in prophecy fulfillment dominate every form of Christian Zionism mentioned above, in no small part due to underlying Pentecostal theological convictions. Though Timothy Weber tries to explain this move from passivity to advocacy as simply irresistible—theological convictions to the contrary—it seems wiser to recognize that such a move is typical of the transition from the once staunchly separatist American fundamentalist movement to the advocacy-promoting theology of

54. Regina S. Sharif, *Non-Jewish Zionism: Its Roots in Western History* (London: Zed, 1983); and Donald M. Lewis, *The Origins of Christian Zionism: Lord Shaftesbury and Evangelical Support for a Jewish Homeland* (Cambridge: Cambridge University Press, 2010).

the Religious Right in the late 1970s.[55] Much of conservative Christianity has largely cast off its asceticism in favor of a world-embracing, victorious-minded theology—whether in the form of modified (progressive) dispensationalism,[56] the Word of Faith movement, or the more radical New Apostolic Reformation. Kenneth Copeland, a popular teacher in the Word of Faith movement, has cleverly called such inherited forms of "hands-off" theology *"religious correctness,"* which, like political correctness, must be jettisoned by true believers in favor of access to truth and victory. This Christian Zionism is probably more accurately described as the foreign policy arm of the Religious Right, with abortion and same-sex rights comprising much of the domestic agenda. This is conservative Christianity in a modern modality: progressive in its triumphalism in regard to human achievement, often arrogant in regard to those who do not share its convictions, and technocratic in regard to achieving its ends. It is a religious form of imperialism, which trumpets the reconstitution of Israel in the land of the Bible as nothing short of proof of the existence of God.

DayStar has claimed a global reach of 2 billion viewers. TBN beams its programs by satellite in many languages (including a dedicated Arabic channel) across nearly the entire planet. Access to so many Israeli households, politically and prophetically significant studio locations, and sustained efforts toward Jewish evangelization within Israel seem likely to have led to a gold rush for Christian television. Given the global reach of the networks and, as reported in a 2006 Pew study, the dominance of Christian Zionism among global

55. Timothy P. Weber, *On the Road to Armageddon: How Evangelicals Became Israel's Best Friend* (Grand Rapids: Baker Academic, 2004).
56. Darrell L. Bock, Walter C. Kaiser, and Craig A. Blaising, *Dispensationalism, Israel and the Church: The Search for Definition* (Grand Rapids: Zondervan, 1992). Progressive dispensationalism also advocates for a more immanent eschatology; see R. Todd Mangum, *The Dispensational-Covenantal Rift: The Fissuring of American Evangelical Theology from 1936 to 1944* (Eugene, OR: Wipf & Stock, 2007), 18 n. 67.

Pentecostals, the Israeli government's granting of permits and land to both DayStar and TBN is sure to have an enormous and sustained impact on the shape of global Christian Zionism for years to come. The effects, though they cannot yet be measured, are clearly worth watching.

5

———

Walking in the Mantle of Esther

"Political" Action as "Religious" Practice

Sean Durbin

Do not think that because you are in the king's house you alone of all the Jews will escape. For if you remain silent at this time, relief and deliverance for the Jews will arise from another place, but you and your father's family will perish. And who knows but that you have come to your royal position for such a time as this?

—Esther 4:13-14 (NIV)

And then look at verse fifteen, the first word in my Scripture in verse fifteen is "Then." There's the question mark and then there's the "Then." And there's that little space in between the question mark and the then. And I would submit to you this morning that we are seated at this moment in time in that little space between God's question mark to us, and our answer to Him.

—Robert Stearns, "The Esther Church"

Over the past few decades, the subject of Christian Zionism has attracted a number of critical perspectives.[1] As it has emerged as a seemingly more coherent and cohesive politically oriented movement, particularly since the 1970s in tandem with the American Christian Right, there has been a steady stream of books and articles—both popular and academic—published on the subject. Although some of the more recent work has sought to understand the much longer history and varying nuances of Christian fascination with Israel,[2] with others treating its more contemporary expressions to social scientific enquiry,[3] much of the work on contemporary Christian Zionism remains highly polemical.[4]

1. Portions of this chapter were previously published as Sean Durbin, "'For Such a Time as This': Reading (and Becoming) Esther with Christians United for Israel," *Relegere: Studies in Religion and Reception* 2:1 (2012): 65–90.

2. Shalom Goldman, *Zeal for Zion: Christians, Jews, & the Idea of the Promised Land* (Chapel Hill: University of North Carolina Press, 2009); Donald M. Lewis, *The Origins of Christian Zionism: Lord Shaftesbury and Evangelical Support for a Jewish Homeland* (Cambridge: Cambridge University Press, 2010); Robert O. Smith, *More Desired Than Our Owne Salvation: The Roots of Christian Zionism* (Oxford: Oxford University Press, 2013).

3. Cf. Sean Durbin, "'For Such a Time as This': Reading (and Becoming) Esther with Christians United for Israel," *Relegere: Studies in Religion and Reception* 2:1 (2012): 65–90; Sean Durbin, "'I am an Israeli': Christian Zionism as American Redemption," *Culture and Religion* 14:3 (2013): 324–47; Sean Durbin, "'I Will Bless Those Who Bless You': Christian Zionism, Fetishism, and Unleashing the Blessings of God," *Journal of Contemporary Religion* 28:3 (2013): 507–21; Sean Durbin, "Mediating the Past through the Present and the Present through the Past: The Symbiotic Relationship of American Christian Zionists' Outsider and Insider Enemies," *Political Theology* 15:2 (2014): 110–131; Faydra L. Shapiro, "The Messiah and Rabbi Jesus: Policing the Jewish–Christian Border in Christian Zionism," *Culture and Religion* 12:4 (2011): 463–77; Faydra L. Shapiro, "Taming Tehran: Evangelical Christians and the Iranian Threat to Israel," *Studies in Religion/Sciences Religieuses* 39:3 (2010): 363–77; Faydra L. Shapiro, "'Thank You Israel, for Supporting America': The Transnational Flow of Christian Zionist Resources," *Identities* 19:5 (2012): 616–31; Faydra L. Shapiro, "To the Apple of God's Eye: Christian Zionist Travel to Israel," *Journal of Contemporary Religion* 23:3 (2008): 307–20.

4. Cf. Grace Halsell, *Forcing God's Hand: Why Millions Pray for a Quick Rapture—And Destruction of Planet Earth* (Beltsville, MD: Amana, 1999); Grace Halsell, *Prophecy and Politics: Militant Evangelicals on the Road to Nuclear War* (Westport, CT: Lawrence Hill & Company, 1986); Stephen Sizer, "The Bible and Christian Zionism: Roadmap to Armageddon?" *Transformation: An International Journal of Holistic Mission Studies* 27:2 (2010): 122–32; Stephen Sizer, *Christian Zionism: Road Map to Armageddon?* (Leicester, England: Inter-Varsity, 2004); Stephen Sizer,

As one might surmise from the titles of these latter works, a large part of these authors' various critiques is related to the theology of dispensational premillennialism, popularized in the 1970s through the writing of Hal Lindsey[5] and given a more dramatized account beginning in the 1990s through Tim LaHaye and Jerry Jenkins's *Left Behind* series of novels. While the nuances of this theology have been well documented,[6] one of its popular variants stipulates that within a generation of the reestablishment of Israel as a Jewish-controlled territory it will be the victim of a violent attack from Iran, Russia, and other neighboring countries.[7] This attack will be followed by the rapture of the church—the miraculous event that instantaneously removes all "believing" Christians from the earth—and a seven-year period known as the great tribulation, during which God turns his attention back to Israel. During the first three-and-a-half years of the tribulation, a benevolent leader who will later reveal himself as the antichrist will broker a false peace between Israel and its neighbors. In the final three-and-a-half years, the antichrist will reveal his true identity, declare himself God, and initiate a program aimed at the destruction of Israel and the Jewish people. At the culmination of the great tribulation, before the Jewish population can be destroyed, Jesus

Zion's Christian Soldiers? The Bible, Israel and the Church (Nottingham, England: Inter-Varsity, 2007); Donald E. Wagner, *Anxious for Armageddon: A Call to Partnership for Middle Eastern and Western Christians* (Scottdale, PA: Herald, 1995); Barbara R. Rossing, *The Rapture Exposed: The Message of Hope in the Book of Revelation* (New York: Basic, 2005); Victoria Clark, *Allies for Armageddon: The Rise of Christian Zionism* (New Haven, CT: Yale University Press, 2007); Rammy M. Haija, "The Armageddon Lobby: Dispensationalist Christian Zionism and the Shaping of US Policy Towards Israel-Palestine," *Holy Land Studies: A Multidisciplinary Journal* 5:1 (2006): 75–95; Alistair W. Donaldson, *The Last Days of Dispensationalism: A Scholarly Critique of Popular Misconceptions* (Eugene, OR: Wipf & Stock, 2011). For a more substantial and nuanced discussion of this issue, see Shalom Goldman, "Christians and Zionism: A Review Essay," *American Jewish History* 92:2 (2007): 245–60.

5. Hal Lindsey, *The Late Great Planet Earth*, first Australian ed. (Melbourne: S. John Bacon, 1972).
6. Perhaps the best overview of the historical development of dispensationalism and its establishment in America can be found in Timothy P. Weber, *On the Road to Armageddon: How Evangelicals Became Israel's Best Friend* (Grand Rapids: Baker Academic, 2004).
7. Based on a particular reading of Ezek. 38–39.

will return with the raptured church, cast the antichrist into a lake of fire, bind Satan, throw him into a bottomless pit, judge the nations for their historic treatment of Israel, and establish his kingdom on earth where he will rule from Jerusalem for 1,000 years of uninterrupted peace.

In many respects, it is this theological schema that has been attached to Christian Zionism since it has become a distinguished political presence in American politics. Accordingly, much of the previous work on Christian Zionism has tended to treat it as a monolithic whole and critiqued it along two distinct lines, thus producing a static notion of what Christian Zionism *is*. First, and perhaps most pervasive, is the criticism that because Christian Zionists are said to read the Bible "literally," inclusive of the series of events described above, their political activities are uniformly and consciously based on the desire to "force God's hand" or "hasten God's timetable."[8]

A second line of criticism, often expressed in conjunction with the first, might be vaguely characterized as a form of historical criticism, although it remains steeped in certain normative theological and ideological assumptions. This criticism generally comes from other evangelicals, mainline Protestants, or liberal humanists who find fault with dispensational theology and thus represent it as "unbiblical"—often by providing a taken-for-granted approach as to how the Bible *should* be read,[9] irrespective of the fact that there never has been one particular way to read the Bible.

While it might be well for these critics to point out the relatively recent construction of dispensational hermeneutics, or to argue that

---

8. Sizer, *Christian Zionism*; Sizer, *Zion's Christian Soldiers?*; Halsell, *Forcing God's Hand*; Halsell, *Prophecy and Politics*; Rossing, *The Rapture Exposed*.
9. Sizer, *Zion's Christian Soldiers?*; Rossing, *The Rapture Exposed*; Donaldson, *The Last Days of Dispensationalism*.

the doctrine of the rapture is "fictional," simply asserting that Christian Zionists have it "wrong" achieves little in the way of social-scientific enquiry. Attempting to adjudicate the validity of particular readings of the Bible does not help us understand Christian Zionism as a cultural phenomenon, nor does it shed light on the various ways in which the modern State of Israel continues to occupy an important symbolic space among self-identified Christian Zionists. Rather, what these arguments tend to do is revalorize the authors' own political and theological positions as more "authentic," thus safeguarding them from the same critical scrutiny to which they subject Christian Zionism.

The purpose of this essay, then, is to consider an alternative approach to understanding the relationship between Christian Zionists' "religious" commitments and their "political" activities. Rather than reinscribing the notion that politics is something logically separate from "religion," I examine the way in which seemingly mundane political activities can become reconstituted as acts of "religious" devotion through particular discursive practices. In particular, I focus on the relationship between what is often asserted to be Christian Zionists' "literal" reading of Scripture, the rigid beliefs that are said to stem from that reading, and the purported direct influence such beliefs have on the political activity that these so-called scriptural literalists are engaged in. Moreover, I trouble the notion that "literalism" is in fact a stable form of reading, and instead argue that what counts as a "literal reading" is achieved through a variety of discursive practices. Rather than dictating what actions Christian Zionists might take in the world, a claim to "literal" or "plain meaning" is in fact a discursive tool used to transform ordinary political activity into "religious practice," and thus protect those activities from critical scrutiny.

To do so, I briefly examine the political activities of the Christian Zionist lobby group Christians United for Israel (CUFI) in relation to Iran, and the way CUFI has discursively established "the Iranian threat" as the most pressing issue of its time, as well as the way in which critics have represented or questioned the authenticity of CUFI's support for Israel. After considering some of the problems with an emphasis on what Christian Zionists are said to "believe" as the determining factor in guiding Christian Zionist political activities, I point to some alternative ways of understanding the eschatological disposition of some Christian Zionists, particularly as it relates to the construction of identity. I pay particular attention to a reading of the book of Esther, which is used as a tool to constitute contemporary Christian Zionists as the typological heirs of the book's protagonists, while the Iranian government, in particular Mahmoud Ahmadinejad, is constituted as the typological heir to the book's antagonists as representatives of Satan and his desire to thwart the final redemption of the world.

Christians United for Israel, the "Iranian Threat," and the Problem with "Belief"

At the forefront of contemporary American Christian Zionism is the lobby group Christians United for Israel, which was founded in 2006 by the Texan televangelist John Hagee. Since its inception, CUFI has contended with ongoing criticism[10] regarding the relationship between its leaders' dispensational theology, on the one hand, and its support for Israel on the other. From the outset, one of CUFI's primary emphases has been highlighting the threats it asserts stem from Iran and its government's work toward developing nuclear

10. Criticism that has taken a similar form to the "forcing God's hand" argument outlined above.

capabilities. While the Iranian government asserts its right to develop nuclear capabilities for peaceful purposes, CUFI and other observers accuse it of working toward developing nuclear weapons. They highlight Iran's former president Mahmoud Ahmadinejad's statements concerning a "world without Zionism" as evidence of Iran's desire to "wipe Israel off the map."[11] As Hagee told David Horowitz of *The Jerusalem Post* in 2006:

> I believe that Iran is a threat to Western civilization. I believe their president means it when he says "Israel should be wiped off the map."
>
> I believe that we are exactly where we were in the middle 30s when Hitler was talking about the world without Jews. We have a new Hitler, in the Middle East. He's the president of Iran. We need to take him very seriously.
>
> I would hope the United States would join Israel in a military preemptive strike to take out the nuclear capability of Iran for the salvation of Western civilization. It is as important to America as it is to Israel.[12]

In spite of these comments, many critics have tended to focus on a Christian Zionist reading of Ezek. 38–39 (which many assert depicts an attack on Israel by Iran) in their assessment of Christian Zionist support for Israel and their corresponding concern over Iran.

Around the time of CUFI's establishment, Hagee's detractors sought to expose the influence that prophetic speculation was having on purportedly more transparent politics. The blogger Sarah Posner, for example, argued:

> When addressing audiences receptive to Scriptural prophecy . . . Hagee welcomes the coming confrontation. He argues that a strike against Iran will cause Arab nations to unite under Russia's leadership, as outlined

11. For further discussion on Iran and Christian Zionism, see Shapiro, "Taming Tehran."
12. David Horowitz, "Evangelicals Seeing the Error of 'Replacement Theology,'" *The Jerusalem Post,* March 20, 2006.

in chapters 38 and 39 of the Book of Ezekiel . . . "plunging the world toward Armageddon."[13]

Another blogger, Bruce Wilson, picked up on similar themes, arguing that Hagee finds this and other scenarios, including a possible nuclear strike on the United States, "thrilling."[14] While it is no secret that Hagee is a dispensationalist who asserts his belief in Israel's eschatological significance, as well as a prophesied attack on Israel by Iran,[15] he also maintains that CUFI's support for Israel has nothing to do with hastening the end times. In 2007, Hagee stated, "Our support of Israel has nothing to do with end-times prophecy. It has absolutely nothing to do with eschatology."[16] One year later, at CUFI's annual Washington Summit, Hagee expanded on the topic: "We don't believe that we can speed up the end of days one second. Why? Because we believe that God is sovereign. That he has set the time. We are powerless to change God's timetable. That's what makes him God."[17]

Although critics might cry foul and argue that the denial of any relationship between "hastening Armageddon" and Christian support for Israel is merely a point of political expediency, it is also, from an emic perspective, ostensibly true. For Christian Zionists, it is not about "hastening the end times," primarily because, as many (particularly CUFI's Christian leadership) understand it, those times are upon us. Hagee, I suggest, is not being disingenuous when he claims that Christian Zionists do not believe they can speed up God's

---

13. Sarah Posner, "Pastor Strangelove," *The American Prospect*, May 21, 2006, http://prospect.org/article/pastor-strangelove.
14. Bruce Wilson, "McCain Endorser Pastor Hagee's 'Thrilling' Scenario Includes Nuclear Strike on US Coasts," *Talk to Action*, May 2, 2008, http://www.talk2action.org/story/2008/5/2/92739/11686 (accessed January 25, 2014).
15. See, for example, John Hagee, *Jerusalem Countdown* (Lake Mary, FL: FrontLine, 2006).
16. Quoted in Max Blumenthal, "Rapture Ready: The Christians United for Israel Tour," July 26, 2007, http://www.youtube.com/watch?v=mjMRgT5o-Ig.
17. Quoted in: Shapiro, "Taming Tehran," 370.

timetable. Christians do not get God to act for them; God gets Christians to act for him. However, their knowledge that God is getting them to act for him is not based on a charismatic leader or on pristine motives that emerge out of nothing, but rather on an interaction between social and political events, on the one hand, and a particular habitus on the other.

Thus Christian Zionists are not solely driven by an apocalyptic reading of biblical texts that many (no doubt sincerely) believe predict the future. Instead, they appear to act on a particular reading that is mediated through, and made relevant by, local social and political situations. It is these situations that enable particular texts and particular readings of texts to become relevant and interpreted and authorized as moments in which humans are not acting on their own but are being called by God. And, at times of crisis (whether real or manufactured), it is those called by God who must act. Accordingly, as Christian Zionists find themselves at a critical juncture on God's timetable, they can side with God and submit to the plans that he has for them (as they understand them) or they can remain silent and side with evil.

It is on this point, arguably, that some of the critics I noted above have fallen short. That is, in my reading, both Posner's and Wilson's arguments over Hagee's hawkish position on Iran, as well as those put forth in much of the earlier work on Christian Zionism, have a tendency to take the reasons for Christian support for Israel as settled. Christian support for Israel is generally construed solely as the result of a literal biblical hermeneutic that is *prior to* and directly determines what it is that Christian Zionists do in the world. If one looks, for example, at Barbara Rossing's *The Rapture Exposed: The Message of Hope in the Book of Revelation,* the synopsis on the rear flap reveals to prospective readers that the dispensationalist interpretation of Scripture "guides the daily acts of millions of people worldwide."[18]

Similarly, as Stephen Sizer sees it, Christian Zionists are united by an "ultra-literal"[19] biblical hermeneutic that induces them to, among other things, become "anxious for Armageddon."[20]

What strikes me as problematic in these arguments is their intrinsic idealism and the notion that Christian Zionists' political activities are derived solely from an (erroneous) "literal" reading of the Bible, without considering the wider social contexts and discursive practices that enable Christian Zionists to make their activities *meaningful* in the first place. For example, as Abby Day points out, beliefs are "performative"; they cannot be timeless or universal, but rather "must be brought into being in specific contexts, times and places."[21] Accordingly (and particularly important when thinking about dispensationalist beliefs and their relationship to political action for reasons that I will explicate below), beliefs are not "static or universal, but must respond, collectively, to changing circumstances."[22] Moreover, with reference to Talal Asad's critique of the interiority that comes with many idealist definitions of religion,[23] Bruce Lincoln argues that one must also recognize, as Emile Durkheim did, that "religious subjects are also bound in their moral communities that enjoy their allegiance and serve as a base for their identity."[24] Not

18. Rossing, *The Rapture Exposed.*
19. Describing Christian Zionists' hermeneutic as "ultra-literal" is a fascinating classificatory move in itself, as it allows Sizer to differentiate himself from Christian Zionists while at times allowing him to use his own "literal" hermeneutic if necessary.
20. Sizer, "The Bible and Christian Zionism," 122–30. For similar readings that emphasize a certain infectious nature to dispensational hermenuetics and their direct relationship to shaping political policy, see Haija, "The Armageddon Lobby"; Donaldson, *The Last Days of Dispensationalism*; Halsell, *Forcing God's Hand*; Halsell, *Prophecy and Politics.*
21. Abby Day, "Propositions and Performativity: Relocating Belief to the Social," *Culture and Religion* 11:1 (2010): 14.
22. Ibid.
23. Talal Asad, "Anthropological Conceptions of Religion: Reflections on Geertz," *Man* 18:2 (1983): 237–59; Talal Asad, *Genealogies of Religion: Discipline and Reasons of Power in Christianity and Islam* (Baltimore: Johns Hopkins University Press, 1993), 27–54.
24. Bruce Lincoln, *Holy Terrors: Thinking About Religion after September 11*, 2nd ed. (Chicago: University of Chicago Press, 2006), 5.

recognizing how Christian Zionists understand and continually constitute themselves as part of a moral community—an imagined community that enables them to construct a particular identity—prevents a greater and more nuanced understanding of their political work. An approach that takes the reasons for Christian Zionists' political activity as settled based on a purportedly unchanging method of reading the Bible "literally" does not help us understand which texts are emphasized or how they become "canon within the canon," and therefore how they can be constructed and referenced as a "plain" or "literal" reading when in fact their meanings and emphases are products of social and historical processes.[25]

This is not to say that Christian Zionists do not appeal to the notion that they are reading the Bible "literally" and are simply acting on its "plain" meaning. Nor is it to suggest that beliefs about Israel's eschatological significance are nonexistent, or that Christian Zionists have little interest in Jesus' second coming. I am arguing that political activity that is purportedly produced by a "plain" reading of Scripture is a rhetorical device used by Christian Zionists to protect that activity from further scrutiny. This is an example of what William Arnal and Russell McCutcheon have described as the politics of the category "religion."[26]

This is what makes a critical examination of the use of Esther as a template for political action particularly illuminating. The book of

---

25. For a more detailed discussion and critique of the emphasis on "belief" in earlier work on Christian Zionism, see Sean Durbin, "The Revelation of John (Hagee): American Christian Zionism, 'Religion,' 'Politics,' and Identity" (unpublished PhD dissertation, Macquarie University, 2013), 1–42. For broader discussions on the problem with belief in the study of religion in general, see Russell T. McCutcheon, "I Have a Hunch," *Method and Theory in the Study of Religion* 24:1 (2012): 81–92; Donald S. Lopez, "Belief," in *Critical Terms for Religious Studies*, ed. Mark C. Taylor (Chicago: University of Chicago Press, 1998); Abby Day and Gordon Lynch, "Introduction: Belief as Cultural Performance," *Journal of Contemporary Religion* 28:2 (2013): 199–206; and Day, "Propositions and Performativity."
26. See: William E. Arnal and Russell T. McCutcheon, *The Sacred Is the Profane: The Political Nature of "Religion"* (New York: Oxford University Press, 2013).

Esther is neither prophetic nor apocalyptic. It does not in any "literal" sense prescribe or describe future events that Christian Zionists might look to in relation to current events, in contrast to the way prophetic books like Ezekiel or Revelation are sometimes read. Yet it is amenable to a particular kind of polyvalent interpretation by which it can be applied to a variety of events and situations that *are* read as prophetically mandated. It provides what Gregory Dawes describes as a "paradigmatic explanation." As a paradigmatic text, Esther defines a pattern that can be applied to new contexts while remaining indeterminate with regard to the context of its original application.[27]

As we will see, Christian Zionists approach Esther in a way that shows how God uses ordinary people to do his will on earth. No overtly supernatural events occur in its narrative; God's will and punishment are meted out entirely by human actors. However, this reading and the inspiration that Christian Zionists derive from it does not occur in a vacuum; religiously motivated political action—that is, activity that is attached to larger, cosmic order—is not based on a simplistic or "literalist" reading of Scripture that induces individuals to act *ex nihilo*. Rather, Esther's contextual application is underwritten by the current social and political moment that Christian Zionists find themselves in *and* the larger cosmological superstructure within which these events are interpreted.

For Christian Zionists, the activities of Iran, Hezbollah, and Hamas, which organizations like CUFI alert them to, and which they assert comprise a unified existential threat to modern Israel, the United States, and thus the redemption of the world, is significant. Iran in particular is significant because of its identification with ancient Persia, the setting of the biblical story of Esther. Mahmoud Ahmadinejad is charged with the same aspirations as the Jews'

---

27. Gregory W. Dawes, "Paradigmatic Explanations: Strauss's Dangerous Idea," *Louvain Studies* 32 (2008): 67–80.

antagonists in Esther's day because of his statements regarding a "world without Zionism" and threats to destroy the State of Israel, coupled with Iran's nuclear program. Moreover, Ahmadinejad's aspirations are attributed to the same demonic sources as those of Esther's antagonists. Thus Esther provides a paradigmatic explanation for the current political situation in the Middle East, where God's chosen people are once again threatened with annihilation at the hands of a Persian ruler—one who, it is said, is not merely acting out of his own desire for political power, but rather out of Satan's ongoing desire to destroy the Jews as God's human instruments that he will use for the final redemption of the world. Hagee explained it to his congregation in these terms in a sermon on Esther:

> Now, a politician by the name of Haman . . . is plotting at this exact time to have all of the Jews of Persia slaughtered. Understand again, for those of you who are just watching it on television, all the Jews of the world were in Persia, and had he been successful, he would have prevented the birth of Jesus Christ.[28]

In this reading, just as Satan used Haman to attempt to prevent Jesus' *first* coming by destroying all the Jews in the world, Ahmadinejad's threats to destroy Israel are connected with Satan's desire to prevent Jesus' *second* coming, which for Christian Zionists is intimately connected to a Jewish Jerusalem.

I deal with these issues in more systematic detail below, where I adopt a close reading of a sermon on "Becoming an Esther Church" by Robert Stearns. This sermon demonstrates the paradigmatic lines that are drawn between a particular reading of the biblical text, Christian Zionists' representation of the current political climate in the Middle East, and the role they ascribe themselves in this context. Before we can get to this discussion, however, it is important to

28. John Hagee, "Desperate Housewives of the Bible: Esther: Crowned in Crisis" (San Antonio, TX: Cornerstone Church, March 11, 2011).

consider one way Christian Zionists use a larger biblical panorama to cultivate a sense of moral identity and community, and how this sense of identity ascribes "religious" meaning to what are otherwise very ordinary forms of political action.

Constructing a Moral Identity in the Last Days

When dealing with conservative Christian Zionism and its apocalyptic impetus, in particular the violent imagery conjured up by the interpretations of texts such as Ezekiel and Revelation, critics often overlook the fact that for Christian Zionists these texts can also provide messages of hope.[29] Indeed, the entire biblical panorama, as read or understood by Christian Zionists, is one of hope. In Stephen O'Leary's words, it is a "mythic theodicy" that provides optimism for a persecuted church awash in a sea of evil. Moreover, it engenders a sense of temporal urgency in "true" believers who, although destined to undergo persecution in their defense of "truth," are also certain in their future triumph alongside God.[30]

Yet Christian Zionists do not merely look to the "end" of the story in Revelation. For evangelicals, the Bible is not a disparate set of texts; it is a cohesive whole that reveals the nature of God, humanity, the unfolding of time, and the purpose of history.[31] For Christian Zionists more specifically, this is the story of God's experiment with Israel and humanity from Genesis to Revelation and everything in between. The text, in conjunction with contemporary history, therefore presents Christian Zionists with two kinds of history: prophecy

29. See Rossing, *The Rapture Exposed*. While Rossing herself finds hope in Revelation, she finds it in contradistinction to her own interpretation of dispensational hermeneutics, which she criticizes for their "escapism."

30. Stephen D. O'Leary, *Arguing the Apocalypse: A Theory of Millennial Rhetoric* (New York: Oxford University Press, 1994), 63.

31. James S. Bielo, *Words Upon the Word: An Ethnography of Evangelical Group Bible Study* (New York: NYU Press, 2009), 64.

fulfilled—what outsiders or moderns might consider "secular" history; and prophecy to be fulfilled—the history of the future.[32]

Through such a reading, Christian Zionists are able to cultivate a moral identity that is modeled after their understanding of God and his work in history—the ongoing reality of which is most readily visible in the history, trials, and survival of the modern State of Israel. This understanding is helpfully explained by Robert Alter, who argues that the implicit theology of the Hebrew Bible identifies a God whose purposes are working through history but remain dependent on the acts of individuals for their continuing realization. These individuals, in Alter's reading, are God's "chosen medium for His experiment with Israel and history."[33]

Reading the text in this way, we can see that although Christian Zionists attribute complete sovereignty to God,[34] there are times when God uses human instruments to help him carry out his will. A practical prayer manual distributed to CUFI members in preparation for a tour of Israel in 2012 describes God's use of humans explicitly: "We bless you for choosing to obey the divine trumpet call to The Church in this hour, to be 'co-laborers with God' for His purposes and plans to manifest in this strategic place and people."[35]

Invoking this sense of "use" and instrumentality, it is possible to understand how tension between Christian action and the ultimate sovereignty of God is resolved. It also enables Christian Zionists to reframe what are otherwise ordinary political activities. In performing these activities, they are not active agents attempting to

---

32. See Susan Friend Harding, "Imagining the Last Days: The Politics of Apocalyptic Language," *Bulletin of the American Academy of Arts and Sciences* 48:3 (1994): 14–44.

33. Robert Alter, *The Art of Biblical Narrative* (New York: Basic, 2011), 12–13.

34. Recall Hagee's statement from CUFI's 2008 Washington Summit quoted above: "We don't believe that we can speed up the end of days one second. Why? Because we believe that God is sovereign. That he has set the time. We are powerless to change God's timetable. That's what makes him God."

35. Robert Stearns, *Watchmen on the Wall: A Practical Guide to Prayer for Jerusalem and Her People* (Clarence, NY: Kairos, 2005), viii.

get God to act for them, but submissive subjects whom God calls to work for him. But as Alter points out, biblical characters are not passive agents in history. God's purposes are always dependent on the acts of individuals.[36] As I will show below, Esther is a paradigmatic example of an individual whom God used to save his chosen people from destruction and further reveal himself in history. She is also an example that Christian Zionists today invoke to attach their own work to what they construe as a similarly urgent call.

Yet just as biblical characters are not passive agents in history, neither are contemporary Christian Zionists passive readers of the text. Rather, their understanding of the Bible and world events is formed in what Stanley Fish calls "interpretive communities," reading the way they do because of their participation in defined communities of practice.[37] The result of Christian Zionists' participation in these communities is the development of what, drawing on Pierre Bourdieu, I describe as a "Christian Zionist habitus," which helps define the relationship that Christian Zionists have with Israel and helps them orient themselves in the world. As Bourdieu describes it, the habitus is comprised of systems of certain dispositions that

> generate and organize practices and representations that can be objectively adapted to their outcomes without presupposing a *conscious* aiming at ends or an express mastery of the operations necessary to attain them. Objectively "regulated" and "regular" without being in any way the product of obedience to rules, they can be collectively orchestrated without being the product of the organizing action of a conductor.[38]

---

36. Alter, *The Art of Biblical Narrative*, 12–13.

37. Stanley Fish, *Is There a Text in This Class? The Authority of Interpretive Communities* (Cambridge, MA: Harvard University Press, 1980); Bielo, *Words Upon the Word*, 13.

38. Pierre Bourdieu, *The Logic of Practice* (Cambridge: Polity, 1990), 53, emphasis added.

Bourdieu's analysis is useful in reconsidering the arguments frequently made regarding Christian Zionists' support for Israel, which often presuppose that *conscious* aiming underpins why Christians "really" support Israel, as I discussed above. For Bourdieu, the habitus predisposes individuals to act in particular ways or pursue certain goals, not because they consciously assent to these goals in a calculated way, but rather because they are the products of particular histories that endure within the habitus.

Whether or not CUFI members self-identify as dispensationalists (and many do not), contemporary Christian Zionism is shaped by particular histories that have been substantially influenced by dispensational hermeneutics,[39] and more generally teleological views of history that do not necessarily require explicit recourse or conscious assent to these truth claims. It is worth pursuing this point further to glean a better understanding of how this helps conceptualize the way Christian Zionists approach historical and contemporary "events," and how they become events of significance in the first place.

In *The Islands of History*, Marshall Sahlins argues that "an event is indeed a happening of significance, and *as significance* it is dependent on the structure for its existence and effect." He clarifies further that "an event is not just a happening in the world; it is a *relation* between a certain happening and a given symbolic system." Thus, while an event may have its own more "objective" origins, its effect and significance are achieved through its relationship to a particular cultural scheme.[40] Through this argument, Sahlins helps open up

---

39. See for example, Yaakov Ariel, *On Behalf of Israel: American Fundamentalist Attitudes Towards Jews, Judaism, and Zionism, 1865–1945* (Brooklyn: Carlson, 1991); Yaakov Ariel, "An Unexpected Alliance: Christian Zionism and Its Historical Significance," *Modern Judaism* 26:1 (2006): 74–100; Weber, *On the Road to Armageddon.*
40. Marshall Sahlins, *The Islands of History* (Chicago: University of Chicago Press, 1985), 153, emphasis original.

a more subtle space for thinking about the relationship between ideas and practice, and the failure of what he calls an "objectified distinction between cultural concepts and practical activities." Such a distinction, he argues, obstructs the fact that "all *praxis* is theoretical. It begins always in concepts of the actors and of the objects of their existence, the cultural segmentations and values of an *a priori* system."[41] Thus, according to Sahlins,

> Events . . . cannot be understood apart from the values attributed to them: the significance that transforms a mere happening into a fateful conjecture. What is for some people a radical event may appear to others as a date for lunch . . . the human symbolic fact is: no event *sans* system.[42]

Sahlins's argument, in conjunction with Bourdieu's notion of the habitus, is useful when thinking about the relationship between Christian Zionists' apocalyptic beliefs and political praxis because it draws a much more nuanced line between the two. Christian Zionists' habitus prompts them to act in certain ways and pursue certain goals, specifically those related to their symbolic relationship to Israel. On the one hand, the habitus is mapped by the long history of Christian fascination with Israel, the contemporary manifestation of which has been significantly shaped by dispensational hermeneutics, even if only obliquely. Through this history there has developed what Sahlins might refer to as a particular structure or *system* that helps organize events as they relate to Israel's known future. On the other, there is also the history of interpreting current events through that lens—events that, with recourse to Sahlins' argument once more, are made important precisely because of their ability to fit into Christian Zionists' particular cosmological system. It is this kind of two-tiered history that has contributed to the formation

---

41. Ibid., 154, emphasis original.
42. Ibid., emphasis original.

of certain communities of practice and contributed to the way readers approach a particular text or event in the world, creating what James Bielo refers to as "textual ideologies."[43] The historically constructed importance of Israel and its necessity for the future consummation of God's plans, as well as the fact that it remains in physical and ideological conflict with its neighbors and others, enables Christian Zionists to continually reaffirm their moral standing toward Israel in what is otherwise construed as a demonically inspired world.

Explaining Christian Zionism is not a black and white activity. One cannot account for Christian support for Israel solely by looking at the Bible, as Shalom Goldman has pointed out,[44] or by simply citing their claims of a "literal" reading of particular texts without further theorization. However, it is equally important not to argue that an emphasis on the end times and a claim to literalism has no bearing on the shape that Christian Zionist praxis takes.

We must think about Christian Zionists' political work in more subtle terms, in relation to structure and event. Dispensational hermeneutics have provided a kind of cultural scheme or structure for thinking about the world. This makes particular emphases or courses of action available for Christian Zionists to "think" them into significance. In order to understand some of the efficacy of CUFI's political appeals, then, it is important to understand how Christian Zionists become reconstituted cultural subjects—no longer merely women and men, but instruments of God—through aspects of evangelical pedagogy.

43. Bielo, *Words Upon the Word*, 51.
44. Shalom Goldman, "U. S.-Israel Relations," *Jewish Quarterly Review* 99:4 (2009): 604.

Having a "Heart" for Israel

Evangelical pedagogy, though sermons, literature, and other educational resources, is littered with references to the "heart" and the use of one's "heart knowledge" over and above one's "head knowledge." Evangelicals consistently appeal to the distinction between heart and head knowledge,[45] and the need to "have a heart for Israel" is a phrase frequently invoked at CUFI events and within its affiliated churches. According to James Bielo's work with born-again Christians, "It is through the heart that the comprehension of spiritual matters is possible."[46] Or, as Melani McAlister elaborates, "Since at least the mid-1990s 'having a heart' has been used to evoke a passion that goes beyond mere predilection: it suggests an unplanned moment of contact with an issue that leads the believer to an understanding of the particular walk God has in mind for her." Such a notion, according to McAlister, enables a variety of evangelical political commitments. These commitments are constituted by practice more so than by belief, but are simultaneously oriented by certain regulatory devices, such as belief, without necessarily producing those practices.[47] Moreover, "To give your heart to God," according to Bielo, "means to recognize God's sovereignty over your life and to commit to place your relationship with God before all else."[48]

Rather than attempting to define the moment in which someone's "heart" is "touched" by God, let alone suggest that there is anything stable in what constitutes "heart knowledge," we can see this as a rhetorical strategy that places particular practices within the realm

45. See Melani McAlister, "What Is Your Heart For? Affect and Internationalism in the Evangelical Public Sphere," *American Literary History* 20:4 (2008): 870–95.
46. James S. Bielo, "Walking in the Spirit of Blood: Moral Identity among Born-Again Christians," *Ethnology* 43:3 (2004): 274.
47. McAlister, "What Is Your Heart For?" 870.
48. Bielo, "Walking in the Spirit of Blood," 274.

of God's sovereignty rather than the individual's. Thus "heart knowledge" is most usefully understood in contrast with "head knowledge"—knowledge that is associated with the flesh and fallible human beings. Because the flesh is part of the fundamentally immoral self, this knowledge is therefore at odds with God's will.[49] For Christian Zionists, and evangelicals more generally, the immorality of the flesh is extrapolated out to the immorality of the world. The perception that "the world" is against Israel, combined with Israel's cosmic significance in God's plans for the redemption of the world, enables Christian Zionists to discern their place in this narrative. If Christian Zionists want to be on the side of God, they need to be on the side of Israel, no matter what "the world" or popular opinion might tell them. As the pastor George Morrison put it to a group of CUFI members in 2010:

A long time ago I learned that you need to get on God's side if you expect anything to happen. And if you're in opposition to what God is trying to do in the world, you're just not going to succeed in a personal way, or in ministry. The only way we're going to succeed is if we align ourselves. I fear there's something happening even within what we call the circle of Christianity, and that is that more Christians, I'm finding out, are being moved by what they're logically seeing happening there [in Israel/Palestine], and by their emotions, and therefore standing in opposition against [sic] what God is doing, not understanding all the purposes of God. We cannot afford to be moved by our emotions; we have to be moved by the Word of God and what the Word of God tells us. It's a mandate. It's not one of those ministry things you can choose to do and not to do. But the nation of Israel, supporting the nation of Israel, is a mandate that comes from the very throne of God.[50]

Their habitus predisposes Christian Zionists to place Israel at the center of their hearts because it is at the center of God's. Moreover,

49. Ibid., 276.
50. George Morrison, "Why We Stand with Israel" (speech delivered at Christians United for Israel 5th Annual Washington, DC, Summit, July 20–22, 2010).

their knowledge of Israel's future in God's plans for the world means that they are privy to knowledge that the world is blind to because "the world" uses "head knowledge" to explain the conflict in the Middle East, attributing to it political rather than cosmic origins. Thus Morrison continued: "We are the watchmen that God has placed on the walls, to call out for God, to move on behalf of the nation of Israel, in protecting it, in guiding it, in giving it wisdom. *We who are Christian—not Jewish—but Christian, move not by emotions, but move by the Word of God.*"[51] Morrison's reference to Isa. 62:6 ("watchmen . . . on the walls") is frequently cited by Christian Zionists and provides a way for them to locate themselves in the biblical text as those whom God has called to protect Israel at this critical hour. By becoming watchmen and taking part in the active protection of Israel, Christian Zionists can see that God remains active in history and that he will keep his word to Israel. In the process, it helps strengthen Christian Zionists' faith (and thus their moral identity) that God will not forsake the promises that he has made to them, either. Morrison explained this clearly to his own congregation on another occasion:

> The study of prophecy, if for no other reason, is valuable to us as believers because it increases [our] faith. It builds my faith up to know that if God is faithful to His Word, down to the manipulation of nations and bringing them into existence at the right time for the right reasons, for the right purposes to be fulfilled, I mean, God's gonna take care of me. And He has the power to do it.[52]

To have a heart for Israel and the Jewish people, to contribute to the protection of Israel through prayer, financial donations, or political lobbying, helps to construct and strengthen Christian Zionists' moral

---

51. Ibid., emphasis added.
52. George Morrison, "Truth Matters . . . About the End Times," sermon delivered at Faith Bible Chapel, Arvada, CO, May 23, 2010.

identity. Such acts, when prefaced with various scriptural references, can act to redefine individuals as "watchmen on the wall," inserting them into the biblical text as divinely inspired subjects whom God has chosen to help further his will at this juncture in history.

Writing the Self into Scripture: A Dialectic of Submission and Volition

The figural association with characters from the Hebrew Bible is all the more compelling for Christian Zionists today because of that text's focus on God's will for the ancient Israelites, who, for Christian Zionists, are synonymous with modern Israelis. During the same sermon cited above, George Morrison helped define how biblical characters relate to Christians today, and therefore how Christians should relate to biblical characters:

> We have to try and put ourselves in their place; where they find themselves when these stories are unfolding. *Because, you see, the advantage we have is that we see the end of it.* ... There are things happening in our life right now that sometimes we throw up our hands and we say "I can't see any purpose in this whatsoever. I don't understand why this is happening to me." Our reaction to it is negative, and we find ourselves stumbling through life trying to work it out. *But that's where we have to trust, and that's why we have these messages so that we can glean from the experiences of others that have gone through it with God and we can learn ourselves.*[53]

The two emphasized sentences are instructive of the disposition wrought by what I have called the Christian Zionist habitus. The advantage of seeing the end of the story of a particular character is the advantage of seeing the end of the story of all characters—one that culminates in the establishment of God's kingdom. As a result,

---

53. Ibid., emphasis added.

members of the congregation become characters in that story, too. The reconstitution of contemporary Christian Zionists into Bible characters—actors in sacred history—further defines their habitus.

It is through the application of "heart knowledge" that women and men are called to submit to the will of God. If we think back to the position of Hagee quoted above regarding the inability of Christians to do anything to speed up God's timetable, and relate that to a reading of the Bible as the history of God using women and men to further his will on earth at certain critical points of danger, then it is possible to reconcile what seems to be a paradox between "forcing God's hand" and submitting to God's will.

Robert Alter argues that the portrayal of human nature in the Bible is caught in a "powerful interplay" between a "double dialectic of design and disorder, providence and freedom" whereby biblical narratives can be seen as "forming a spectrum between opposing extremes of disorder and design."[54] This dialectic is prevalent in the futurism that informs some of the prophetic elements of Christian Zionism. On the one hand, the future *is* known. On the other, the Bible remains silent regarding the present and the way those future events will unfold. Thus all that can be known about the present, in many respects, is its relation to the known future—its potential to fit within the structure discussed above.

Christian Zionists are, in many respects, caught in what I call "a dialectic of submission and volition." This dialectic is facilitated by their "heart knowledge," or their habitus, which orients and presents "events" that individuals can become active participants in, surrendering to what they understand as God's will for them, based on the orienting capacity of the habitus and their understanding of God's design for the world. On the one hand, Christians are called

54. Alter, *The Art of Biblical Narrative*, 12–13, 38.

to submit to what are described as God's plans for them, and this helps typify and give meaning to their political activities. On the other, there is an element of volition regarding the path they take, once again constrained and oriented by the habitus from which they view the world and through which events become significant. The trajectory of this volition is therefore historically determined through the habitus and continually shaped by current events, which become meaningful events (in the sense Sahlins described) by their potential to fit into a particular prophetic system.

Thus, while many observers might render a flattened interpretation of Christian Zionists' political activity that stipulates a direct line of causality from ostensibly fixed "beliefs" to action, the reality is more subtle and complex. It is thus more fitting to view political activities as what Max Weber might have described as Christian Zionists' "calling,"[55] a submission to God's plans (as understood through their orienting system) for the church in the end times. For the Christian Zionists with whom this essay is concerned, the fact that we are living in the liminal space between the passing away of current history and the establishment of Christ's kingdom stimulates and orients a search for signs and ways to actively participate in (and thus submit to) God's plans.

Reading the rhetoric of Christian Zionists on their own terms in relation to their understanding of our place on God's prophetic timetable—while at the same time redescribing this rhetoric—yields a more dynamic, multidimensional understanding of the relationship between Christian Zionists' interest in prophecy and their political activity. Although the prophetic timetable is nowhere near as fixed as Christian Zionists—or their sharpest critics—might assert, it does act, in a sense, as a backdrop or orienting structure against which

---

55. Max Weber, *The Protestant Ethic and the Spirit of Capitalism*, trans. Peter Baehr and Gordon C. Wells (London: Penguin, 2002).

faith is strengthened, a moral identity is cultivated, and God's will for individuals, through historical happenings, is discerned and continuously "revealed." Christian Zionists' habitus is at once receptive to these ideas and also shaped and further defined as a result of them and the products of history that they absorb. Moreover, the typological enactment of Scripture is conducive to exercising and bringing into existence one's heart knowledge or moral identity, the construction of which also paradoxically helps shape how and for what purposes stories are invoked in the first place.

With this understanding in mind, we can now turn to the book of Esther and the claims by Christian Zionists and their supporters that they have been called "for such a time as this." By examining the book, we can see how invocations of "for such a time as this" and the themes discussed above are rhetorically produced. This story and others like it become models of divine action undertaken by human instruments, and to follow them is to walk out the will of God. Along the way, we will see how ordinary, "profane" activities, such as political lobbying are reconstituted as a form of "sacred" or "religious" practice.

You Are Esther; Esther Is You

I noted above that the book of Esther has a relevant paradigmatic application for Christian Zionists though it is neither prophetic nor apocalyptic, troubling the notion that Christian Zionists act out of a purely literal interpretation of prophetic and apocalyptic texts. In what follows, I want to examine one way Esther is used to attach and transform the political work of contemporary Christian Zionists to what is described as God's will.

When members attend CUFI's annual meeting in Washington, DC, as I did in 2010 and 2011, they are greeted by banners that

juxtapose Isa. 62:6 ("I have posted watchmen on your walls, O
Jerusalem," NIV 1984) with Esther 4:14 ("For such a time as this"). As
many CUFI representatives would have it, that time is now. I have
also heard CUFI officials assert that the creation of the organization
was itself an act of God; although CUFI is said to have existed since
the "beginning of time," it has been loosed through intercessory
prayer to act as God's instrument in the world due to Israel's current
crisis. Yet rather than focus on the political work that flows out of
CUFI summits and other events, or what effect this work is having
in the supposedly irreligious domain of "secular" politics, I want
to examine what occurs before members arrive in Washington and
why a banner, or a speaker's reference to Esther 4:14, might inspire
a particular understanding in members taking part in what might
otherwise be considered the "profane" act of political lobbying. That
is, it is important to examine how Christian Zionists attach their
political work to what they assert is the much larger picture of God's
plans for the world in a way that enables them to further articulate
their moral identity.[56]

Biblical narrators of the past and present are skilled in their ability
to link one story to another. As Susan Harding points out, narrators
engaged in this kind of oratory tie together "tissues, sinews of divine
purpose, design and will that join concrete events across millennia."[57]
Thus when Robert Stearns told members of Faith Bible Chapel[58]
that "God sent me to Denver . . . to tell you there's a new breed of

56. For other examples of the use of Esther in this way, see Robert Stearns, *The Cry of Mordecai*
(Shippensburg, PA: Destiny Image, 2009); Larry Christenson, *The Mantle of Esther: Discovering
the Power of Intercession* (Grand Rapids: Chosen, 2008). While I am using Robert Stearns's
sermon on Esther here as the indicative example, one can also hear (as I did during my own
research) Esther used in the same manner throughout CUFI's constituent churches.
57. Susan Friend Harding, *The Book of Jerry Falwell: Fundamentalist Language and Politics* (Princeton,
NJ: Princeton University Press, 2000), 110.
58. Faith Bible Chapel is a nondenominational megachurch in Arvada, Colorado. Its pastors,
George and Cheryl Morrison, serve on the executive board of CUFI.

Christian that is rising up in the earth . . . and they are strong with the Lord and in the power of his might,"[59] and to share the story of Esther with them, it was not merely to share a parable that might relate to their lives in some way. Rather, it was to tell a historical story that typifies the modern church—one that, in his telling, the church needs to reenact if they are to submit to God and remain faithful to the purposes he has for them and, ultimately, the world. Stearns's language, in this respect, was performative. It was a prediction that made a claim about things as they "naturally are," and also brought about its utterance through the very act of speaking it.[60] Accordingly, Stearns's words placed him in the role of a modern prophet, an anointed speaker whom God was using to translate into practical terms what he had in mind for the American church.

The story of Esther tells of an ordinary Jewish woman who poses as a Gentile in order to replace the dethroned queen of Persia. Shortly after taking the throne, Esther's uncle Mordecai tells her of a plot devised by a government official named Haman to destroy all of the Jews in Persia because of their devotion to the God of Abraham, Isaac, and Jacob, and hence their unwillingness to abide by all the king's laws.[61] Although Mordecai warns Esther of the threats facing her people, she is initially unreceptive to his warnings; alerting the king to Haman's plans might compromise Esther's own life, so she remains silent. Finally, after numerous pleas from Mordecai, Esther accepts his challenge, noting that it might result in her own death ("If I perish, I perish," Esther 4:16). As a result, Esther saves the Jews of Persia[62] from

---

59. Unless otherwise indicated, the quotations that follow are all taken from Robert Stearns, "Becoming an Esther Church," sermon delivered at Faith Bible Chapel, Arvada, CO, October 18, 2009.

60. Pierre Bourdieu, *Language and Symbolic Power*, ed. John B. Thompson, trans. Gino Raymond and Matthew Adamson (Cambridge: Polity, 1991), 127–28.

61. This aspect of the story is another instance of "head knowledge" and worldly government attempting to silence true believers in the God of Israel who refuse to submit to its laws, which they argue are in conflict with those laws passed down by God.

62. And, in Hagee's telling of the story referenced above, the Jews of the entire world at the time.

their impending annihilation. The king ensures that the plot Haman hatched against the Jews is brought back on his own head; he and his sons are executed through the exact means by which they had intended to murder the Jews (Esther 9:25). Consequently, the Jewish holiday of Purim was established to celebrate the deliverance of these Persian Jews.

Yet as it is narrated by Christian Zionists, the story of Esther is more complex.[63] For the Christian Zionists whom I studied, Esther is not simply about a historical event that demonstrates and celebrates the deliverance of God's chosen people; it is also about human instrumentality, spiritual warfare, and the assertion that any ordinary individual can become a pivotal actor in God's plans. At a cosmic level, this was a plot to eradicate the lineage of the future Messiah, Jesus, and therefore the consummation of God's plans and the redemption of the world. Moreover, it is another historical confirmation of God's promise to bless those who bless his chosen people and curse those who curse them, evidenced by Haman's gruesome death at the place where he plotted Mordecai's demise.[64]

This interpretation, as well as what aspects of the story are emphasized and embellished, is far more complex than a simple "literal reading." While it is taken literally—that these events are historically accurate and happened as they were recorded—Christian Zionists find an additional, and perhaps more important, message about the nature of God and their relationship with him. As Simon Coleman argues, "The application of so-called literalism and doctrines of inerrancy in relation to the Bible is as much about embodying and 'living out' the text in a self-reinforcing process of

---

63. As it certainly is for other stripes of Christians and Jews. Naturally, however, my interest is in the emphasis Christian Zionists place on the story.

64. This is according to a Christian Zionist interpretation of Gen. 12:3. For further discussion on the Christian Zionist emphasis on "blessing" and interpretations/invocations of Gen. 12:3, see Durbin, "'I am an Israeli'"; Durbin, "'I Will Bless Those Who Bless You.'"

spiritual authentication as it is about the verbalized assertion that everything the Bible says is unproblematically 'true.'"[65] Moreover, the effective deployment of performative utterances in relation to the typological reenactment of Scripture occurs "at the crucial junctures in the lives of heroes," and is a "means of attaching that moment to a larger pattern of historical and theological meaning."[66] Keeping such insights in mind, it is worth considering how Stearns narrated the story of Esther—not only *to* his audience, but also how he narrated his audience *into* the story.

Stearns began by announcing that "Esther's life and Esther's example has never been more pertinent or applicable for the people of God than it is in this moment in time." By announcing the importance of Esther as a moral exemplar, the first thing Stearns established in his sermon was his audience's close relationship with her, allowing him, in Harding's words, to "enlist the listener"[67] and demarcate his role and authority, as well as his relationship to those in the audience. Enlisting the listener helps bring them into the story; it invites participation and binds the audience to the speaker in a relationship of dependence.[68] Again, appealing to (and thus producing and reinforcing) his audience's close relationship with Esther, Stearns told them that Esther:

> understood what it felt like to be on the outside. Unpopular, unwanted, not accepted. . . . Chances are there are some people here this morning who . . . would have written things a little differently than it seems like God has written for you.
>
> There was nothing in Esther's life . . . that would say "most likely to

65. Simon Coleman, *The Globalisation of Charismatic Christianity: Spreading the Gospel of Prosperity*, (Cambridge: Cambridge University Press, 2000), 118.
66. Alter, *The Art of Biblical Narrative*, 60, 72; Susan Friend Harding, "Convicted by the Holy Spirit: The Rhetoric of Fundamental Baptist Conversion," *American Ethnologist* 14:1 (1987): 172.
67. Harding, "Convicted by the Holy Spirit," 172.
68. Ibid.

succeed." There was nothing about her that would say: "Here's someone that would be written into the pages of history. Here's someone whose life is going to make a great difference." ... She was an average, ordinary, everyday person who life had not dealt a good hand to.

But God—aren't you glad this morning that we serve a God that says, "Your past does not equal your future"? Aren't you glad that we serve a God this morning who says, "My plans for you are greater than the plans that others may have spoken over your life"? And God had a plan for Esther—she didn't fully understand it, she didn't fully see it—you may not fully see this morning, the story that God is writing over the challenges of your life. But I promise you this morning if you're here ... God has a plan, a purpose, a destiny for your life.

Although Stearns emphasized Esther's ordinary identity and related it to the congregation's own concerns about money, status, and family issues, his emphasis on their shared identity performed a greater feat. Through their mutual ordinariness, they became extraordinary. Despite any feelings of failure or lack that they might hold, God wanted to use them for a greater purpose, just as he had used Esther; all they had to do was allow him. Moreover, Christian Zionists' self-understanding as persecuted was reinforced, in turn reinforcing their identity as a moral community committed to truth:

> Beloved, we are living in a moment in time where it is not popular to believe in the God of the Bible. We are living in a moment in time when it seems that all hell itself is arrayed against those who believe in this book. And the twin forces of secular humanism on one hand, and radical Islam on the other, are assaulting the very foundations of our faith.

However, just as this persecution did not matter for Esther, Stearns's implication was that it should not matter for Christians today. More importantly, Stearns emphasized the fact that Esther did not know *how* she would be used, just as individual Christians today do not necessarily know how God will use them. This does not matter because God knows how he will use them, and so long as they submit to God and privilege their heart knowledge over their head knowledge, God will guide them in the right direction:

And so Esther is transported into opulence and splendor.... She's enjoying the blessings . . . of the king.

While out here . . . Mordecai is off in a place called Susa. And Mordecai is aware that there is trouble brewing in Susa . . . that threatens all of the Jewish people. Haman has hatched his deadly plot. And over here in Susa or *Gaza*, or *Tehran* . . . Mordecai begins to try and get a message across to Esther: "Esther, there's danger for your people! Esther, I need your attention, there's problems here; you really need to listen, Esther!" But Esther is here and she's just so happy. She's just so blessed. And she can't hear Mordecai's message. Oh, she hears it; but she doesn't *hear* it. Church, there is a huge difference between hearing God's voice, and *hearing* God's voice.

And she says: "Mordecai, I really can't get involved . . . and I'm sorry for what's happening over there in the Middle East . . . but I'm really doing fine and things are secure, the economy's good, the military is strong and I'm protected and I'm doing well; I just can't get involved." . . . WHY couldn't Esther *hear* the voice of Mordecai? Why do we sometimes not *hear* the voice of the Holy Spirit warning us as we enjoy the blessings of the king?

[There are] two things that I suggest block our hearing that blocked Esther's hearing. Number one, I think Esther was distracted. . . . Esther was enjoying all the *stuff*; she was enjoying all the blessings. . . . *Esther didn't realize that she had been blessed unto a greater purpose.* The blessings were not simply there for her to enjoy. While God has blessed the American church . . . we can get distracted by the stuff. *And we can fail to realize that there's a greater purpose that God is writing us into.* And we've been blessed, and with blessing comes responsibility—"to whom much has been given, much is required."

The second reason I believe Esther couldn't hear the message of Mordecai, the message of the Spirit, was denial. I think Esther simply refused to believe that things could possibly be that bad. She simply refused to believe that it possibly could be so bad. Why? Because she worked all her life to just feel good. And she finally was feeling good and she didn't want to have to deal with the fact that there was a real threat that was finding her in the palace. . . . What did Esther not realize? Her life was already in danger. Precious American Church brothers and sisters, we had better wake up to the fact that our perceived security in America is a thin veneer. We had better wake up to the fact that Israel's battle is our battle in this moment. We had better stop being in denial and just thinking that everything's gonna continue to go on as it always has been and that we don't need to be vigilant about maintaining liberty in our nation. It is time for the Church to arise and to awaken.

So Esther is there in distraction and Esther is there in denial and Mordecai sends back this message, as I believe the Mordecai voice of the Holy Spirit is sending to us today: "Esther, do not think that because you're in the king's house"—don't think because you're in America—"that you alone will escape, for if you remain silent at this time, relief and deliverance will come from another place. But you and your father's family will perish. And who knows but that you, yes Esther, you"—poorly educated, unconnected, orphaned, not qualified, average ordinary you and me, who somehow say yes to God and God somehow decides to take our yes seriously—"Who knows, Esther, but that you have come to the kingdom for such a time as this?"

And now I want to show you what has become one of my all-time favorite places in all of Scripture . . . look at it please, the end of verse fourteen, do you see the word "this" and the question mark —"who knows that you have come to the kingdom for such a time as this?" Do you see that question mark? And then look at verse fifteen, the first word in my Scripture in verse fifteen is "Then." There's the question mark and then there's the "Then." And there's that little space in between the question mark and the "Then." And I would submit to you this morning that we are seated at this moment in time in that little space between God's question mark to us, and our answer to him. And Esther finally allowed the voice of Mordecai to penetrate her reality and she finally understood that it was not all about her; it was about a bigger plan, a bigger purpose, a bigger destiny.

Beloved, I'm here to tell you this morning, my prayer for you is that you will never be a nice local church. America does not need another nice local church. What we need is an embassy for the kingdom of God, to move and advance God's purposes and God's kingdom in this hour because we are in a moment of extraordinary battle.

Through this narration, the American church becomes Esther, and Esther becomes the American church. Ordinary Esther is transported into luxury, just as American Christians, while ordinary on the one hand, are also aware of their material and spiritual blessings. Yet as a result of these blessings, the church, according to Stearns, has become lazy. Thus when Stearns caricatured Esther ("Mordecai, I really can't get involved . . . and I'm sorry for what's happening over there in the Middle East . . . but I'm really doing fine and things are secure"), he was also speaking about the American church and their contemporary political moment, employing language ambiguous enough to refer to both. He placed concerns about the economy, military strength, and the Middle East into Esther's mouth before returning explicitly to the church: "Precious American church brothers and sisters, we had better wake up to the fact that our perceived security in America is a thin veneer." Significantly, Susa is now "Gaza, or Tehran," thus attaching the current political moment to the book of Esther, and vice versa, at once dissolving any contingent historical reality and investing in the conflict a sense of timeless universality. Those unwilling to recognize the reality of the Middle East—that Islam is a demonically inspired religion not only bent on destroying "Judeo-Christian" society but also on the cusp of succeeding—are therefore, like Esther prior to her transformation, in denial.

In this way, Stearns's sermon and others like it contribute to and help produce Christian Zionists' understanding of their role in the world, their instrumentality, and their need to submit to the plans into which, they are told, God is writing them. The emphasis on submission to God's plans, then, is crucial—how do Christian Zionists "know" what God's plans are for them? In a way, like Esther, they don't. This is what makes moments of particular urgency significant, whereby spontaneity and urgency are transformed into "heart knowledge" and a call from God. Moreover, because they do know "the end of the story," they are also imparted knowledge through people like Stearns who engender what Bourdieu calls "symbolic capital"[69] as men and women anointed by God. Such symbolic capital is not the result of something "special" inherent in a particular individual; rather, their audience attributes it to them. Preachers achieve this by situating their message in such a way that it is understood to be a direct mediation of the word of God and at the same time situating their listeners within that word. For many of their listeners, preachers like Stearns do not "interpret" the Bible; they merely convey what the author of a given biblical text—and by extension, God—is telling them.[70] The use of typology by contemporary Christian Zionist narrators frees biblical books from the time period in which they were written; their words, as God's words, are timeless. Accordingly, for his audience, Stearns did not interpret Esther; he merely conveyed what God was trying to tell the church through the "Mordecai voice of the Holy Spirit": that at this point in history, this crucial juncture in their lives as heroes, *in between the question mark and the then,* they were being called to be his instruments.

By using speech that is considered to emanate directly from the word of God, speakers—in this case Stearns, although it could be any of the thousands of pastors who share this oratory—ostensibly erase themselves and humble themselves, in turn evoking a similar sense of submission from the audience. This then creates a paradox

69. Pierre Bourdieu, *Outline of a Theory of Practice* (Cambridge: Cambridge University Press, 1977), 171.
70. Recall, for example, Hagee's sermon that resulted in John McCain rejecting Hagee's endorsement for his presidential bid in 2008. In the sermon, Hagee used Jeremiah to argue that God used Hitler as a "hunter" to force Jews back to Israel after the Holocaust, and then argued: "And that will be offensive to some people. Well, dear heart, be offended. I didn't write it, Jeremiah wrote it. It was the truth and it is the truth." In this way, Hagee takes himself out of the act of interpretation and merely portrays what God was and is apparently saying through the words of Jeremiah.

that enables speakers to invert the terms of their relationship to their listeners and the wider community and reproach those who speak for themselves. As Bourdieu puts it, "The right of reprimanding other people and making them feel guilty is one advantage enjoyed by the militant."[71] Moreover, this rhetorical act creates a sense that to not submit to God's word, in any setting with a speaker who commands biblical authority, would be to place human reasoning (head knowledge) over a divine calling (heart knowledge) and therefore be arrogant in the face of God. Stearns sums this up succinctly in his book upon which this sermon is based: "Life isn't always about what you choose; more often than not, it's about what chooses you."[72]

It would be remiss, however, to see this merely as a form of manipulation on Stearns's or any other Christian Zionist speaker's part, galvanizing political support by manipulating preexisting or somehow more pristine religious symbols. As Asad argues, determining what counts as orthodoxy amid change and disruption—in this case, social contests over the true meaning of Christianity and the threats (whether real or perceived) posed by Iran, Islam, and secular humanism, as Stearns characterized them[73]—requires the representation of the present "within an authoritative narrative that includes positive evaluations of past events and persons."[74] Importantly, this authority is not merely created by speakers filling their listeners with ideas, as though they were empty vessels willing to accept all that they hear. Rather, Asad continues, "Because such authority is a collaborative achievement between the narrator and audience, the former cannot speak in total freedom:

71. Bourdieu, *Language and Symbolic Power*, 211.
72. Stearns, *The Cry of Mordecai*, 204.
73. For more on this, see Durbin, "Mediating the Past through the Present and the Present through the Past."
74. Asad, *Genealogies of Religion*, 210.

there are conceptual and institutional conditions that must be attended to if discourses are to be persuasive."[75] It is for this reason that

> attempts ... at rendering such discourses as instances of local leaders manipulating religious symbols to legitimize their social power should be viewed skeptically ... because [such an approach] introduces the notion of a deliberative, rationalistic stance into descriptions of relationships where that notion is not appropriate.[76]

Asad's insights are useful in illuminating one way the Christian Zionist habitus works. The people Stearns was speaking to were not empty vessels but a receptive audience, products of a history that enabled him to provoke or challenge them while remaining within the parameters of acceptable discourse in order to attach a hostile stance toward Iran to a moment of divine triumph. In the process, he transformed this stance into one that was not only an acceptable form of Christian action in the world, but an obligatory one.

Similarly, as Harding puts it, this form of rhetoric and the narration of biblical stories to contemporary audiences is just as much about the listeners as it is about the characters. The speakers locate listeners and themselves between God and the biblical figures.[77] Just as Stearns listened to God and went to Denver to share the message of Esther, the same way Esther had listened to God and fulfilled the role that she had been written into, Stearns's story was also about his listeners. They too were characters in the story, and it was just as much about them as it was about Esther. It is this rhetoric, Harding argues, that gives this kind of preaching its efficacy. It is "not just a monologue that constitutes its speaker as a culturally specific person; it is also a dialogue that reconstitutes its listeners."[78] Although Harding's

---

75. Ibid.
76. Ibid., 210–11.
77. Harding, "Convicted by the Holy Spirit," 173.

concern is with the rhetoric of conversion and the transformation of "unsaved" listeners who appropriate the language of the speaker and become invested with a specific mode of organizing and interpreting experience, the effect here, on predominantly "saved" listeners, is similar. Stearns invested his listeners with a particular identity: they became sacred actors in the biblical narrative whom God was calling to act on his behalf at an important historical moment.

In this instance, Stearns brought the world into the text of Esther and at the same time used Esther as a device to frame and make significant a particular social and political moment. Again, Alter's point is illuminated through Stearns's performative speech. Through his sermon, Stearns situated Christians as the heroes at a critical juncture in history. He used the story of Esther to view Esther's actions as a type that fit into a larger pattern of historical and typological agency that has to be enacted in the present to ensure God's will is done in the world.

Conclusion:
"Political" Action as "Religious" Practice

Thinking about this particular reception and deployment of the book of Esther provides an interesting way of rethinking the relationship between Christian Zionists' "beliefs" and their political action in the world, in particular the notion that an unchanging "literal" reading of the Bible both precedes and plays a determinative role in terms of what activities are undertaken in the world. By focusing on Esther—a nonprophetic and nonapocalyptic text—I have shown that it is not an uncritical reception of dispensational theology, or the "literal" reading of texts like Revelation and Ezekiel—which *are* read

78. Ibid., 167.

prophetically—that compels Christian Zionists to "force God's hand." By examining the way aspects of Esther are emphasized and related to contemporary Christian Zionists today, we can see how Christian Zionists' political praxis is about constituting a moral identity, imagining oneself as having a special part in God's plans, and binding individuals into a larger moral community, thus producing and authenticating particular beliefs in the process.

By engaging with Christian Zionists on some of their own terms, while at the same time remaining unyielding in terms of critical scrutiny, we can see how the interpretation of a given text is dependent on a complex array of social, political, historical, and cultural factors. In this instance, Stearns brought the world into the text of Esther and at the same time used Esther as a device to frame and make significant the current social and political moment. On the one hand, this is achieved through the kinds of authoritative narration that make the text relevant to the present. On the other, its reception is not based on a sui generis, psychological impulse, a simple "literal" interpretation, or a process of calculated manipulation, but rather a historically constructed disposition to accept certain modes of knowing as divine truth.

It is through such analysis that we can reframe and rethink the relationship between the apocalyptic outlook of many Christian Zionists and their political action. Christian Zionist activities are arguably not about "hastening Armageddon" or the end times, as many critics would have it, precisely because—at least for the Christian leaders of CUFI—those times are upon us. Rather, these activities are about acting as God's instruments and blocking activities that might impede God's plans for the world.

This is the way that we might consider how apocalyptic "beliefs" relate to political action. Many Christian Zionist activities—lobbying for tougher sanctions on Iran, asserting Israel's right to a preemptive military strike on Iran, or attempting to obstruct the election of officials who might take a "hard line" against Israel or a "softer" line with Iran—are not about actively making things happen. Prophetically minded Christian Zionists do not necessarily do things purely out of their own volition in a calculated attempt to enact what needs to occur through their prophetic readings. Rather, they respond to events that fit in the larger structure or lens—their habitus—that makes events in the world significant in the first place. In this sense, it is about clearing the way for God's will to be worked out in the world as the end times unfold. And it is through this work that ostensibly ordinary political action becomes reconstituted as a form of "religious" practice. Christian Zionists are not "forcing God's hand" through their political efforts but are rather, as one pastor put it to a group preparing to lobby congress in 2010, "walking in the mantle of Esther."

6

———

Christian Zionism at Jerusalén Church in Copán Ruinas, Honduras, an "Out-of-the-Way" Place

William Girard

Studies of Christian Zionism have almost exclusively focused on how this movement emerged in Great Britain and the United States and later came to have powerful consequences for the Middle East. This attention to Great Britain and the United States makes a great deal of sense, especially for those of us concerned about Christian Zionism's effects in the Middle East. However, as Protestant churches (largely Pentecostal and charismatic) rapidly expand in Asia, Africa, and Latin America, many of them are translating Christian Zionism into diverse spaces and cultures. In order to gain a clear picture of the variety of Christian Zionisms that exist today, scholars must begin to examine its distinct manifestations and consequences in what anthropologist Anna Tsing has called "out-of-the-way" places.[1] We need to ask how Christian Zionism has taken shape in places with different histories than the United States or Great Britain. For example, does Christian Zionism look different in countries that were never colonial powers? What effects have secular states' relationships with Israel had on the forms of Christian Zionism that have taken root within those countries? Does Christian Zionism have a different expression in Haiti (where Israel recently sent a large number of doctors and medical supplies in the wake of a devastating earthquake) than in Nicaragua (where Israel armed the brutal right-wing Contra forces during the 1980s)? Further, the role of Christian Zionists in the United States and Great Britain in shaping the Middle East have now been well documented,[2] but have Christian Zionists from other countries had an impact on the Middle East? That is, should Christian Zionism in El Salvador matter to anyone besides Salvadoran Christian Zionists? Should it matter, for example, to Palestinians?

These are difficult questions to answer. My aim in this chapter is to take a modest step toward answering some of them. As an anthropologist, I begin this investigation through grounded attention to congregants' daily practices in a single Pentecostal church, *Jerusalén*, in the small town of Copán Ruinas, Honduras. Overall, I suggest the importance of both (1) a particular racial and ethnic history in Honduras and (2) the geographic imaginary of the nation

---

1. A. L. Tsing, *In the Realm of the Diamond Queen: Marginality in an Out-of-the-Way Place* (Princeton, NJ: Princeton University Press, 1993).
2. See, for example, Victoria Clark, *Allies of Armageddon: The Rise of Christian Zionism* (New Haven, CT: Yale University Press, 2007); Stephen Sizer, *Christian Zionism: Road Map to Armageddon?* (Leicester: Inter-Varsity, 2004); and Timothy P. Weber, *On the Road to Armageddon: How Evangelicals Became Israel's Best Friend* (Grand Rapids: Baker Academic, 2004).

as a single, independent unit for the ways in which Christian Zionism is remade within *Jerusalén* Church.

Jerusalén in Honduras

Jerusalén is one of around eighteen churches that are currently active in the small town of Copán Ruinas. The vast majority of these churches are both Pentecostal and Christian Zionist. *Jerusalén's* church structure is located a bit outside of town and across the Copán River, the result of a specific effort by the church leadership to put both physical and symbolic distance between it and the rest of the community. This decision is not lost on the general population of Copán. By and large, adults in the church form part of Copán's small middle class: they are schoolteachers, work in banks, or own their own modest businesses.

My first experience with Christian Zionism took place in the summer of 2006 when I was renting a room with the Rodriguez family—prominent members of *Jerusalén*—as part of my preliminary fieldwork. Early in my visit, I was chatting over dinner with Enrique, the husband and father of the family, when, no doubt in response to my endless questions about his Pentecostal beliefs, he asked about my own religious background. A little nervous about how he would respond, I explained that I had been raised in a Jewish household. Upon hearing this, Enrique slowly stood up, threw his arms out, and exclaimed, "Welcome to my home!" He told me that his family prayed for Israel every night, and that they consider Jews to be their *hermanos* (brothers). Normally calm in his demeanor, Enrique became quite excited as he walked over to my side of the table and sat down next to me. "You know, I wasn't sure if renting out that room was the right thing to do, but now that there is a Jew staying there, I know it was the right choice."[3]

Enrique's response was the first of many experiences during my fieldwork in which members of *Jerusalén* displayed incredible affection for me based on my Jewish heritage. The flip side of this warmth was displayed in the malicious comments I would often hear members of the community make about Muslims, Arabs, and particularly Palestinians. As with many Christian Zionists, the *Jerusalén* community maintains that God blesses Jews because they are the descendants of Isaac (Abraham's son with his wife Sarah, a son God promised to Abraham), while Muslims are seen as cursed and under the control of Satan as the spiritual descendants of Ishmael (Abraham's son with Sarah's handmaiden Hagar). *Jerusalén*'s pastor would often preach that Palestinians are the equivalent of beasts, that they live completely in the flesh, and that their jealousy over the blessings that God has given to the Jews overwhelms their consciences. A number of times the pastor claimed that "Kill a Jew, go to heaven" is a common phase among Palestinians in the Middle East.

While this antipathy toward Arabs and Palestinians is not uncommon among Christian Zionists, in Honduras these sentiments emerge within a particular history of racial and ethnic formation. Honduras has a significant population of people of Palestinian descent. In fact, since the early twentieth century Palestinian immigrants to Honduras (often called *Turcos* because they carried Ottoman passports when they first began to arrive) have asserted significant control over large-scale commerce and, especially, the import and export commercial sector in the North Coast department of Cortés.[4] Hence, while numerically Honduran Palestinians

3. All quotes in this chapter are reconstructions from field notes, which were often taken shortly after the events occurred.

constitute a small minority of the population, their presence has had significant consequences for the country.[5] There is also a small (around 100 families in a nation of 7.3 million) but economically powerful community of Honduran Jews whose ancestors immigrated to Honduras at the same time as the Palestinians and who occupy similar positions within the national economy.

Both Jews and Arabs in Honduras are situated as others in relation to the national body. They are distinct from both the formerly hegemonic discourse of *mestizaje*, which imagined all Hondurans as the descendants of both the Spanish and indigenous population, and the contemporary discourse of multiculturalism, an attempt to include what have often been considered "uncivilized," marginal peoples (primarily Afro-Hondurans and the indigenous) as full members of the Honduran nation. Common stereotypes of both Honduran Palestinians and Jews portray them as obsessed with money, cheap, and unconcerned about the well-being of other Hondurans.

La crisis and the End Times

Before exploring further the ways in which Christian Zionism is remade in *Jerusalén*, it is important to consider a bit of recent Honduran history. In the early morning of June 28, 2009, soldiers from the Honduran military stormed the president's residence on orders from the country's Supreme Court to arrest President Manuel

4. See D. A. Euraque, *Reinterpreting the Banana Republic: Region and State in Honduras, 1870–1972.* Chapel Hill: University of North Carolina Press, 1996), 30–35; and N. L. S. González, *Dollar, Dove, and Eagle: One Hundred Years of Palestinian Migration to Honduras* (Ann Arbor: University of Michigan Press, 1992), 68–72, 99.
5. Based on surveys from 1989, D. A. Euraque, *Conversaciones Históricas con el Mestizaje y Su Identidad Nacional en Honduras* (San Pedro Sula, Honduras: Centro Editorial, 2004), argues that perhaps 4 percent of Honduras are "of Palestinian decent" (*de descendencia Palestina*) (94).

Zelaya. The soldiers overwhelmed Zelaya's personal guard, took him into custody, and had him flown to Costa Rica. The immediate reason for this first successful coup d'état in Latin America since the end of the Cold War was a nationwide, nonbinding vote Zelaya was sponsoring to gauge popular opinion about whether a constitutional assembly should be called to rewrite the Honduran constitution, a move that the Supreme Court ruled was illegal.

While the referendum was the immediate reason for the coup d'état, it was part of a history in which, after campaigning and then governing for two years as a moderate, Zelaya angered the national elite when he moved sharply to the political left, developing close relationships with other leftist Latin American leaders such as Hugo Chávez and raising the Honduran minimum wage by 60 percent. Following the coup, after two attempts to reenter Honduras, Zelaya suddenly appeared in late September 2009 at the Brazilian embassy in the nation's capital, Tegucigalpa. The Honduran military and police quickly surrounded the embassy, and Zelaya was unable to leave the building for fear of being arrested.

The period leading up to the national referendum and the months that followed the coup were filled with incredible tension. *La crisis*, as it was called, was always the first topic of conversation when you ran into someone on the street. No one knew what was going to happen, but the realm of the possible had grown much larger. Most people never thought the coup would happen, but then it did. What other possibilities had been mistakenly judged as impossible?

Beginning a few weeks before the proposed referendum and continuing for a couple months after the coup, the *Jerusalén* pastor gave a series of sermons laying out a scenario for the end times. These sermons provided little information that the congregation would not have heard before, but the content was presented with an order and clarity that I had never encountered. The most relevant aspect of these sermons for Christian Zionism in the church was the way the pastor divided the western hemisphere according to a Manichaean-type dualism. On one side of the geographic and ideological split were the socialist (and even left of center) countries throughout Latin America: Venezuela, Nicaragua, Bolivia, Brazil, and now, with Barack Obama as president, the United States as well. On the other side were the countries with governments to the right of center, most prominently Colombia.

Both sides of this division were then associated with a parallel geographic and religious binary in the Middle East: the left with Muslims, the right with Israel. Particularly through references to Hugo Chávez's relationship with the president of Iran, Mahmoud Ahmadinejad, the pastor maintained that a socialist–Muslim alliance[6] would soon provide the armies of the Antichrist during the end times. In contrast, the pastor asserted that countries that continued to support Israel would receive divine blessings. Before the coup, the pastor rhetorically positioned Honduras as dangerously close to becoming part of the socialist–Muslim alliance. After the coup, when the conservative head of the Honduran Congress, Roberto Micheletti, replaced Zelaya, he described Honduras as in a liminal space between the two sides. The church's responsibility would be to pray for God to once again firmly situate Honduras on the right-wing/Israel/God side of the binary.

Israeli Radiation?

Christian Zionists were not the only people who considered Israel and the Jews relevant to those extraordinary times. A few days after

---

6. This is not an uncommon association made by Christian Zionists. Also, since his presidential campaign, many on the right in the United States have argued that Barack Obama is both a socialist and a secret Muslim.

his return to Honduras, while still trapped in the Brazilian embassy, former president Zelaya conducted an interview with *The Miami Herald* in which he claimed that Israeli mercenaries were torturing him and others in the embassy with "high-frequency radiation."[7] The next day on the leftist radio station, Radio Globo, the station's executive director, David Romero, used Zelaya's statement as a launching pad to assert, "There are times when I ask myself if Hitler was or was not correct in finishing with that race with the famous Holocaust. If there are people that do damage in this country, they are Jewish, the Israelis."[8]

These comments caught the attention of major media outlets in Honduras and the United States, including *The New York Times* and the Associated Press. The statements drew sharp condemnation from Jewish institutions, including the Anti-Defamation League and the Simon Wiesenthal Center, as well as right-wing Zionist blogs from Israel and the United States. In most of these sources, whether from the United States, Israel, or Honduras, Zelaya's claims that Israeli mercenaries were involved in the Honduran crisis were depicted as fantastic, the result of the deposed president's deepening paranoia. In addition, their clear concern was that these comments would lead to discrimination or possibly even violence directed at the tiny Honduran Jewish community.

While most sources in the Honduran and English-language media dismissed the idea that Israeli mercenaries were involved in the crisis, the members of *Jerusalén* were certain that the Israeli military *was* involved, not only at the Brazilian embassy, but also in providing the

7. F. Robles, "'They're torturing me, Honduras' Manuel Zelaya claims," *The Miami Herald,* September 24, 2009.
8. D. Romero, "Jews As Scapegoats in the Honduras Political Stalemate: Anti-Semitic Statements," Anti-Defamation League (September 25, 2009), available online at http://archive.adl.org/main_Anti_Semitism_International/Jews_Scapegoats_Honduras.htm?Multi_page_sections=sHeading_3 (accessed June 18, 2013).

Honduran military with training and intelligence. According to the *Jerusalén* community, Israel became involved in the crisis as the result of Honduras's support for Israel. That is, Israel was seen as paying Honduras back for both its political support and the prayers that came from churches like *Jerusalén.*

In addition, while I am certain that the members of *Jerusalén* were concerned about the consequences of Romero's comments for the Jewish minority in Honduras, they never mentioned them. Rather, their anxiety was specifically a matter of what these comments might mean for the future of Honduras as a whole. Just as Honduras could be blessed if it blessed Israel, it could also be cursed if it turned against Israel. Honduras was now in a liminal state, but it could quickly end up back on the left-wing/Muslim/Antichrist side of the binary. Indeed, the scale of the nation-state and a concomitant geopolitical imaginary whereby nations are viewed as autonomous actors with their own agency and character as friends and enemies[9] was the dominant way that the *Jerusalén* community described the situation. It was not only individuals' futures that Zelaya and Romero's comments would affect, but also the whole of Honduras.

Honduran Palestinians and the Civilized/Barbarian Divide

Based on the previous description of *Jerusalén's* members' sentiments toward *Palestininas,* one might expect that they would routinely blast the Honduran Palestinian minority as an internal threat that places Honduras's relationship with Israel and its fate during the end times in danger. This was certainly my expectation. Yet as I conducted my fieldwork, I waited for the pastor or members of the congregation to

---

9. See J. Agnew, *Geopolitics: Re-visioning World Politics* (New York: Routledge, 2003); and S. Dalby, "Calling 911: Geopolitics, Security and America's New War," in *Geopolitics* 8:3 (2003): 61–86.

discuss Honduran Palestinians, but it never happened. Finally, after hearing nothing for months, I started to ask members of *Jerusalén* about Honduran Palestinians, explaining that I often heard them talk about Palestinians in the Middle East but never about Palestinians in Honduras.

The answers I received were not uniform. Even the same person would give different responses at different times. Nevertheless, while these views were quite diverse, they did follow some common Pentecostal tropes or scripts. First, there was the trope of the internal enemy that I had expected. "The *turcos* here are always against Israel. They carry with them the same spirit of the Enemy [like those in the Middle East]," one member of the community told me. Second, there was also the trope of development, which lauded the presence of Palestinians in the country: "They've brought a lot of progress to Honduras, and a lot of money." Finally, they expressed the trope of individual salvation: "It depends on the person. If he has been born again he will be like any other Christian."

What accounts for this diversity of views about Palestinians within Honduras as opposed to the unitary vision of Palestinians in the Middle East? One option is that the vast majority of Palestinians who immigrated to Honduras were not Muslims, but rather Orthodox Christians, with many of them later converting to Catholicism. However, while this might be part of the story, the *Jerusalén* community often does not make a clear division between the categories of religion and ethnicity. For example, someone with Jewish ancestry (a descendant of Isaac) would still receive divine blessings even if—like me—she or he were not a practicing Jew. In this way, even if a person of Arab or Palestinian descent were Catholic, he or she would still be considered a descendant of Ishmael (only the experience of being born again is regarded as capable of transforming this aspect of one's heritage).

Another option, and one I consider more important, is that Honduran Palestinians do not fit well with the visions of hierarchy within the *Jerusalén* community. Members of *Jerusalén* tend to view wealth as a blessing from God. Unlike popular representations of Palestinians in the Middle East, Honduran Palestinians have a reputation for being wealthy. As a result, they do not fit well with the church's imaginary of people who go against the will of God. Further, unlike indigenous and black Hondurans, Honduran Palestinians are generally regarded as falling on the "civilized" rather then the "barbarian" side of a civilized/barbarian binary that is alive within *mestizo* culture. Or put another way, Honduran Palestinians were never viewed as a racial or ethnic group that held back national progress.

Anti-Palestinian Sentiment

In this chapter, I have argued for the importance of considering the diverse ways that Christian Zionism has been remade outside Great Britain and the United States, suggesting the scholars interested in Christian Zionism also turn their attention to its diverse manifestations and consequences in other places. As a step in this direction, I have detailed how Christian Zionism was translated into one church in Copán Ruinas, Honduras, focusing on both a geographical imaginary of the nation as an autonomous actor and a specific history of ethnic and racial formation in Honduras. My hope is that this modest attempt will encourage others to think about Christian Zionism in a range of "out-of-the-way" places.

7

Christian Zionist Pilgrimage in the Twenty-first Century

The "Holy" in the "Holy Land"

Curtis Hutt

What is "holy" about the "Holy Land" to diverse groups of Christian Zionist pilgrims in the twenty-first century? In this chapter,[1] I present the results of two paths of research—one historical, the other anthropological. In addition to comparing predominant Christian Zionist responses to this question with that of Christian forebears, I correlate these answers to those derived from anthropological investigation of Christian pilgrimage to the Holy Land in the present. Attending to context, recent developments are placed side by side with those encountered upon examination of local Palestinian

---

1. I want to thank the following University of the Holy Land graduate students (past and present) for their contributions to this text: Rachel Faisst, Laura Hull, Samuel Martin, and the late Shigeko Rakosi.

Christian pilgrimage as well as Jewish and Islamic pilgrimage to religious sites in Israel and the Occupied Territories.

Even though some contemporary Christian Zionists have argued that their practices and beliefs are based on historical precedents established by earlier "Bible-believing" Christians and biblical traditions, comparison of their practices and beliefs with those of earlier Christians reveals the novelty of their approach to pilgrimage to the Holy Land. In addition to contrasting Christian Zionist religious travel to Israel with that of Roman Catholic, Eastern Orthodox, and Oriental Orthodox pilgrimage in the present, I will compare it to journeys made—and intentionally not made—by earlier Protestants. When Christian Zionists who travel to and sometimes take up long-term residency in Jerusalem frequent traditional Christian sites like the Church of the Resurrection/Holy Sepulchre and the Church of the Nativity, they oftentimes resemble non-Christian tourists who do not acknowledge the sacredness of these traditional places of worship. However, this is not always because they share the iconoclasm of earlier Protestants. In many cases, present-day Christian Zionists have substituted new Christian pilgrimage destinations for old ones in this new Holy Land.

Before beginning a review of graduate fieldwork on Christian Zionist pilgrimage in the present, I want to set the stage by examining historical Christian answers to the question, What is "holy" about the "Holy Land?"—or, at least for Christian forebears living prior to the Crusades, "holy sites" found in this geographical location.[2] This chapter is thereby an exercise in comparative

2. As noted by Tomaž Mastnak in *Crusading Peace: Christendom, the Muslim World, and Western Political Order* (Berkeley: University of California Press, 2002), 119–20, the "Holy Land" (*terra sancta*) was a "crusading invention." Prior to the Crusades, sacred space in the area of the Eastern Mediterranean was—as evidenced in the enforcement of purity regulations—limited to specific temples, shrines, and sometimes cities. Entire "lands" or "countries" were never considered "holy." Hebrew and Greek etymological equivalents for the Medieval Latin "*terra sancta*" are not found in the Tanakh or Christian New Testament.

sacramentalism, similar to and building upon work done by other scholars but with an expanded scope.[3]

Below is a scale measuring the degree of iconoclasm in Christian theological traditions (see table). By examining the degree of iconoclasm in different Christian groups, I believe that we can assess major differences in the approach of various pilgrims to the Holy Land. My main focus is on the religious convictions and propensities that pilgrims bring with them on their journeys. There is typically great variety among self-identified members of what sometimes appear to be unified historical Christian traditions; therefore, designations do not occupy single points along the iconoclasm scale but a range of positions. Given the human tendency to posit supernatural causes for peculiar phenomena and produce anthropomorphisms, one must acknowledge that there are always exceptions to these general ratings. As controls, I supply general references to Jewish, Muslim, and nonreligious iconoclasm. I have then divided the Christian world into three main groups—Oriental Orthodox miaphysites, Roman Catholic and Eastern Orthodox diophysites, and Protestant diophysites.

By *iconoclasm* I refer to the rejection in ideology and practice of images (*eikona*) understood by others to be sacred—whether these are specific paintings or statues, individuals or groups of people, or locations. Iconoclasts deny that an image, person, or place can encapsulate the divine. Note that by this definition, all Christians—at least those who affirm the statement of faith adopted at the Council

3. See, for example, Faydra Shapiro's "To the Apple of God's Eye: Christian Zionist Travel to Israel," *Journal of Contemporary Religion* 23.3 (2008), 307–20, and Glenn Bowman's "Christian Ideology and the Image of the Holy Land: The Place of Jerusalem Pilgrimage in the Various Christianities," in *Contesting the Sacred: The Anthropology of Christian Pilgrimage*, ed. John Eade and Michael Sallnow (London: Routledge, 1991), 98–121. In this chapter, I explore a greater variety of Christian Zionist pilgrimage to Israel than is addressed in Shapiro's article and, complementing Bowman's work on this topic, make comparisons to a wider range of historical Christian pilgrimage traditions.

of Nicea—are, to one degree or another, not iconoclastic. Whether they believe Jesus to be the son of God or that different saints or more generally all humans are images of the divine, Christians are markedly less iconoclastic than atheists as well as many Jews and Muslims. Most atheists, of course, deny the existence of the divine, supernatural, and sacred in the world. In Judaism and Islam, images of the divine are forbidden. Synagogues and mosques are not houses of the divine. Religious leaders and specialists are recognized to be flawed humans. There are exceptions to these generalizations—notably the sacred nature of the Torah and Qu'ran, the special character of key pilgrimage sites like that of the former Jerusalem temple and the Ka'aba, and some highly esteemed Jewish miracle workers (*baalei mofet*) like Rabbi Yisrael Abuhatzeira as well as the twelfth Shia imam. Acknowledging this variety of belief and practice in these non-Christian and Christian assemblages, one can still plot out with relative ease A, J, and I on the table below.

Christianity and Iconoclasm

Before plotting out Christian Zionist understandings of the "holy" in the "Holy Land," I will examine the different historical views of various Christian groups on sacred images, people, and places. First, I will quickly review the respective christologies of miaphysites (less tolerably titled "monophysites") and diophysites—the two main approaches to the topic of Jesus Christ's divinity and humanity across diverse Christian theological traditions. While miaphysites and diophysites agree that Jesus was the divine son of God, exactly what they mean by this parallels and sets precedents for their iconoclasm or lack thereof.

Miaphysite Christians—like Egyptian and Ethiopian Copts, Armenians, and Oriental Orthodox Christians from Syria to

India—reject the view adopted at the Council of Chalcedon that Christ was a "hypostasis" of two distinct natures (divine and human) joined in a single person. Instead, Christ was dominated by one nature as the divine spirit flooded his humanity. The alternative diophysite position allowed Chalcedonian Orthodox communities as well as Roman Catholics and Protestants to explain theological conundrums like how Christ could suffer and die (this was his human legacy). To explain in the simplest terms a complicated theological debate that raged across decades and patriarchates in Christian antiquity, rather than being fully divine and completely subjugated by one nature, Christ was both fully human *and* fully divine.

Following similar reasoning, diophysites came to maintain that sacred images, people, and places had two natures—they were weak, finite vessels that at the same time contained the divine spirit. Through these material bodies, and in spite of them, religious truths were revealed. Icons and statues, while transmitting sacred revelations and teachings, were not materially holy. Churches and the altars contained therein were understood in the same way. Religious leaders, furthermore, were still capable of sinful action in spite of the sacred office they held. Sainthood could only be bestowed on persons after the death of their corporal forms.

Miaphysite Christians, on the other hand, have maintained the least iconoclastic positions—along with the most "superstitious" members of other traditions of popular Christian piety—plotted on the iconoclasm scale located at the end of this chapter. Provoking the criticism and sometimes wrath of diophysite Christians[4] and iconoclastic Muslims alike, they consider icons to be not simply teaching tools but holy objects—actual portals to the divine through

4. This very rudimentary account of Chalcedonian "sacramentalism" is complicated by the work of diophysite thinkers like John of Damascus who defend the use of holy icons in Christian worship.

which miracles might occur (e.g., the "Image Not-Made-By-Hands" of King Abgar). Likewise, their crosses are often considered not simply symbols of the faith but powerful sacred objects. The sanctity of their sanctuaries is utterly inviolable. Just as Jesus was considered fully holy in body as well as soul, miaphysite Christians famously show unconditional respect and deference to their religious leaders. Saints are so named in life, not only upon death.[5] See the designations DC, MC, and P below.

Christian Zionism originally emerged among some of the most iconoclastic of Protestant radical reformers—nonconformist/free churches found throughout the English speaking world as well as the descendants of Anabaptism in the nineteenth century. Not only did these Protestant Christians reject the holy fathers of the Roman Catholics, but the ordained leaders of state churches like the Church of England and several Lutheran bodies as well. Generally speaking, they recognized no space as more holy than others. The holiness of religious rites like the commemoration of the Lord's Supper depended not upon the sacred nature of the altar, apostolic succession, or the actual transformation of bread and wine into body and blood. Instead, the significance was symbolic or spiritual. Pilgrimage to sacred sites in the Holy Land was in no way a priority as it was for Roman Catholics, Eastern Orthodox, and miaphysite Christians. Like Martin Luther, many equated pilgrimage to Rome, Santiago de Compostela, and Jerusalem with idolatry. In the same vein as John Calvin in Geneva, several conceived of their own communities as the new Jerusalem. In some Protestant countries, pilgrimage was banned entirely, as it was from the sixteenth to the twentieth century in Lutheran Sweden. One might be fully Christian without traveling to

5. See Peter Brown's work on the origin of this cult of saints in ancient Syria and Egypt in texts like *The Body and Society* (New York: Columbia University Press, 1988) and *Society and the Holy in Late Antiquity* (Berkeley: University of California Press, 1989).

traditional holy sites in the Near East and elsewhere. The indwelling of the Holy Spirit might occur just as easily in Akron, Ohio as Jerusalem. Spiritual rebirth, or being "born again" as emphasized by early Anabaptists and many thereafter, could happen anywhere. In fact, the importance of making pilgrimage to sacred locations like the Church of the Resurrection/Holy Sepulchre faded away entirely for many Protestant reformers. These traditions are plotted out as NC, AB, R, L, and ACE on the iconoclasm scale.

The relationships between Christian Zionists and Jews in the nineteenth century were also extraordinarily different from those of other Christians at the same time and before them. For example, while early Christian Zionists were deeply involved in proselytizing the Jewish people, their mission was different from those who focused on extending political/cultural hegemony or carrying out acts of mercy. The dispensational premillennialist goal of converting and/ or returning Jews to Jerusalem in preparation for the messianic age is markedly absent as a motivational factor for many nineteenth-century Christian missionary groups. As shown by John Conway, missions to the Jews in the Protestant world during this time—like those of Roman Catholics preceding them—were often aimed at extending European (e.g., Anglo-Saxon) "cultural imperialism."[6] Others, like the Roman Catholic founders of the Sisters of Sion, Theodor and Maria Alphonse Ratisbonne, missionized Jews in Jerusalem with the intention of saving them—not necessarily to usher in the millennial age. Even when the founders of Christian missions to the Jews like Franz Delitzsch were inclined toward premillenialism, they oftentimes didn't believe Jewish return to the Holy Land was a realistic option.[7]

---

6. See John Conway, "Protestant Missions to the Jews 1810–1980: Ecclesiastical Imperialism or Theological Aberration?" *Holocaust and Genocide Studies* 1 (1986): 127–46.
7. Franz Delitzsch, an ardent Christian defender of Judaism who founded the Evangelical Lutheran Central Society for Missions among Israel in 1869 and Institutum Judaicum in

There were several catalysts for Christian advocacy of Jewish return to the Holy Land among generally iconoclastic groups in the nineteenth century. First and foremost was the belief, brought on by a commitment to dispensational premillennialism, that the end times were near. At times, this was combined with: (a) the promotion of "original exemplars" from early Judaizing forms of Christianity; (b) political agendas; and (c) popular experientalist forms of Christianity. Such amalgamations are not always present, though. Rarely, Christian advocacy of Jewish restoration to the land has relied solely on one of the latter catalysts.

Most importantly, those advocating the return of Jews to their ancient homeland felt little compulsion to engage in or promote large-scale Christian pilgrimage to the Holy Land. This is not to say that Protestant Christians who believed, for example, that the end of the world was nigh or that it could be speeded up did not travel to the Holy Land during this time. Several of the oldest Christian Zionist groups did precisely this—but not, at least primarily, to make pilgrimage to Christian holy sites. Their goal instead was to hurry the return of the Messiah by converting Jews and aiding their return to their biblical homeland.

Such dispensational premillennialism had a huge effect on English, Scottish, and Irish nonconformist Christians like the Plymouth Brethren movement of John Nelson Darby and American evangelicals like D. L. Moody and William Eugene Blackstone. Influenced by the latter, the Spafford family founded the American Colony in Jerusalem in 1881 with the help of Swedish premillennialists. While mainstream Anglicans, Lutherans, and Calvinists were not as influenced by such end-times thinking, these

1880, did not believe that Jewish return to the land was a real possibility, as evidenced in his nonliteralist reading of Ezek. 37:21. See Carl Friedrich Kiel and Franz Delitzsch, *Biblischer Commentar über das Alte Testament* 3.3 (Leipzig: Dörffling & Franke, 1868).

traditions were not free from such sentiments. For example, an independent Anglican missionary society founded in 1809 known as the London Society for Promoting Christianity Amongst the Jews (today titled CMJ: The Church's Ministry Among Jewish People) was perhaps the earliest of such groups active in Jerusalem. In 1873, the Temple Society—an offshoot of pietistic Lutherans—founded the German Colony in Jerusalem out of millenarian motivations. It was not traditional Christian sacred sites that attracted these groups to the Holy Land but the promise of a future new Jerusalem once the Jewish people were returned to their land and reconciled with the risen son of God.

Less well known, Judaizing Christian groups—sometimes holding premillennialist beliefs and missionary agendas but sometimes not—have supported and even joined Jewish migration to the Holy Land. Whereas during the medieval period Christian pilgrimage to the Holy Land was often associated with violent anti-Semitic activity,[8] groups from Eastern Europe like the Transylvanian Szekler Sabbatarians and Russian Subbotniki adopted Jewish religious practices and joined Jews emigrating to Israel. From the time of Elizabeth I, Sabbatarianism made its way to Western Europe and the British Isles via Dutch Anabaptists, Polish Brethren, Socinians, and some members of Reformed churches. From here it traveled throughout the British Empire, influencing Judaizing Christians of a number of stripes and underpinning subsequent large-scale support of Zionist initiatives in the late nineteenth and early twentieth centuries. In the United States, a combination of Millerite dispensational premillennialism and Sabbatarianism produced the Seventh Day Adventists, whose communities in Israel today number twenty-nine.[9] Sabbatarian Christians protected Jews from Nazi

---

8. See Alexander M. Shapiro, "Jews and Christians in the Period of the Crusades—A Commentary on the First Holocaust," *Journal of Ecumenical Studies* 9 (1972): 725–49

persecution and in many cases promoted Jewish restorationism, though not necessarily its political manifestation. Most relevantly, these Judaizing communities tended to be iconoclastic. Not only did they reject the use of images during worship, but some went so far as to reject Trinitarianism and even, like the Jehovah's Witnesses, traditional Christian holidays.

Christian Zionism in the nineteenth century was also sometimes nourished by the less iconoclastic belief that members of an ethnic group—while not specifically "Jewish"—were themselves the descendants of biblical Israelites and therefore had related rights to the Holy Land. In England and throughout its colonies, "British Israelites" claimed to be descended from lost tribes via Ephraim. The British royalty itself was considered heir to the throne of King David. While British Israelites did not always support plans for restoring the Jews to the Holy Land, especially if they concerned the return of the descendants of Judah alone, preoccupation with this narrative made the English-speaking world fertile ground for nascent Christian Zionism.[10] Advocacy for the "restoration of Israel" was for the most part connected with political aspirations.

In the United States, sometimes this writing of one's own ethnic-political-religious community into sacred histories was merged with belief in the imminent return of the Messiah and Judaizing practices such as Sabbatarianism—as found, for example, in the Armstrongism of the Worldwide Church of God. Earlier, members of the Church of Jesus Christ of Latter-day Saints, in addition to maintaining a focus on the existence of the lost tribes of Israel in the modern world, also espoused a form of dispensational premillennialism and described themselves as returning to the earliest Judaized Christian forms of

9. These Seventh Day Adventist congregations in Israel have 980 members; see http://www.sdaisrael.org/seventhday-adventists-in-israel (accessed October 18, 2011).

10. This is the argument of Michael Polowetsky in *Jerusalem Recovered: Victorian Intellectuals and the Birth of Modern Zionism* (Westport, CT: Praeger, 1995). See especially the introduction.

worship. Notably, each criticized other traditional Christian churches like the Roman Catholics for having succumbed to paganization and apostasy. In this sense, their teachings are relatively iconoclastic—but not as much as one might expect from religious groups with extremely iconoclastic roots and those following Jewish sacramentalist exemplars. Insistence that the leaders of these groups were inspired as the apostles/saints of old, as is found in many Pentecostal/charismatic groups today like those associated with the New Apostolic Reformation, sets a limit on their iconoclasm, as does their eschatological foci on the return of Jews to a very "holy" Holy Land and the future construction of a third Jewish temple prior to or during (depending upon one's view) the millennial age. See JC and ECZ below.

Christian Zionist Pilgrimage:
The "Holy" in the Holy Land Today

In 2007, I began teaching graduate courses part-time at the University of the Holy Land (UHL) in Jerusalem. The institution had already been studying Christian pilgrimage to the Holy Land for several years. In the late 1990s, this labor culminated in the construction of a database of Christian pilgrimage for the Israel Ministry of Tourism. My work, with the assistance of UHL students, has primarily focused on recent developments and adding a new component to the mix—a review of local Palestinian Christian pilgrimage. I have especially attended to situating changes in Christian pilgrimage within the greater context of what has occurred with religious pilgrims from Jewish and Islamic traditions as well. UHL attracts many students who identify themselves as Christian Zionists, and a primary concern of UHL graduate students is contemporary Christian Zionist pilgrimage. Fleshing out exactly what this means has been an important topic of five Anthropology of Pilgrimage graduate seminars as well as research conducted on focus groups composed of self-identified Christian Zionists in Jerusalem.

Before turning to some of our findings, it is essential to briefly review developments within Islamic, Jewish, and Christian pilgrimage to Holy Land sites since 1948. This material was presented at the 2010 World Congress of the International Association of Historians of Religion in Toronto and is published elsewhere.[11] In brief, the central argument is that change over the last hundred years in diverse Christian pilgrimages mirrors what is found on examination of Jewish and Islamic travel to and within the Holy Land. There has been a large increase in the number of active Jewish pilgrimages, pilgrims, and "sacred sites" since 1948 and 1967.[12] At the same time, Islamic pilgrimages have suffered decline. Paralleling these developments, some international Christian pilgrimages have prospered in the last several decades, with explicit support of the Israeli government, while Palestinian Christian pilgrimage has declined—especially to and from the Occupied Territories. For example, at the same time that access to Aboud on the West Bank for the Feast of Saint Barbara has been severely limited to Christians from Israel, and travel to Jerusalem on Palm Sunday and Lod for the Feast of St. George by traditional feeder communities of local Christians on the West Bank has been often curtailed (and to a much greater extent for the 450,000 descendants of Palestinian Christian refugees living outside the Holy Land), several international pilgrimages have dramatically grown in size and importance.[13] This is especially the

---

11. Curtis Hutt, "Pilgrimage in Turbulent Contexts: One Hundred Years of Pilgrimage to the Holy Land," *ID: International Dialogue* 2 (2012): 34–64.

12. Doron Bar, "Reconstructing the Past: The Creation of Jewish Sacred Space in the State of Israel, 1948–1967," *Israel Studies* 13:3 (2008): 1–21. See also "Re-Creating Jewish Sanctity in Jerusalem: The Case of Mount Zion and David's Tomb Between 1948–1967," *The Journal of Israeli History* 23 (2004): 233–51.

case where pilgrims' political support for Israel is explicit and/or some degree of government patronage is clear—as is the case with Christian Zionist pilgrimage. Another notable example of this is the lifting of visa requirements for Russian citizens traveling to Israel on September 20, 2008. This led to a huge upsurge in Russian Orthodox Christian pilgrims to holy sites, who now are second in number only to religious visitors from the United States.[14]

In the last several decades, there has been a large increase in pilgrimage to the Holy Land by diverse groups of Christian Zionists—including *a*dispensationalists, dispensationalists, and Judaizing Christians. In the next few pages, I will present the results of fieldwork on all three general groupings. I will begin with a discussion of the new Christian pilgrimage sponsored by the powerful International Christian Embassy in Jerusalem (ICEJ) with the explicit patronage of the Israeli government: the "Feast of Tabernacles." This Christian celebration of the Jewish holiday of Sukkot, which brings together Christian Zionist pilgrims from a variety of nations and church backgrounds, lasts for one week and has been held now for over thirty years. Every year, either or both the president and prime minister of Israel have addressed the pilgrims.[15] In recent years, members of the Knesset Christian Allies Caucus have also been part of the program. The Israeli government's support of nontraditional pilgrimage by Christian Zionists is not new; Uri Bialer has outlined this for the years 1948 to 1967 in his book *Cross on the Star of David.*[16] In recent years, it has continued most visibly in

---

13. These findings are evident from the fieldwork performed by UHL graduate students Laura Hull (Palm Sunday, Aboud/Jerusalem) and Samuel Martin (Feast of St. George, Lod).

14. In 2011, visa requirements for Ukrainian pilgrims were canceled as well.

15. One notable exception was in 2005, when Prime Minister Ariel Sharon refused to address Christian pilgrims to the Feast of Tabernacles because many of the groups represented did not support the Israeli disengagement from Gaza.

16. Uri Bialer, *Cross on the Star of David: The Christian World in Israel's Foreign Policy 1948–1967* (Bloomington: Indiana University Press, 2005), 94.

the approval of the establishment of Brigham Young University's Jerusalem Center on premium real estate next to Hebrew University's Mount Scopus Campus.

Review of the past schedules of events by UHL graduate students has revealed that pilgrims organized by ICEJ, including large numbers of evangelical and New Apostolic Christians, at first glance appear quite iconoclastic relative to other traditional Christian pilgrims. Travel to sites like the Church of the Resurrection/Holy Sepulchre, the Church of the Nativity in Bethlehem, and Church of the Annunciation in Nazareth, or even pilgrimage centers like Nazareth Village is not promoted. If Christian Zionist pilgrims visit these places, they often do so as tourists without any "spiritual" connections to these sites. Instead, the *al-Haram al-Sharif*—presumed site of the future third Jewish temple—is a central symbol and focal point for pilgrims who envision themselves to be making pilgrimage to Jerusalem as directed by Zech. 14:16 to celebrate this feast at the time of the return of the Messiah. When leaving Jerusalem, pilgrims are often brought to the Dead Sea region, with several regularly traveling to Masada and Qumran. Additional bus tours, such as in 2011, took pilgrims on tours of the pre-1967 Green Line, "flashpoints" in Jerusalem, and the Sderot/Gaza border area as well as a home for Holocaust survivors and Yad Vashem. In 2012, highlights included a visit to the Center for Jewish-Christian Understanding and Cooperation in the settlement of Efrat, which included a talk on the "end of days" as well as an "aid" mission to Nitzan, a community established in 2005 to house Jewish evacuees forcefully expelled from Gush Katif in Gaza by the "unfortunate" Israeli disengagement plan.

The Holy Land is not holy in the same way for ICEJ pilgrims as it is for Oriental Orthodox, Greek Orthodox, or Roman Catholic Christians. According to "Land Promise" theology, the land formerly known as Canaan has been given by God for all time to the Jews. The

Jewish people, moreover, are a special "chosen" people—an integral part of the divine plan of God as understood by Christian Zionists. This is one of the primary reasons for its special character—though whether it is holy, according to members of Christian Zionist focus groups queried, was a matter of how the term was defined. One might easily surmise from the actions of these Christian Zionist pilgrims organized by ICEJ, however, that the site of the future Jewish temple is holy in some strong sense—akin to how other Christians look at the Church of the Resurrection/Holy Sepulchre. As the location of the future new Jerusalem and home of the prophesied premillennial Jewish state of Israel, the Holy Land itself is distinctive.

ICEJ is careful in its official publications not to overtly support a dispensational premillennialist agenda. Its mission is to provide "comfort" to the Jewish people in keeping with Isa. 40:1-2. This comfort is quite different from that extended to Jews by Christians in the nineteenth century like Theodor and Maria Alphonse Ratisbonne; it is explicitly tied to support for a Jewish state and, more circumspectly, to the presumed imminent return of the Messiah. In spite of carefully worded denials that their Christian Zionism is tied to dispensational premillennialist commitments, given ICEJ's sponsorship of the Feast of Tabernacles pilgrimage such a connection is hard to deny.

Other Christian Zionist groups, like John Hagee's Christians United for Israel (CUFI), walk a similar adispensationalist tightrope, also unconvincingly. Whereas several nondispensationalist Protestants from, for example, Congregationalist, Presbyterian, Lutheran, and Friends (Quaker) traditions as well as Roman Catholics have identified themselves as Christian Zionists on account of their advocacy for a Jewish homeland—based on the need to provide often-persecuted Jewish minority communities with a refuge from longstanding Christian and now Islamic aggression—this is not, upon close analysis, the case with CUFI. In official CUFI publications and statements of purpose, it is true that "blessing" Israel is carefully separated from the belief that the end of the world is nigh. The State of Israel deserves Christian support on account of the fact that the land was given to the Jews by God as a "royal land grant." The majority of Christian Zionist pilgrims from CUFI and other Christian Zionist groups polled have expressed their belief that the return of the Messiah is not far away. Given the high percentage (58 percent) of white evangelicals in the United States who believe that Jesus will return in the near future,[17] this is not surprising. Christian Zionism and millenarianism often merge.

As might be inferred from the support given above to Christian pilgrimage organized by ICEJ by the Israeli government, Christian Zionists are often indistinguishable from Israeli ultranationalists. This is clear not only from the tours organized for Feast of Tabernacles participants, but every time a bus from CUFI shows up in East Jerusalem neighborhoods like Sheikh Jarrah or Silwan in support of Jewish settler activity by groups like the El'ad Association. In the extreme, Christian Zionist pilgrims have identified the spot at the Hyatt Hotel marking the assassination of Israeli Minister of Tourism Rehavam Ze'evi, proponent of transferring the Palestinian population of Israel and the West Bank to Jordan, as "sacred ground."[18]

Another example of a newly transformed sense of the "holy" in the Holy Land evident in Christian Zionist pilgrimage can be found in the activities of pilgrims associated with the New Apostolic Reformation. This fast-growing form of Protestantism associated with Pentecostal and charismatic movements—with a few exceptions—holds strongly to dispensational premillennialism. As

---

17. Pew Study, June 22, 2010.
18. Yaniv Belhassen and Carla Almeida Santos, "An Evangelical Pilgrimage to Israel: A Case Study on Politics and Triangulation," *Journal of Travel Research* 44 (2006): 435.

with the ICEJ, the central focus of their pilgrimages is not traditional Christian holy sites but the presumed location of the future third Jewish temple. They have regularly joined ICEJ's Feast of Tabernacles celebrations, and on the thirtieth anniversary of the pilgrimage the featured speaker was Apostle Reinhard Bonnke. Communities identifying with the New Apostolic movement (like those associated with the International Coalition of Apostles), in comparison with traditional Protestant Christians, are far less iconoclastic when it comes to the status of their leadership. Central to their beliefs is the restoration of the leadership positions of "apostle" and "prophet" in the contemporary church. New Apostolic leaders are often involved in the performing of miracles like healing and prophesying the future.[19]

A study on comparative Christian pilgrimage on Palm Sunday in Jerusalem by UHL graduate students compared the activities of the Jerusalem House of Prayer for All Nations (JHOP) on the Mount of Olives, led by Apostle Tom Hess (affiliated with the International House of Prayer in Kansas City as well as the International Coalition of Apostles), with those of pilgrims participating in the ancient Saturday of Lazarus feast and Palm Sunday procession from Bethpage down the Mount of Olives. As witnessed in the Byzantine Rite (followed by Orthodox and Eastern Catholics), the Armenian Rite, and the fourth and fifth century writings of John Chrysostom and Augustine, the celebration of the resurrection of Lazarus and triumphant procession of Jesus into Jerusalem on Palm Sunday is arguably the oldest of all Christian pilgrimages.[20] Today, Palestinian

---

19. Through the ministry of Apostle Bonnke, for example, Nigerian Pastor Daniel Ekechukwu was allegedly raised from the dead. The son of Apostle and Prophetess Karen Dunham, leader of the Living Bread International Church in Jerusalem and Jericho, was also reputedly "resurrected from the dead"; see http://www.livingbreadchurch.com/ (accessed October 18, 2011). Dunham is unusual among those associated with the New Apostolic Reformation in Jerusalem, as her ministry is directed primarily at Arabic-speaking refugees in the Occupied Territories.

Christians from the West Bank and Israel, together with international Christian pilgrims from a variety of backgrounds including Roman Catholic, Eastern and Oriental Orthodox, and many from Anglican and Lutheran traditions, pass from Bethpage to the Church of St. Anne in the Old City of Jerusalem on dates corresponding to their usage of the Julian and Gregorian calendars. Travel to Jerusalem at this time is particularly difficult for Palestinian Christians from the West Bank.

This is not the case, though, for international Christians associated with the New Apostolic Reformation—whether affiliated with the ICEJ, CUFI, or the major 24/7 houses of prayer in Jerusalem (JHOP and Succat Hallel in West Jerusalem). These self-described interdenominational Christians do not formally participate in the age-old Palm Sunday procession. Instead, Christians associated with JHOP gather on Saturday evening before Palm Sunday on the Mount of Olives. Then in the predawn hours they approach the Golden Gate onto the *al-Haram al-Sharif* or Temple Mount through which the returning Messiah is to pass. Here, away from the gaze of onlookers, they hold a prayer vigil entreating the divine for the return of Jesus and the rebuilding of the Jewish temple at the beginning of the millennial age.[21] What is "holy" in the Holy Land is focused on the role of the Jewish people in the millennial age and, specifically, the presumed site of the future third Jewish temple. Apostle Tom Hess and the worldwide 24/7 House of Prayer movement's single-minded focus on the imminent return of the Messiah has notably not quenched the Israeli government's support for this Christian mission on the Mount of Olives. The Knesset's Christian Allies Caucus has repeatedly joined with the All Nations Convocations and

20. For an account of the first Palm Sunday procession (and its politics!), see Marcus Borg and John Dominic Crossan, *The Last Week: A Day-by-Day Account of Jesus's Final Week in Jerusalem* (New York: HarperCollins, 2006).
21. Details have been provided by UHL graduate student Shigeko Rakosi.

Watchmen's Tour of Apostle Hess to bring Christian political leaders to Israel in support of a "unified and undivided Jerusalem."

JHOP is not the only millenarian Christian community in Jerusalem that receives the backing of the Knesset's Christian Allies Caucus. Christine Darg, of Exploits Ministry and Covenant Alliance, while claiming to have congenial relations with Christians from Palestinian and non-Palestinian backgrounds, devotes much of her work to outlining a Judeo-Christian strategy for supporting Israel in the messianic age. In addition to supporting the ICEJ's Feast of Tabernacles pilgrimage, Covenant Alliance has organized with the help of the Knesset Christian Allies Caucus four "Christian Jerusalem Assemblies" where international Christian leaders meet with Israeli government officials (including a VIP reception at the Knesset itself) for the purpose of securing backing for Israeli control of Jerusalem. Darg's admitted proselytizing of Jews, along with that of many other millenarian Christians such as those associated with the New Apostolic Reformation, has outraged many Israelis. However, according to Darg, it is the presence of a Jewish state in the Holy Land that makes Israel special today—as opposed to one hundred years ago. In spite of the claims made by these Christian Zionists influenced by dispensational premillennialist commitments that their beliefs and activities are a return to past biblical forms of Christianity or the result of renewed divine inspiration in the present, they are plainly new forms of Christian conduct.

The final group of Christian Zionist pilgrims that we investigated at UHL is Messianic/Jewish Christians. These groups are often prototypically iconoclastic, rejecting the use of images in worship. Likewise, they often identify their leaders as rabbis—rejecting, though not in all cases, the view that they embody the authority of restored apostles. The main difference between these Christian groups and other Judaizing Christians like the members of Seventh

Day Adventists in Israel is the insistence that they are ethnically and religiously Jewish—in spite of their devotion to Jesus (Yeshua) as rabbi, Messiah, or even the son of God. According to the US State Department's 2010 International Religious Freedom Report, this often-persecuted (e.g., by Yad L'Achim)[22] collection of diverse groups numbered anywhere between 8,000 and 15,000 members. In the same report filed in 2012, the number of Messianic Jews was estimated at 20,000. These figures are difficult to confirm, as Messianic Jews surveyed by UHL graduate students are often reluctant to advertise their faith. Some, such as Revive Israel's Asher Intrater—leader of one of the most-attended Christian churches in Jerusalem, Ahavat Yeshua—are more vocal, not only advocating for "revival" among Jews living in Israel but speaking out against the "pre-meditated attacks" against Messianic Jewish believers by "a fringe minority of ultra-Orthodox Jews."[23] Messianic congregations in Israel and settlements on the West Bank number, by our count, approximately two hundred. These Christians who are ethnically Jewish, moreover, have the support of a large and growing international community, especially in the United States.[24]

Self-identified Messianic/Jewish Christians today are often overtly Zionist, though they are not uniformly committed to dispensational premillennialism. As we learned through open-ended individual and focus group interviews, while many Messianic/Jewish Christians

---

22. Groups like Yad L'Achim have been connected with acts of violence against Messianic/Jewish Christians. See, for example, *Time Magazine* article on the topic, June 6, 2008.

23. See Asher Intrater's response to Rabbi Shlomo Riskin's article "Dialogue: The Messianic Movement" in *The Jerusalem Post*, August 27, 2010 which can be found online at http://roshpinaproject.com/2010/09/09/asher-intrater-responds-to-rabbi-riskin/ (accessed October 18, 2011).

24. The CEO of the Messianic Jewish Alliance of America, Joel Chernoff, makes the incendiary though largely unsubstantiated claim that there are between one and two million Messianic Jews living in the United States alone. This can be found on his blog at http://joelchernoff.wordpress.com/tag/messianic-jewish-revival/ (accessed October 18, 2011). To my knowledge, no systematic, comprehensive count of this clearly growing, dynamic, and diverse set of Christian communities has been undertaken or published to date.

believe that they are living in the end times; others were primarily committed to practicing "original forms" of Jewish Christianity that had not been corrupted or paganized by Greco-Roman religious practices. These two convictions are often merged. Messianic/Jewish Christians are almost always Zionists maintaining some version of Land Promise theology—that is, the belief that Scripture grounds Jewish claims to the Holy Land.

Unlike other Christians attending Sukkot celebrations, Messianic/Jewish Christians participate as Jews—not the "righteous" from among the gentile nations. Often, Jewish and Judaizing Christians worship together and/or support each other's communities. For example, arguably the most regularly attended Christian church in Jerusalem over the last few decades, notably not a local Palestinian congregation, is the "Messianic" King of Kings Community located in the Clal Building ("The Jerusalem Prayer Tower") on Davidka Square in West Jerusalem. This Christian church is composed of both non-Jewish Judaizing Christians linked to the New Apostolic Reformation and Messianic/Jewish Christians. According to their core values statement, "Jewish and non-Jewish disciples serve together." While King of Kings leader Pastor Wayne Hilsden—in spite of the criticism of many Christian Zionist and Messianic/Jewish Christians—did participate in Bethlehem Bible College's 2012 "Christ at the Checkpoint" conference as part of outreach to local Palestinian Christians, his congregation is openly committed to "proclaiming the Good News . . . primarily to Jewish People." [25]

25. See the King of Kings Community's statement of "Vision and Core Values" at http://www.kkcj.org/about/vision-and-core-values (accessed October 18, 2011).

Conclusion

In closing, I will note where the just-reviewed Christian Zionist groups fall on the iconoclasm scale (see CZ, aD, D, and D NA) and make a provocative though carefully considered claim. First, I have plotted on the table below different varieties of Christian Zionists in the following ways—again, allowing for variability in specific positions. Several Christian Zionist groups, I assert, have pushed beyond conventional theological limits associated with the often-Protestant groups from whence they have historically emerged. Dispensational premillennialist groups, in light of their belief in the imminent return of the Messiah, the perceived special nature of the Jewish people in the divine plan, and establishment of a new messianic temple in Jerusalem, are registered as less iconoclastic—in territory traditionally marked out by Roman Catholics, Greek Orthodox, and even miaphysite Christians. The land and specific sites within it like the Temple Mount are holy, or will soon become holy as the site of the new millennial kingdom and third Jewish temple. On the other hand, Judaizing Christian Zionists and Messianic/ Jewish Christians are often more iconoclastic, especially when it comes to their view of "holy individuals" and representations of the divine. Often, however, such groups are drawn in the opposite direction—something clearly correlated with their adoption of dispensational premillennialist beliefs. Christian Zionist groups influenced by the New Apostolic movement, including Messianic/ Jewish Christians, are even further predisposed toward the least iconoclastic position. The presence of modern-day apostles and prophets in their midst is reminiscent of the traditional miaphysite belief concerning the sacred nature of their spiritual leaders.

Second, for the Christian theologian generally removed from or unaware of contemporary developments in evangelical, charismatic, and Messianic/Jewish Christian theologies, the plotting exhibited below may come as a surprise. It many ways it represents a sea change in contemporary Protestant Christian theology, implanted on the ground in Jerusalem—a city where local Palestinian Christians are arguably a minority compared to New Apostolic, millenarian, and Messianic/Jewish Christians.[26] In a city where the rise and fall of great empires, civilizations, and world religions can be seen inscribed on its stones, a new development in the history of Christianities is being written. Religious studies scholars and others would do well to take notice.

---

26. While the Israeli Central Bureau of Statistics in 2010 officially counted 11,576 Arab Christian and 3,029 non-Arab Christian residents of Jerusalem, these numbers are by no means the final word. This is especially the case in light of the desire of many Christians not to be counted as such. The largest active congregations and most numerous "denominations" (though oftentimes the groups analyzed above deplore the use of this terminology) are no longer Palestinian Greek Orthodox, Roman Catholic, Greek Catholic, Anglican, or Lutheran. The list of Christian communities, for example, found on the webpage of the Christian Information Centre, run by the Franciscan Custodia Terrae Sanctae, is not comprehensive. Notable omissions include 24/7 houses of prayer, South Korean, African, and Jewish-Christian communities. This population shift among Christian communities in Jerusalem, moreover, is accelerating.

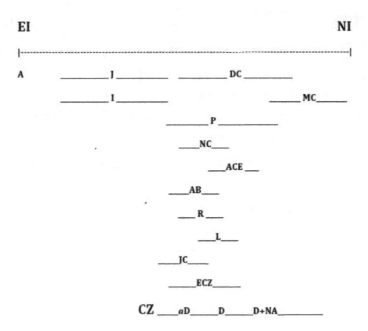

Table: Iconoclasm Scale

Table Key

* EI=extremely iconoclastic; NI=not iconoclastic at all
A=atheism; J=Jewish traditions; I=Islamic traditions
DC=Diophysite Christians, Roman Catholics, and Eastern Orthodox
MC=Miaphysite Christians, Coptic/Syrian/Armenian Oriental Orthodox
P=Protestants; NC=Nonconformist/free churches; AB=Anabaptists
R=Reformed churches; L=Lutherans; ACE=Anglicanism
JC=Judaizing Christians; ECZ=Expected Christian Zionists
CZ=Christian Zionists: aD=adispensationalists, D=dispensationalists
D NA=New Apostolic dispensationalists

8

Living in the Hour of Restoration

Christian Zionism, Immigration, and Aliyah

Faydra L. Shapiro

It is exciting to know that I wasn't born 500 years ago, or 1,000 years ago, but I'm actually living in the hour of the restoration of Israel and the returning of the Jewish people, and there's a role for me to play. And not only for me to play, but to encourage other non-Jewish people to participate . . . encouraging Jewish people who might not be aware of their own role, being in a Diaspora so long, not realizing that God might ultimately have a role for them back in Israel. And to be able to know the times, to be able to share with them that God might have a plan for them in Israel is exciting.

— Pastor Smith[1]

Christian Zionism is a general label for a specific orientation and

---

1. Identities of interviewees are protected in this chapter with pseudonyms.

emphasis within evangelicalism that ascribes vital theological, and often eschatological, importance to the Jews living in Israel. Christian Zionists are distinguished from evangelicals more broadly by two intense and intertwined emphases: Israel and the Jews. Those two passions bring together Christians across the evangelical spectrum into both broad, international parachurch ministries, like the International Christian Embassy Jerusalem (ICEJ) or Christians United for Israel (CUFI), and local organizations and smaller ministries. Christian Zionists see their Zionism as a logical extension of their commitment to God and his word. In their reading of the Bible, God has decreed a special role and status for the Jews, sealed in an eternal covenant, with a promise to restore them to their land. Thus Christian Zionists see their solidarity with the Jews and the modern State of Israel as paying homage to the God of Israel.

This chapter examines Christian Zionist attitudes toward immigration, specifically Jewish immigration to Israel (*aliyah*). In an effort to make sense of Christian Zionist support for *aliyah*, this chapter strives to assess its uniqueness. Does Christian Zionist support for Jewish immigration to Israel reflect a broader evangelical attitude toward immigration generally, Jewish Zionist attitudes toward *aliyah*, or simply an uncritical attitude toward Israeli public policy? I will argue that Christian Zionist support for *aliyah* has several unique components, reflecting its specific combination of transnational and theological focus on Israel.

Transnationalism

Christian Zionism is a phenomenon defined by its transnationalism. It is a worldwide but locally rooted movement with an overwhelming material, symbolic, and spiritual focus on Israel. Its members are evangelicals who are embedded in their local countries but at the same time constantly participating in Israel in ways that include prayer, repeat tourism, financial support, political activism, and volunteer efforts.

Christian Zionists constitute a Christian community in the land of Israel in a manner that is rather different than historic Christian presence in the Holy Land. Protestant groups sometimes do not have the institutional and organizational infrastructure enjoyed by the Orthodox and Catholic churches. This is even more so in the case of evangelicals, whose adherents form a loose collection of many different denominations and often belong to nondenominational fellowships and churches. Evangelicals have no single organization, leader, or church that can speak for all of them, making it impossible for the State of Israel to establish any formal ties with them as a recognized church. Evangelical Christian Zionists are almost entirely foreigners and only rarely live in Israel with any permanent status. Yet they are deeply invested in Israel from afar, as regular and returning visitors and volunteers, as political supporters abroad, and as contributors of critical financial resources that power some of the country's most pressing social services.

Perhaps as a result of its popularity, transnationalism is a category whose boundaries are sometimes troublingly elastic.[2] It is a term productively distinguished from globalization, which

> refers to social, economic, cultural, and demographic processes that take place within nations but also transcend them. . . . Transnationalism overlaps globalization but typically has a more limited purview. Whereas global processes are largely decentered from specific national territories and take place in a global space, transnational processes are anchored in and transcend one or more nation-states.[3]

2. For a more in-depth investigation of transnationalism and Christian Zionism, see Faydra Shapiro, "Thank You Israel, for Supporting America': the Transnational Flow of Christian Zionist Resources," *Identities: Global Studies in Culture and Power* 19:5 (2012): 616–31.

Transnationalism, then, is primarily about dynamic connections across national boundaries, flows of resources that can include people, money, cultural forms, information, and language. These specific transnational flows do not exist in a vacuum, and they both influence and are influenced by larger global dynamics.

Aliyah

No doubt Christian Zionism's most significant transnational activity is its production and promotion of other transnationals in the form of Jewish migration to Israel. For Christian Zionists, *aliyah*—Jewish immigration to Israel—is one of the most significant events of our time. When it comes to Jews and Israel, Christian Zionists do not simply tolerate immigration; they serve as its active supporters and enthusiastic admirers, encouraging Jewish immigration with money, prayer, and organizations dedicated to aiding both migration and needy immigrants settled in their new country.

Nefesh b'Nefesh, perhaps the best-known private agency whose mission is to facilitate Jewish immigration from English-speaking countries, is supported by millions of dollars from evangelical Christian donors through the International Fellowship of Christians and Jews and John Hagee Ministries. Evangelical Christians run organizations like the Cyrus Foundation, whose work is to encourage *aliyah* from North and South America primarily through financial support for travel and shipping of possessions. The Ebenezer Fund's Operation Exodus and Word of Life's Operation Jabotinsky do the same, although they serve a rather different population and set of needs, primarily working with Jews in the former Soviet Union. In addition, there are several Christian Zionist organizations

---

3. Michael Kearney, "The Local and the Global: The Anthropology of Globalization and Transnationalism," *Annual Review of Anthropology* 24 (1995): 548.

that raise funds to encourage *aliyah* from countries like Ethiopia and India, as well as Christian organizations that offer all kinds of social services to needy immigrants once they have settled in Israel. These organizations have actively and concretely promoted the immigration of hundreds of thousands of Jews to Israel.

Christian Zionist organizations not only support *aliyah* in material terms; they celebrate it spiritually. One ministry where I've done fieldwork, in small-town Ontario, Canada, has a whole wall with pictures of Jews whom they've helped to immigrate to Israel.[4] Prayer and intercession are also vital parts of Christian Zionist support for *aliyah*, including prayers for immigrants, for the state that welcomes them, for the Jews who have not yet heard the "call of return," for the nations of the world to prepare the paths and means for Jews to reach the "promised land," and for the gentile church to awaken to its responsibility to help the Jews home.

Immigration or *Aliyah*?

Significant work has been done on the role of religion in shaping political attitudes, resulting in plenty of data showing that American evangelicals tend to have conservative attitudes toward public policy, including immigration. Researchers have shown that there is an evangelical Christian animus toward immigration on both economic and symbolic levels.[5] A 2006 Pew Research Poll showed that white evangelicals evince a particular concern about immigrants on

---

4. In the interest of full disclosure, a picture of the author's family appears on that wall as Jewish immigrants to Israel. We did not receive any direct financial support from Christian Zionists or Christian Zionist organizations for our immigration. We did receive encouragement and, presumably, prayers for our successful *aliyah*.

5. See B. R. Knoll, "And Who Is My Neighbor? Religion and Immigration Policy Attitudes," *Journal for the Scientific Study of Religion* 48:2 (2009): 313–31; and Eric L. McDaniel, Irfan Nooruddin, and Allyson F. Shortle, "Divine Boundaries: How Religion Shapes Citizens' Attitudes Toward Immigrants," *American Politics Research* 39:1 (2011): 205–33.

economic and cultural bases, with 63 percent feeling that they threaten "traditional American values and customs" and 64 percent seeing immigrants as "a burden because they take our jobs, housing and health care." In both cases, these negative attitudes far outweigh those of the general American population.[6]

A possible factor in Christian Zionist support for Jewish immigration to Israel is that it involves a low amount of risk. There are neither perceived economic threats (immigrants will threaten my own interests) nor ostensible symbolic threats (immigrants don't understand our American values) in supporting Jewish immigration to Israel. Simply put, it seems easy and romantic to support immigration to a country in which one does not live since the personal risks are few, if any.

Eric McDaniel, Irfan Nooruddin, and Allyson F. Shortle have also explored the role of Christian nationalism in making sense of evangelical Christian ambivalence about immigration, focusing on immigration as a potential threat to the evangelical sense of American exceptionalism. They suggest that "the importance of the United States of America in God's plan should make those who adhere to this belief system highly attentive to who is part of the nation."[7] Thus evangelical Christian Zionist support for *aliyah* ought not to be taken for granted, given the anti-immigration bias of much of American evangelicalism.

A significant subset of evangelicals, both in America and around the world, have a specific focus on Israel as a "true north" that brings with it a distinctive orientation. While not all evangelicals are active Christian Zionists, the majority of the estimated 60 million evangelicals in the United States are indeed supporters of Israel. Some

---

6. Gregory A. Smith, "Attitudes Toward Immigration: In the Pulpit and the Pew," http://www.pewresearch.org/2006/04/25/attitudes-toward-immigration-in-the-pulpit-and-the-pew/ (accessed May 19, 2013).

7. McDaniel et al., 212.

of the best-known American evangelical figures of the twentieth century, including Jerry Falwell, Billy Graham, and Pat Robertson, have been outspoken in their Zionism. Christian organizations that enthusiastically support the State of Israel and the return of the Jews to their ancestral homeland are active in many countries around the globe, including South Africa, Nigeria, Brazil, South Korea, and throughout Europe and North America.

In contrast to the Christian nationalism that McDaniel and his colleagues argue is at the heart of American evangelical ambivalence toward immigrants, Christian Zionism is defined by its transnationalism, in which the exceptionalism of America is superseded only by the exceptionalism of Israel. It was the restorationist activity of William Blackstone that really set the stage for America to serve in the form of a gentile "redeemer nation" that should facilitate the realization of God's plan for the Jews. In his "Memorial" of 1891, Blackstone offered the United States—and specifically President Harrison—this very role:

> There seem to be many evidences to show that we have reached the period in the great roll of centuries, when the everlasting God of Abraham, Isaac and Jacob, is lifting up His hand to the Gentiles (Isa 49:22) to bring His sons and his daughters from far, that he may plant them again in their own land, Ezekiel 34, etc. Not for twenty-four centuries, since the days of Cyrus, King of Persia, has there been offered to any mortal such a privileged opportunity to further the purposes of God concerning His ancient people.[8]

Years later, President Truman would refer to himself as Cyrus in light of his efforts to establish the State of Israel. These references to the biblical Cyrus mobilize an image of a gentile power that helps

8. William E. Blackstone, "Palestine for the Jews: A Copy of the Memorial Presented to President Harrison, March 5, 1891," reprinted in *Christian Protagonists for Jewish Restoration: An Original Anthology,* ed. Adolf Augustus Berle (New York: Arno, 1977), 17.

to materialize God's plan in restoring the Jews to their promised homeland.

So while Christian Zionists are indeed keenly concerned with America, they believe that its success—and the success of all gentile nations—comes from the degree to which it supports or impedes God's plan for Israel. This enables Christian Zionists to focus less on immigrant threats to America and more on the divine blessing that America will receive for enabling Jewish immigration to Israel.

It might be tempting to suggest that Christian Zionist support for *aliyah* is simply a function of an uncritical approach to the State of Israel, and that as a policy of this much-vaunted state its support by evangelical Christians is to be expected. However, this is not the case: Christian Zionists have no difficulty criticizing particular policies, choices, and actions of the Israeli state when they are felt to contradict the will of God. Notwithstanding its unique supernatural status, Israel is also imperfect and subject to all the vicissitudes of the modern democratic nation-state. The State of Israel can—and often does—make wrong choices, making political decisions and tolerating social practices deemed by Christian Zionists to run contrary to God's will and as such have severe national and spiritual implications. Thus Christian Zionists find themselves free—and even compelled—to speak out against particular policies of the State of Israel such as access to abortion, permission for a gay pride parade to pass through the streets of Jerusalem, and the 2005 disengagement from Gaza. Clearly, support for *aliyah* is not a function of the uncritical, blind support for Israel that Christian Zionists are often accused of by their critics.

Christian Zionist Narratives of *Aliyah*: Restoration, Reconciliation, Redemption

For Christian Zionists, it is axiomatic that the contemporary nation-state of Israel sits on the same territory as the land promised to

Abraham's descendants in the Hebrew Bible. It is equally taken for granted that those descendants are the Jews of today, all over the world.

What might appear to be "just" a political engagement with Israel is an expression of a deeply held religious belief in the divinely ordained connection between the Jewish people and the land. In a 2001 statement to the United States Senate, Sen. James Inhofe (R-OK) explained the link between the political appearance and the religious truth at its base:

> I believe very strongly that we ought to support Israel; that it has a right to the land. This is the most important reason: Because God said so . . . look it up in the book of Genesis. . . . That is God talking. The Bible says that Abram removed his tent and came and dwelt in the plain of Mamre, which is in Hebron, and built there an altar before the Lord. Hebron is in the West Bank. It is at this place where God appeared to Abram and said, "I am giving you this land," the West Bank. This is not a political battle at all. It is a contest over whether or not the word of God is true.[9]

For Christian Zionists, Israel is exceptional, by divine fiat. It is the only nation-state in the world that matters, supernaturally speaking. The land itself is felt to be cosmically aligned with forces of good. Israel is viewed as God's land, the one he called out and bordered in a special way as an inheritance for a chosen people to realize their distinctive mission. It is unique by virtue of its origin and role, such that "all other nations were created by an act of men, but Israel was created by an act of God! The Royal Land Grant that was given to Abraham and his seed through Isaac and Jacob with an everlasting and unconditional covenant."[10] It is "the only piece of land on earth

9. James M. Inhofe, "Senate Floor Statement of Senator Inhofe: America's Stake in Israel's War on Terrorism," (December 4, 2001).
10. John Hagee Ministries, "Why Christians Should Support Israel," http://www.jhm.org/Home/About/WhySupportIsrael (accessed June 5, 2014).

God considered so precious, so valuable, that He included it, along with His children, in an eternal covenant."[11]

While the land, for Christian Zionists, possesses an inherent power by virtue of its chosenness by God, the fact that Israel regained her political independence as a specifically Jewish state in the twentieth century is nothing short of a miracle, functioning as the vital connection point between the past and future. The return of the Jewish people to Israel is taken as evidence for the belief that God is keeping his past promises to his chosen people. In this way, *aliyah* serves as proof of God's trustworthiness about what is to come both for individuals and the world. For Christian Zionists, Jewish immigration to Israel is not a matter of public policy, but rather an issue of divine prophecy. As Pastor Smith, a Christian Zionist leader in Canada, explained to me:

> When I think of restoration, it's the fact that God spoke his word, and he keeps his word, and now he's returning his people back to the land of Israel just as his word foretold. He's returned, he's restoring the ancient ruins, just as his word foretold. And for me this is excitement. It's excitement to be alive in an hour in which so much of his holy word is actually being fulfilled to give evidence that he is the God of Abraham, Isaac, and Jacob, he is the God of Israel. He's the God who speaks his word and fulfills his word.

In contrast with classical Christian thinkers such as Justin Martyr and Augustine who saw the exile as God's punishment for the Jews' rejection of Jesus, Christian Zionists mobilize different images, more explicitly calling on the Hebrew Bible. Pastor Harris is a popular Christian Zionist commentator on contemporary political and social issues in Israel. As he explained to me:

> According to the prophets . . . after the Diaspora, after the dispersion of the Jewish people, who were dispersed not because they were unfaithful

11. Tommy Waller, "HaYovel Update: The Freeze," *HaYovel Newsletter*, November 2010.

to Jesus but because they were unfaithful to God . . . you [Jews] were driven out all over the world for a long time. At the end of a period of time, God said he would bring you [Jews] back. Physically restore you [Jews].

For Christian Zionists, the migration of Jews to a sovereign State of Israel is taken as evidence of a God who keeps his promises and serves as proof of the eternal truth of God's word. Their reading of biblical prophecy, using a futurist hermeneutic, allows the words of Hosea, Zachariah, and Ezekiel to refer to events thousands of years in the future in the contemporary State of Israel. Mr. Quinn, who has worked for many years in Israel at a major Christian Zionist organization, explained that

> there's a biblical pattern of return to the land. Moses brings the people out of Egypt and Joshua came into the land. The first thing he had to do once he was back in the land was hold a repentance service and build an altar to the Lord, and have the nation gather, repent, and get in right relationship with God. When they came back from Babylon, the first thing they did is rebuilt the house of the Lord. In Nehemiah's chapter 9 you read their prayer of repentance before God. . . . So there's a pattern of return. And Israel hasn't come to this place yet. . . . I don't know exactly where the Jewish people stand with God right now, but I do see a return—a promised, a divine appointment between God and the Jewish people, between you and your beloved, in a place where only Jewish people are allowed. This is from Hosea, it's from Zechariah 4, it's from Job 2, and not just the New Testament Scriptures. The prophets actually promise. The redemptive process that we're in today is a physical return to the land, and a spiritual return to God. That "I'll bring you back to the land and then I'll sprinkle you with clean water." That's Ezekiel. Jeremiah says, "I'll bring you back to the land, and then I will make a new covenant with you." There's some divine appointment that God has with the Jewish people.

One instrumental image in Christian Zionist restorationist thinking comes from the vision of the valley of the dry bones of Ezekiel 37. The picture of bones being brought together physically before becoming animated spiritually has been critical for justifying why Jews could be restored to the promised land in their unbelief. Christian Zionists maintain that the physical return of Jews to Israel is simply a precursor to a spiritual revival. The physical return of the Jews to the State of Israel is only the first part of a multi-act drama. As Pastor Harris said, exploring this imagery with me,

> God says he's going to first reach out his hand with tenderness and love and compassion; he is going to draw back the Jews physically. Put the bones together, as Ezekiel says—and physically reconstruct the nation. First the bones, then the sinews, then the flesh and the skin. Then there's a kind of stop to the story, because they're still dead. They have no *ruach*, no spirit ... after their physical restoration, there is a spiritual awakening—not here and there a convert. Not here and there a *baal teshuvah* [penitent], but as a nation.

The physical and anticipated spiritual restoration of the Jews is thought to have far-reaching effects. Beyond the Jewish people and their ostensible relationship with the divine, Christian Zionist support for Jewish migration to Israel reflects a standard Christian concern with the universal rather than the particular. *Aliyah* is believed to have effects for the whole world, Jews and gentiles alike. When Pastor Smith spoke to his Christian Zionist tour group at the grave of David Ben-Gurion, Israel's first prime minister, Ben-Gurion was described as a visionary who actualized God's plan for the Jews' return to Israel. Of special interest was the fact that Ben-Gurion himself emigrated to Israel (then Ottoman Palestine) in 1906. This event was presented to the group as intimately related to the 1906 Azusa Street Revival, which is the most important revival of the twentieth century and began the Pentecostal movement. That the Latter Rain Revival began in 1948—the year that Israel gained her political independence—and the Jesus Movement emerged in 1967—the year of "miraculous" victory in the Six-Day War and territorial expansion—could hardly, in the eyes of Pastor Smith and his tour group, be coincidental. As he explained:

> Everything that happens in Israel is directly related to what's happening in the church. Because, as you see, as Israel comes into its restoration, the church is coming into greater power and understanding. . . . We need to realize that Israel's restoration directly effects something great for the gentiles. . . . Anytime anything happens for the restoration for Israel, bring one more Jewish person to this land, it's like the heavens look down and say, "Hey, we can do something more among the gentiles."

Later, in an interview, Pastor Smith expanded on this idea, underscoring the idea that the Jews "in place" (Israel) is really about the Jews in a restored relationship with God, and ultimately is about all people playing their established roles in the cosmic drama.

> Ultimately I don't believe that God just wants to bring the Jewish people back to the land of Israel so that they can build houses over there. I believe that, ultimately, he's calling them back to his own heart and that they would love him and they would worship him and . . . we see the fullness of his word coming to pass for all of us. . . . Because ultimately, God is not just in love with Jewish people, he's in love with many other people. He has chosen the Jewish people to bring this revelation to the entire earth. And so the Jewish people kick things off, gentiles take their role.

In contrast to immigrant narratives that tend to emphasize themes of rupture and displacement, *aliyah* is framed by Christian Zionists in utterly opposite terms: as things coming (back) together, about coming (back) to their right place. Thus rather than migrants, who are narratively "out of place," *Olim*—Jewish immigrants to Israel—are felt to be returning to their divinely ordained, true place in the land promised to the descendants of Abraham. Jewish immigration to Israel, for Christian Zionists, is part of a theological vision of restoration and reconciliation in which the mundane details of migrant experience are overlooked in favor of the perceived cosmic significance of the immigration itself. Immigration of Jews to the Jewish state is never about what Louise Rorabacher identified as "all the elements of human experience inevitable in the migratory process, the homesickness, the painful adjustments, the bitter disappointments, the ultimate successes and failures."[12]

Jewish Zionism and *Aliyah*

Christian Zionists are hardly alone in espousing the idea that Jewish immigration to Israel is unique. Indeed, while at one level *aliyah* is simply a rhetorically charged form of immigration, it does have some special features, functioning as a basic platform of the state both structurally and ideologically. The Jewish immigrant to Israel receives certain privileges as incentives, including immediate citizenship, financial support, and tailored services.

Israeli public discourse and policy reinforce the idea of a Jewish return to an ancestral homeland as something unique. As Judith Shuval points out, "From its earliest stages, the notion of migration to Israel has been socially constructed as a unique phenomenon."[13] This is clear in the use of Hebrew: Jewish immigrants to Israel are *Olim* who are engaged in the act of *aliyah,* or "ascent." Jewish emigration from Israel is colored as *yerida,* or "descent." All other generic forms of immigration, including that of non-Jews to Israel, is simply *hagirah,* a word that is never applied to Jews and immigration to Israel. As David Bartram notes, "To describe Jewish migration to Israel as *aliyah,* then, is to approve of it at a fundamental level—as indeed most

12. Louise E. Rorabacher, ed., *Two Ways Meet: Stories of Migrants in Australia* (Melbourne: Cheshire, 1963), 13–14, quoted in Elisa Morera de la Vall, "Looking Through Their Eyes," in Martin Renes, ed., *Lives in Migration: Rupture and Continuity,* http://www.ub.edu/dpfilsa/ebook1contents.html (accessed May 31, 2013).
13. Judith Shuval, "Migration to Israel: The Mythology of Uniqueness," *International Migration* 36:1 (1998): 4.

Israeli Jews do."[14] The state has a great deal invested in the notion that Jewish immigration to Israel is unique.

We must ask, then, whether Christian Zionist support for *aliyah* simply reflects standard Jewish Zionist rhetoric about the uniqueness of Israel as a Jewish homeland. Leaving aside the obviously distinctive Christianity of Christian Zionist support for Israel, it is important to remember that ideas about the meaning and significance of the Jewish state are by no means uncontested among Jews. Seeing any kind of divine redemption in the Jewish State of Israel is anathema for secular Zionists and religious anti-Zionists alike. The Reform movement's early opposition to Zionism is well documented. Unaffiliated and/or uneducated Jews in North America would never think of the Jewish "return" to Israel as a part of the unfolding of God's redemptive plan.

Even within religious Zionism, significant divisions over this issue express themselves in discussions about what kinds of prayers ought to be said and not said on Independence Day. Writing in 1998, Sergio DellaPergola noted the decline of the "ingathering of the exiles" myth for understanding Israeli support for Jewish immigration.[15] Even among recent Jewish immigrants to Israel from North America, whose immigration by choice is distinctive in the number of migrants who identify as "religious," actual motives for *aliyah* are mixed and include significant economic, personal, and political factors.

Clearly, the Christian Zionist idea that *aliyah* is part of God's plan for the restoration and redemption of the Jewish people, not to

---

14. David Bartram, "Migration, Ethnonationalist Destinations and Social Divisions: Non-Jewish Immigrants in Israel," *Ethnopolitics* 10:2 (2011): 237.

15. Sergio DellaPergola, "The Global Context of Migration to Israel," in *Immigration to Israel: Sociological Perspectives*, ed. Elazar Leshem and Judith T. Shuval (New Brunswick: Transaction, 1998), 51–94.

mention God's plan for restoring and redeeming the whole world, is in no way simply a reflection of the broader Zionist beliefs of Jews.

Olim as Immigrants

The question, "Who/what makes a good immigrant?" is not even asked by Christian Zionists when it comes to *aliyah*. All Jewish immigration to Israel is good. Unsurprisingly, Christian Zionist deliberation regarding who is a Jew does not ever rely on halachic Jewish definitions, reflecting a significant ambivalence about rabbinic Judaism. Christian Zionists have little difficulty relying on the state to define Jewishness as per the Law of Return. In this sense, issues that might drive the Israeli rabbinate to distraction are not relevant for Christian Zionists. Jews are those whom the state deems to be Jews for the purposes of citizenship. However, there is a significant exception: Messianic Jews.

Under the 1970 amendment to the Law of Return, a child, grandchild, and spouse of a Jew, as well the spouse of a child and the spouse of a grandchild of a Jew, may claim the rights of an *oleh*. The exception is a Jew who has voluntarily changed his religion.[16] This effectively means that Messianic Jews, except in some very specific circumstances, cannot immigrate to Israel as Jews under the Law of Return.[17]

A 1990 open letter to the Israeli Supreme Court regarding the 1989 decision against Gary and Shirley Beresford, two Messianic Jews from South Africa who sought Israeli citizenship as Jews under

---

16. Other exceptions include Jews deemed dangerous to the welfare of the State of Israel or Jews with a serious criminal history.

17. A successful appeal to the Israeli Supreme Court in 2008 argued that Messianic Jews who are children only of a Jewish father have never been Jews and therefore cannot have been said to have changed their religion.

the Law of Return, argues that singling out Jewish belief in Jesus (Yeshua) as a special problem for Jewish identity is deeply illogical:

> In Israel, one can be an atheist and be Israeli, a Baha'i follower and be Israeli, a Hindu and be Israeli, a Buddhist and be Israeli, or even a murderer and still be Israeli. Yet, if a Jew who truly clings to his national identity and the heritage of his faith happens to believe in the way hundreds and thousands of Jewish people in the first century did, that Yeshua of Nazareth is the Messiah of Israel . . . he is told, "You are not a part of the Israeli nation." . . . [We] humbly request, as fellow Jews, and as fervent followers of the Hebrew Scriptures, that we be accorded the same respect, recognition, and rights as the rest of the nation whose heritage, history, and destiny we share. . . . We are Jews. We were born as Jews, and we will die as Jews.[18]

Gentile Christian Zionists have a great deal in common with Messianic Jews: their support for the State of Israel, their interest in the Jewish roots of Christianity, and their shared evangelical theology. For Christian Zionists, Messianic Jews are both members of the body of Christ and Jews, a combination that mainstream Jews cannot abide. For Israel to deny them citizenship rights as Jews threatens the important belief of evangelical Christianity that one can be an ethnic Jew and believe in Jesus Christ. This rejection of Messianic Jews as Jews for the purposes of citizenship is another example of Israeli state policy that Christian Zionists criticize. However, this criticism is quiet out of a concern that vociferously championing this cause will alienate the mainstream Jewish world both inside and outside Israel, for whom the rejection of Messianic Judaism is clear.

---

18. *The Jerusalem Post*, International Edition, May 5, 1990, 4.

Conclusion

For evangelical Christian supporters of Israel, Jewish immigration to Israel is, simply put, not immigration. The Christian Zionist belief in the uniqueness of Jewish immigration to Israel is not just a reflection of Jewish Zionist thinking about the significance of *aliyah*. It also does not reflect the uncritical attitude toward Israeli policy that some observers might expect from such staunch Israel supporters.

Christian Zionists understand this particular expression of migration within a theological framework that is grounded in earlier restorationist ideas. This framework is rendered powerful for its evangelical adherents by its ostensibly authoritative source (the Bible), its breadth (from Abraham to the second coming), and its scope of influence (the entire world, Jews and gentiles alike).

However, no doubt what makes this view of Jewish migration to Israel most plausible and compelling for contemporary Christian Zionists is that it is, in fact, underway. What for nineteenth-century restorationists was a distant, romantic dream is for Christian Zionists an ongoing project that can be promoted and encouraged, a mission whose fruits can be seen walking the streets of Jerusalem in the hundreds of thousands.

9

Christian Zionism and Mainline Western Christian Churches

Rosemary Radford Ruether

There is a danger in discussing Christian Zionism as if it were only a phenomenon of a particular kind of Christian millenarian fundamentalism, and therefore a viewpoint that mainline churches can dismiss as literalist and fanatical. Equally problematic, and perhaps more important in terms of geopolitical influence, are the more pervasive but unnamed forms of Christian Zionism found in mainline churches. These forms of Christian Zionism are deeply entwined with Western Christian imperialism toward the Middle East, represented by the British Empire and now by American empire.

Christian Zionism is deeply rooted in Britain's and America's identifications of themselves as elect nations, heirs of God's election of Israel. This election is construed as a duty to patronize the Jewish people by restoring them to their national homeland in Palestine under the aegis of global Christian empire, British or American. In the critique of classical Christian supersessionism, this kind of restorationism, rooted in the Puritan tradition, has often been ignored.

In restorationism, the relation of Christianity to the Jews remains one of universalism to particularism. But instead of negating Jewish particularism and demanding that it obliterate itself into Christian universalism, it seeks to restore Jews to their status as a nation in their national land under Christian imperial patronage. It is assumed that thereby they will operate as a collaborator with Christian empire in the Middle Eastern context.

Shaftesbury and British Identity

As Barbara Tuchman has shown, the British have long identified with Israel as God's new elect people.[1] Seventeenth-century English Puritans developed hopes that converted Jews under the patronage of the English would be restored to their homeland in Palestine, thereby becoming the precursor of a coming millennium.[2] These ideas were revived and developed by new evangelical groups, such as the Plymouth Brethren under John Nelson Darby, in mid-nineteenth-century England.[3]

But such views were not only found among sectarian groups. They also shaped an evangelical party in the Anglican Church and became influential in British imperial politics in the Middle East, leading

1. Barbara Tuchman, *The Bible and the Sword: England and Palestine from the Bronze Age to Balfour* (New York: Minerva, 1968).
2. Regina Sharif, *Non-Jewish Zionism: Its Roots in Western History* (London: Zed, 1983).
3. Stephen Sizer, *Christian Zionism: Road Map to Armageddon?* (Leicester: Inter-Varsity, 2004), 50–52.

eventually to the Balfour Declaration in 1917. A key figure here is Anthony Ashley-Cooper, Lord Shaftesbury.[4]

Shaftesbury was an earnest believer in an evangelical interpretation of biblical prophecy in which the restoration of the Jews to their homeland was a prerequisite for the return of Christ and the establishment of the millennium on earth. He worked all his life, from the 1830s to his death in 1885, for this great event. He was also connected with the highest British political leaders of the day, such as Lord Palmerston, the British Foreign Secretary, and sought to translate his enthusiasm for Jewish national restoration in Palestine into terms intended to recommend this to British imperial interests in the Middle East.

Shaftesbury was a leading actor in the Church of England's decision to establish an Anglican bishopric of Jerusalem. Shaftesbury, as a leader in the London Society for Promoting Christianity among the Jews, envisioned a vast redemptive project in which unconverted Jews would return to Palestine, in the process becoming Anglican Christians. These two events would prepare the way for the second advent of Christ. The first incumbent chosen for this Anglican See of Jerusalem was intentionally a converted Jew, the Reverend Dr. Michael Solomon Alexander, professor of Hebrew and Arabic at King's College.

In Shaftesbury's vision of the future age of redemption, Christ would return to reign over a restored Jewish nation of Anglican Christian Jews. The Jews' Society, as it was called, had the restoration of the Jews to their national existence in Palestine as an integral part of their purpose. Shaftesbury also opposed the Emancipation Bill that would have removed restrictions from Jews to full participation in

---

4. This story has been detailed in Donald M. Lewis, *The Origin of Christian Zionism: Lord Shaftesbury and Evangelical Support for a Jewish Homeland* (Cambridge: Cambridge University Press, 2010).

English political and cultural life. Thus his enthusiasm for the return of the Jews to Palestine went hand in hand with his refusal to accept their full equality as citizens in his own nation.

Although Shaftesbury died in 1885 before seeing a restored Jewish nation in Palestine, the influence of Christian restorationist ideas continued into the next generation of British politicians. Lord Arthur Balfour met with leaders of the developing Jewish Zionist movement, such as Chaim Weizmann, and was aware of their demands for Palestine as the only appropriate homeland for Jews. After World War I, the British collaborated with the French to develop mandate territories in the former Ottoman territories in the Middle East. On the eve of British General Allenby's entrance into Jerusalem to establish the headquarters of the British Mandate there, Balfour issued the Balfour Declaration declaring Britain's support for "a national home for the Jewish people."

In defending this decision in 1922 before the House of Lords, Balfour made clear the intertwining of British imperial and Christian religious interests. He proclaimed that the decision sprang not only from its political usefulness but even more from the deep debt of gratitude that Christians such as himself and those of the House of Lords should feel toward the Jews as the progenitors of their religion:

> The policy we initiated is likely to prove a successful policy. But we have never pretended that it was purely from these materialist considerations that the declaration originally sprang. . . . It is in order that we may send a message that will tell them that Christendom is not oblivious to their faith, that it is not unmindful of the service they have rendered to the religions of the world, and most of all to the religion that the majority of Your Lordships' house profess, and that we desire to the best of our ability to give them that opportunity of developing in peace and quietness under British rule, those great gifts which hitherto they have been compelled to bring to fruition in countries that know not their language and belong not to their race. That is the ideal which I desire to see accomplished, that is the aim which lay at the root of the policy I

am trying to defend; and, though it is defensible on every ground, that is the ground that chiefly moves me.[5]

How Palestinians were supposed to feel about this declaration of their homeland as the "national homeland of the Jewish people" is not discussed. The Declaration does say that it is clearly understood that "nothing shall be done which may prejudice the civil and religious rights of the existing non-Jewish communities in Palestine." Yet referring to them only as "non-Jewish" implies that they have no national claims on this land themselves.

The New Elect Nation and the Jewish State

The United States inherited this British support for Palestine as a "national homeland for the Jewish people" and played a critical role in converting it into a Jewish state. Americans also possess a religious-nationalist identification of themselves as a new "elect nation," and the Puritan tradition links this with restoration of the Jews to their national homeland. Groups promoting restoration abounded in the nineteenth-century United States. This movement gave rise to the 1891 Blackstone Memorial organized by William Blackstone, author of the popular apocalyptic book *Jesus Is Coming* (1878), and signed by 413 leading Americans such as John D. Rockefeller, Cyrus McCormick, J. Pierpont Morgan, and leading senators, clergy, and newspaper editors. This memorial was sent to President Harrison recommending that he create a restored state for the Jews in Palestine.[6] Significantly, American Jewish leaders deeply opposed this

---

5. Blanche Dugdale, *Arthur James Balfour* (New York: Putnam, 1937), 2:58.
6. William E. Blackstone, "Palestine for the Jews: A Copy of the Memorial Presented to President Harrison, March 5, 1891," reprinted in *Christian Protagonists for Jewish Restoration: An Original Anthology*, ed. Adolf Augustus Berle (New York: Arno, 1977).

initiative, seeing it as a ploy to divert Jewish refugees fleeing pogroms in Russia from coming to the United States.[7]

But it was after World War II and the Jewish Holocaust that an American president had the opportunity to push forward a resolution in the United Nations partitioning Palestine and giving 55 percent of the land for a Jewish state. The United States also stood by while the 45 percent allotted for a Palestinian state disappeared—28 percent taken into the Jewish state and the rest occupied by Jordan and Egypt, with a million Palestinians dispersed as refugees. The United States has given unstinting support to Israel since that time, both through three to four billion dollars in yearly aid and continual verbal affirmation. Although claiming to be an "honest broker" for the rights of both groups, no one examining this history can doubt that the State of Israel is overwhelmingly America's primary ally and concern.

What is America's interest in this support for Israel, a one-sided support so entrenched in American political culture that virtually no politicians can dare criticize it even slightly without jeopardizing their position? I would argue that here we find a deep intertwining of American political and religious identity and interests. On the one hand, particularly since the 1967 Six-Day War established Israel's military preeminence in the Middle East, the United States has seen Israel as helping to maintain its balance of power in the region. Most importantly, the armies of the two countries are deeply intertwined, with constant sharing of military tactics and armaments. Jeff Halper, Israeli critic of Israel's occupation, sees this close identification of the two military systems as the real "elephant in the room" that ties the two states together.[8]

---

7. Joseph P. Steinstern, "Reform Judaism and Zionism, 1895–1984," in *Herzl Year Book*(New York: Theodor Herzl Foundation, 1963), 5:11–31.

8. This is a phrase I have heard Jeff Halper use often in public talks.

The religious identification of American Christians with Israel as a Jewish state is also very deep. Most American Christians would agree with the statement that God gave the land of Palestine to the Jewish people as a permanent and exclusive donation. This supposedly biblically based claim in effect deprives Palestinians of any national rights to the land. This biblical land claim is the primary basis for American Christian identification with Israel.

This belief has been supplemented, particularly since 1967, with a Christian post-Holocaust theology that claims that Christian responsibility for the Holocaust demands repentance in the form of unstinting support for Israel. This is couched both in terms of a kind of payment or compensation for Christian sins against the Jews, and also as the necessary protection of the Jewish people against any future Holocaust. I think that the exclusivist land claim argument is the primary basis for American Christians' identification with Israel, across the political and religious spectrum, while the guilt and repentance argument has supplemented it primarily among self-critical Christians.[9]

The guilt and repentance argument is particularly important in mainline churches, though it is a lesser compelling factor for millennarian evangelicals attracted by the combination of the exclusivist land claim and the belief that restoration of the Jews is about to usher in the redemptive millennium. The repentance argument typically takes the form of a devastating rebuttal of any effort by Christians who are aware of injustice to the Palestinians and seek to criticize Israel. Any Christians that criticize Israel are typically met with an intense outcry from Jewish spokesmen to the effect that

---

9. For post-Holocaust Christian theology and its relation to Christian Zionism, see Mark Braverman, *Fatal Embrace: Christians, Jews and the Search for Peace in the Holy Land* (Austin, TX: Synergy, 2010), 105–22.

they are "anti-Semitic," threatening the security of the State of Israel, and are even seeking to "destroy" the State of Israel.

Post-Holocaust Jewish-Christian Dialogue

A faction of Christians within mainline churches has reinforced this outcry over the years through Christian-Jewish dialogue and Christian post-Holocaust. Christians calling for some parallel justice for Palestinians are thus either silenced entirely, or else the denomination finally issues a compromised statement that removes any call for real change in Israel frontline projects of occupation and land confiscation while fervently affirming the church's commitment to the security of the State of Israel. Any critique of Israel in Western Christian churches, especially in the United States but also in Canada and Europe, has been effectively silenced by the combination of these two arguments.

However, in the first few years of the twenty-first century this situation of silencing has begun to shift slightly, although not yet decisively. This has been caused by two factors. First, Israel's policies toward the Palestinians in the occupied territories have grown increasingly extreme. The separation wall, which confiscates major sections of land and water inside the 1967 truce line, fragments the Palestinian communities with curfew and checkpoints, making it ever more difficult for them to carry on daily life and making a two-state solution ever less possible by removing the land base for such a state. Those Christians in communication with Palestinians have intensified their efforts to educate other Christians about the dire injustice of this situation for Palestinians.

A second key factor is the emergence of a sector of American Jews alarmed by this growing injustice. These Jews have come to redefine their own allegiance to Israel, seeing that such allegiance must include some deep change on the part of Israel to accommodate Palestinian rights, either in the restoration of land for a possible two-state solution or else by acceptance of a one-state binational solution. For them, Israel is destroying itself by becoming unsustainably aggressive. Transformation of this culture is necessary, both to save Israel and to allow a just solution for the Palestinians.

Critical groups have grown among Israeli Jews. Some of them have become activists in resistance, opposing Palestinian house demolitions. Critical Palestinian Christians have also sought to make their voices heard, developing versions of Palestinian liberation theology. In 2009, they issued a collective Kairos statement enunciating their cry for justice and their vision of a just future for both peoples and three religions in the one land. These four groups—critical Christians and Jews in the United States (and elsewhere in Canada and Europe) and critical Israeli Jews and Palestinian Christians—have bonded and work together. The interconnection of these four groups has begun to create a sufficiently strong common front that has begun to threaten the hold of Christian Zionism in US mainline denominations.

An important voice for this emerging common front is an American Jew, Mark Braverman. In his 2010 book *Fatal Embrace*, Braverman critiques the development of Christian post-Holocaust theology that has distorted the rejection of supersessionism into an uncritical tool of support for the triumphalist policies of the State of Israel. This theology of Christian repentance originated from the best intentions and out of the justified horror of the role Christians have played in oppressing Jews in Europe over the centuries, leading to active promotion or passive acquiescence to the Nazi genocide.

But the theology that these critics shaped in mainline churches to demand repentance of Christians for the Holocaust was turned into a tool to reinforce Israel's aggression against Palestinians and silence any Christian critique. This distortion came come about through a confusion of two different discussions: Jewish-Christian interfaith dialogue and internal and international discussion of the Israeli-Palestinian conflict.

Jewish-Christian interfaith dialogue is primarily a Western discussion, rooted in the centuries of Christian hegemony in the West and the Christian theology toward the Jews shaped in that context. Christians and Jews in the Middle East from the seventh century lived in a totally different context, as minority religions under Islam. Eventually, a Jewish-Christian-Muslim dialogue in the Muslim world might arise, but that is not the issue here.

Rather, a Western Jewish-Christian dialogue started with Christians learning about injustice to Jews by Christians and coming to appreciate a more authentic Judaism, rejecting anti-Semitic supersessionism and affirming the autonomous authenticity of Judaism. However, this dialogue has been constructed in a one-sided way, in which Jews are not expected or intended to learn anything from Christians, but simply to shame Christians into a position of overt or covert acquiescence to Jewish political demands in the Middle East. Braverman, by contrast, sees himself as transformed by conversation with Christians. Jews like himself have come to critique their own hidden ethnic exclusivism and have been called to a more pluralist universalism.

For Braverman, Jewish-Christian interfaith dialogue must no longer be used as a covert tool to silence critique of the State of Israel and its policies toward Palestinians. The Israel-Palestine conflict is not primarily about relations between religions (Jewish, Christian, and Muslim). Rather, it is an issue of relations between peoples, of justice and injustice. All three religions and their cultures have traditions that critique injustice and to call for genuine justice toward peoples. These are the traditions that have to come into play to create a just coexistence between Israeli Jews and Christian and Muslim Palestinians who need to share the historic land of Palestine in peace and justice.

For Braverman, the two conflicts mentioned above and their false confusion came to a head in the General Assembly of the Presbyterian Church meeting in Minneapolis in July 2010.[10] The Presbyterians have developed an increasingly strong group calling for justice for the Palestinians. In 2006, this group called for active disinvestment in those parts of the Israeli economy that served the occupation. This call echoed the successful strategy of disinvestment used against the apartheid state of South Africa in the 1980s. It also repositioned the critique of Israel as a critique of an apartheid state. Jewish defenders of Israel were alarmed and mobilized their Christian Zionist allies among Presbyterians to try to kill this idea of disinvestment.

Breaking Down the Walls

The Presbyterian Middle East Study Commission was commissioned to study this conflict and came up with a carefully worded document, "Breaking Down the Walls," to be voted on in the 2010 General Assembly. A strong group of defenders of Israel, representing the Simon Wiesenthal Center and the Jewish Council on Public Affairs, together with Presbyterians for Middle East Peace, a Christian Zionist group of Presbyterian pastors and seminary professors, worked determinedly to demonize the statement by the study commission. It was decried as anti-Semitic, as betraying the historic friendship of Jews and Presbyterians, and as seeking to destroy the State of Israel. The Palestinian Christian Kairos document, which the

10. See Mark Braverman, "Report from the Presbyterian General Assembly—Part 2, The Jewish Response," http://markbraverman.org/2010/07/report-from-the-presbyterian-general-assembly-part-2-the-jewish-response (July 20, 2010).

study commission recommended for study among Presbyterians, was also decried as anti-Semitic and supersessionist.

But unlike earlier years, this time there was a counter group of Jews attending the Presbyterian Assembly. These were members of the Jewish Voice for Peace, as well as Mark Braverman, who supported the Presbyterian Study document and counteracted the arguments of the Jewish establishment and its Presbyterian defenders. The result? The commission's document, with some modification, passed the Assembly. Presbyterians committed themselves to an effort to end violence on both sides, a call to Israel to relocate the separation wall on the 1967 truce border, equal rights for Palestinian citizens in Israel, and cessation of practices such as collective punishment, home demolitions, and deportation of dissidents. Disinvestment was maintained. The Palestinian Christian Kairos document, as a study document for Presbyterians, also continued to be recommended.

In Braverman's view, the tactics of silencing of Christian critique of Israel through Jewish establishment and Christian Zionist pressure failed. They failed not because Presbyterians have become anti-Semitic, but because many have learned better what is actually happening in Israel-Palestine and have decided where the line between injustice versus justice and possible peace between the two people actually falls. Others see the Presbyterian document that passed as more compromised, and the conflict between those who want to silence the churches and those who want to speak out for justice as still unresolved.

10

Palestinian Christian Reflections on Christian Zionism

Mitri Raheb

Much has been written about Christian Zionism, yet little of it has been by Middle Eastern Christians, though the topic is present in the thoughts and minds of the people in our region. In this chapter, I would like to present a Palestinian Christian perspective, showing how Christian Zionism is seen and evaluated based on the Palestinian Christian understanding of theology in context. I hope that this Palestinian Christian voice will add to the choir of voices from around the world.

Christian Zionism as part of European Colonial History

The seeds for the Israeli-Palestinian conflict were sown over 150 years ago in England. These seeds would not have borne fruit if they had not fallen in that specific place at that specific time. Great Britain was the colonial empire of its time, and fifty years later it had a mandate over Palestine. The mid-nineteenth century was the era of a flourishing Christian Zionism and European nationalism. It was in this context that Lord Shaftesbury wrote in his diary in 1854:

> The Turkish Empire is in rapid decay; every nation is restless; all hearts expect some great things. . . . No one can say that we are anticipating prophecy; the requirements of it (prophecy) seem nearly fulfilled; Syria "is wasted without an inhabitant"; these vast and fertile regions will soon be without a ruler, without a known and acknowledged power to claim domination. The territory must be assigned to someone or other; can it be given to any European potentate? to any American colony? to any Asiatic sovereign or tribe? Are these aspirants from Africa to fasten a demand on the soil from Hamath to the river of Egypt? No, no, no! There is a country without a nation; and God now, in His wisdom and mercy, directs us to a nation without a country. His own once loved, nay, still loved people, the sons of Abraham, of Isaac, and of Jacob.[1]

Already in these words of Lord Shaftesbury we can see how an imperial agenda was woven with religious rhetoric: the goal is clearly stated as replacing the Turkish Empire and claiming domination over Syria. Greater Syria is seen as a fertile land waiting to be exploited and subjugated by European powers—a clearly orientalist lens.

What is interesting here is the ease with which Shaftesbury moved between biblical prophecies and British imperial interests. Colonial interests are packaged in a religious overcoat. England was here seen as the instrument for fulfilling the divine plan. In this orientalist perspective, European Jews belonged to the Orient and were

---

1. Edwin Hodder, *The Life and Work of the Seventh Earl of Shaftesbury, K. G.* (London: Cassell & Co., 1887), 493.

assigned to Palestine by the empire. Fulfilling God's plan and that of the British Empire become two sides of the same coin. Christian Zionism becomes the ideological glue that assigns divine purpose to colonial ambitions.

After the collapse of the Ottoman Empire, this seemingly wild idea of an English lord was made official British policy by another lord. On November 2, 1917, Lord Balfour wrote to Lord Rothschild:

> I have much pleasure in conveying to you, on behalf of His Majesty's Government, the following declaration of sympathy with Jewish Zionist aspirations which has been submitted to, and approved by, the Cabinet. "His Majesty's Government views with favour the establishment in Palestine of a national home for the Jewish people, and will use their best endeavours to facilitate the achievement of this object, it being clearly understood that nothing shall be done which may prejudice the civil and religious rights of existing non-Jewish communities in Palestine, or the rights and political status enjoyed by Jews in any other country."[2]

The timing of the English cabinet decision was not by chance. The British army, stationed in Egypt, was ready to storm southern Palestine. On November 22, 1917, Bethlehem was occupied by the commander-in-chief of the Egyptian Expeditionary Force, Sir Edmund Allenby, to be followed by Jerusalem just two weeks later. A four-century-long Ottoman occupation of Palestine came to an end. Palestine was now under the mandate of the British Empire.

What the words of Lord Shaftesbury and Lord Balfour have in common is that they ignore the native people of the land. While the first describes Palestine as a "country without a nation," the second doesn't mention by name the over 90 percent of the inhabitants of Palestine. Their identity is negatively described as "non-Jewish

---

2. http://www.milestonedocuments.com/documents/view/balfour-declaration/textFor in depth analysis, see Rashid Khalidi, *British Policy Towards Syria & Palestine, 1906–1914: A Study of the Antecedents of the Hussein—the McMahon Correspondence, the Sykes-Picot Agreement, and the Balfour Declaration* (Oxford: Ithaca Press, 1980).

communities" whose civil and religious rights are not to be jeopardized. But they were not seen as a "real" people and therefore did not deserve national rights or a homeland. Thus, historically speaking, Christian Zionism was from day one part and parcel of European colonial history.

Christian Zionism Is to the Right of the Likud Ideology

The year 1967 was a decisive moment in the history of the Middle East in general and Israel-Palestine in particular. The State of Israel occupied the West Bank, the Gaza Strip, and the Golan Heights and decided to continue occupying them. The branding of the state as "biblical Israel" accelerated after 1967. The name chosen for the war—"The Six-Day War"—had a biblical connotation: many branded the victory as little "David" (the State of Israel) defeating the monster "Goliath" (the Arab world). Moreover, the conquest of East Jerusalem became the theme of the song "Jerusalem, City of Gold," which became the hit of the year in 1967, perpetuating the image of two thousand years of longing for the city. In this song, we also see the myth of Israel as coming back to a barren land, to dry fountains, and to the "temple mountain."

The outcome of the 1967 war gave a boost to Jewish religious nationalism and to "messianic" extremist Jewish groups within Israel. These groups started settling in the West Bank, claiming it as ancient "Judea and Samaria." This was not so much a geographical description as a religious claim with a political agenda. The "Judaization" process soon started in the country, with settlers building Jewish settlements on every hill that had a biblical connection. The occupation of the West Bank, Gaza, and East Jerusalem gave a boost to Israeli archaeologists, who shifted their focus to the West Bank in general and to Jerusalem and the "temple" in particular. The appetite of Jewish archaeologists after 1967 was such that many of them, like Moshe Dayan and Yohanan Aharoni, were advocating for a greater Israel with land as extensive as the "Kingdom of David."[3] In this post-1967 discourse, native Palestinian populations were seen as the Canaanites whose land had to be occupied by Israel. The Canaanites could thus be tolerated only as servants and cheap laborers under an almost "divine Jewish race." Some radical Jewish groups openly called for the ethnic cleansing of the Palestinian people based on biblical passages that propagated the extermination of the Canaanites and other native groups of ancient Palestine.

The 1967 victory had a huge impact on Christians worldwide. The David and Goliath myth circulated among many Christian groups, not only in the West. In fact, I remember being told by an Indonesian Christian how his church was praying vehemently during the war for Israel to defeat the Arabs. Many saw the victory as divine intervention. The myth of Israel bringing the "desert to bloom" became widespread in church circles, and a vast number of Christians thought that they were seeing divine history unfold before their eyes.

In this context, Christian Zionism experienced a new revival. The movement got a new ally in the Israeli Likud Party, which came to power in 1977. Likud, as well as the National Religious Party (Mafdal), has much in common with Christian Zionists. They believe that all of historic Palestine has to be and remain part of the State of Israel. Menachem Begin[4] was one of the first Likud leaders to understand the importance of utilizing Christian Zionists for Israeli interests, followed by Natan Shiransky, Benjamin Netanyahu, Moshe Ayalon and others. In fact, the political views of the Christian

3. Shlomo Sand, *The Invention of the Jewish People* (London: Verso, 2009), 112–15.
4. "Profile: Menachem Begin,"
http://www.historycommons.org/entity.jsp?entity=menachem_begin (accessed November 10, 2011).

Zionists are more radical than that of Likud. This is why Prime Minister Sharon's withdrawal from Gaza in 2005 was seen as a sin and his subsequent stroke as divine punishment. Christian Zionists are eager to be "more Roman than the Pope," and more to the right than Likud and Mafdal. Political compromise is not in their vocabulary. If it were up to them, they would like to see Israel occupy the whole region from the Nile to the Euphrates and beyond. The cost of wars is, in their ideology, nothing compared with the glory of end-time Armageddon.

Christian Zionism is a Booming Business

The ties between the Christian Zionist movement and the State of Israel are not only political but economic. It is said that in 1979, Jerry Falwell received a jet airplane from the Israeli Prime Minister, Menachem Begin, in gratitude for his support.[5] Starting in the early '80s, Pat Robertson and other leading Christian Zionists started bringing hundreds of thousands of tourists to Israel. They proved to be a major "travel agency," especially in years that saw a sharp decrease in tourism to Israel. And when John Hagee brags that his organization has sent over $80 million to Israel[6], one can only imagine how economically lucrative this relationship is. It is important to point out that a good chunk of Christian Zionist support to Israel goes toward bringing Jews from Russia to Israel, or supporting the building of settlements in the West Bank, or buying more weapons so as to be ready for Armageddon. The economic dimension of Christian Zionism is something that needs to be studied and researched.

---

5. "Why Does Jerry Falwell Support Israel?" http://www.comeandsee.com/view.php?sid=504 (accessed November 10, 2011).

6. http://www.jhm.org/Home/About/PastorJohnHagee (accessed June 28, 2014).

Christian Zionism is Searching for a "Deus Revelator"

Christian Zionists are obsessed with a God that shows his strength over and over again in history. This is why this theology was part of British imperial theology; this is why it experienced a revival after the war of 1967; and this is why Christian Zionists are anxious for Armageddon. They worship God the warrior. In this, Christian Zionists miss the "Deus Absconditus," the God who reveals himself in the suffering of the cross.

This obsession with a glorious God leads Christian Zionists to overlook the people who are caught in between. They miss seeing the Palestinian Christians, they overlook the Muslims and demonize them, and they do not even take people of Jewish faith seriously. They are interested in them only as part of the divine plan, an instrument in God's end-time scenario. In that sense, Christian Zionist ideology is not only Islamophobic, but also anti-Semitic. Christian Zionists are not interested in relating to any group of people or listening to the suffering of others, but are only interested in seeing God's plan implemented at any cost. So they end up demonizing whole people (Russians, Arabs, Chinese, Persians, and others) and/or sacrificing them (Israeli Jews and Palestinian Christians) on the altar of dangerous hallucinations.

The Role of Christian Zionism Today

The image of Israel today is definitely not what it used to be. The euphoria that resulted from the 1967 war is not there anymore. The promise is turning into a nightmare. The separation wall has given a face to the Israeli occupation. The rapid expansion of settlement in the West Bank is turning even Israel's closest allies against it.

According to international law, the International Court of Justice, the Geneva Convention, and the Universal Declaration of Human Rights, what Israel does in the occupied territories is illegal and a violation of those laws and rights. Israel is becoming more and more isolated. Calls for boycott, divestment, and sanctions(BDS) are increasing. It is becoming more and more difficult to defend the policies of Israel.

In this context, Christian Zionism becomes very important. This movement doesn't care what the human rights charter states because divine rights supersede all other rights. International laws are not important, because divine laws are to be followed. In such a context, Christian Zionists might be the last allies that Israel has. They might be the only group outside the Israeli Right that not only defends Israeli violations, but promotes and supports them. It is no wonder that the Netanyahu government is trying to promote the Christian Zionist allies as the sole voice of Christianity abroad. Especially in the last two years, there has been an attempt by the current Israeli government to silence the voice of the native Palestinian Christian leaders and to replace it with that of Christian Zionists. In that sense, the imperial project that started in the mid-nineteenth century is continuing today.

11

From the Institutum Judaicum to the International Christian Embassy

Christian Zionism with a European Accent

Yaakov Ariel

Contemporary observers identify Christian Zionism with conservative evangelical Christians who hold to a dispensational premillennialist messianic faith and global vision. The support that Christian Zionism receives, at times from the Dutch Reformed in Holland or Lutherans in Finland, is generally overlooked or considered of marginal importance. Historically, however, Reformed and Pietist European Protestants have played an important role in constructing messianic theologies that have placed the return of the Jews to Palestine at the center of the events of the end times. A number of such thinkers and groups did so even before the rise of evangelical Christianity in the English-speaking world at the turn of the nineteenth century. While Pietists did not exercise the same influence in continental Europe as evangelicals would in Britain of the early and mid-nineteenth century and America of the late twentieth and early twenty-first century, their attempts to support Jewish restoration to Palestine is worth investigating. Pietists were essential to the rise of both Christian and Jewish Zionism, influencing evangelical opinions and actions and often cooperating with evangelical Christian Zionists on mutual projects. Like evangelicals, who followed in their footsteps, their ideas about and interactions with the Jews have gone beyond political aspirations and included evangelism, philanthropy, and extensive literature.

Early Christian Zionism

The beginnings of Christian Zionist attitudes can be traced to Protestant groups and thinkers in the sixteenth and seventeenth centuries who advocated a new understanding of the Jews and their role in history. While most Protestants at the time agreed with the traditional Christian claim that Christianity inherited God's covenant with Israel, some did not. Within the ranks of Protestantism, both in the radical, left wing of the Reformation and among a number of mainline thinkers, a new understanding of the Jews developed. While not fully devoid of elements of anger and bitterness, such Protestants often looked on the Jews of their generation as heirs to the covenant between God and Israel and objects of biblical prophecies about a restored Davidic kingdom in the land of Israel. John Calvin, the father of Reformed theology, took special interest in biblical codices of law and psalms with messianic overtones in his commentaries on a number of books or chapters in the Hebrew Bible.[1]

---

1. See John Calvin's major theological work, *Institutes of the Christian Religion*, trans. F. L. Battles, ed. J. McNeil, 2 vols. (Philadelphia: Westminster, 1960); William Sourmee, *John Calvin: A Sixteenth Century Portrait* (New York: Oxford University Press, 1988).

Like many Reformed thinkers, Calvin's thoughts about the Jews wandered between rejection and appreciation, anger and sympathy. When it suited his arguments, he regarded Jewish regulations based on biblical commandments as adequate and commendable, such as when he discussed the Sabbath or the prohibition on images.[2] While he was less than pleased with the Jewish refusal to accept the Christian faith, Calvin nonetheless argued that when the Bible spoke about the sinfulness of the Jews, it referred to that nation as symbolizing all people. Not only Jews but all of humanity stood guilty before the Lord, and what happened to the Jews, he warned his readers, could also happen to Christians.[3] Unlike most Christian thinkers before him, who believed that the role of the Jewish people, as an entity separate from Christianity, had come to an end, Calvin and a number of other Reformed theologians believed that while God was angry with the Jews, they could still be redeemed as a nation.[4] This idea would become a cornerstone of Reformed, Pietist, and evangelical attitudes toward the Jews. At the same time, Calvin pursued the historical dispute between Christianity and Judaism. He wrote a dialogue in which he argued with a (probably imaginary) Jewish polemicist.[5]

Theodore Beza, Calvin's heir in Geneva, was more emphatic in his sympathy for the Jews. While he held the view that the Jews were rightly punished, he prayed daily for their redemption. While often mixed and ambivalent, Reformed attitudes toward the Jews were more positive than traditional Christian understandings of the Jews or those of other mainline groups at the time. Reformed thinkers

2. Calvin, *Institutes of the Christian Religion*, book 2, chapter 30.
3. Salo Wittmayer Baron, "John Calvin and the Jews," in *Harry Austryn Wolfson Jubilee Volume*, ed. Saul Lieberman (Jerusalem: American Academy for Jewish Research 1964), 2:141–63.
4. Calvin's commentary on Matt. 27:25.
5. *Ad Questiones et Obiecta Iudaei cuisdam Responsio Ioannis Calvini* [Response to Questions and Objections of a Certain Jew], in *Corpus Reformatorum* (Brunswick: Schwetschke & Son, 1870), 37:653–74.

in England, Holland, France, and Switzerland, as well as in those parts of the New World where Reformed theology gained influence, often expressed hope for the Jews' national restoration as well as for their eventual conversion to Christianity.[6] A number of Reformed theologians who viewed the Jews as the chosen people closely followed developments such as the rise of a large Jewish messianic movement in the mid-seventeenth century, stirred by Shabttai Zvi's claim to be the Messiah, hoping that the Jews would return to Palestine to build a commonwealth there.[7]

In the late seventeenth century and the early eighteenth century, Christian Pietist groups in Central Europe constructed similar ideas about Jews. Often operating in Lutheran environments, Pietists advocated a private inner religious experience as well as the need to live committed Christian lives on both the personal and communal levels. They read the Bible more literally and emphasized missionary work, becoming, in effect, pioneers of global Protestant evangelism. Many Pietist thinkers were also messianically inclined and convinced that the Jews would again play a central role as God's chosen people.[8] They took special interest in the prospect of the conversion of the Jews, considering it to be an essential step toward the advancement of the messianic age.

6. Myriam Yardeni, *Huguenots and Jews* (Jerusalem: Zalman Shazar Center, 1998), 83–112; J. van den Berg, "Eschatological Expectations Concerning the Conversion of the Jews in the Netherlands During the Seventeenth Century," in *Puritans, the Millennium and the Future of Israel: Puritan Eschatology, 1600–1660*, ed. Peter Toon (Cambridge: James Clarke, 1970), 137–39; Frank E. Manuel, *The Broken Staff: Judaism Through Christian Eyes* (Cambridge: Harvard University Press, 1992), 92–98.

7. Gershom Sholem, *Shabbtai Zvi, The Mystical Messiah* (New York: Schocken, 1972).

8. Walter Beltz, "Gemeinsame kulturelle Codes in koexistierenden Religionsgemeinschaften, dargestellt und untersucht an Beispielen der Messiasdiskurse in den Reisetagebüchern des Institutum Judaicum J. H. Callenbergs," in *Sprache Und Geist: Peter Nagel Zum 65 Geburtstag, Hallesche Betrage zur Orientwissenschaft 35* (Halle [Saale]: Martin-Luther-Univ. Halle-Wittenberg, 2003), 11–20; and Christoph Rymatzki, *Hallischer Pietismus und Judenmission: Johann Heinrich Callenbergs Institutum Judaicum und dessen Freundeskreis (1728–1736)* (Tübingen: Niemeyer, 2004).

Pietists were pioneers in the realm of evangelization of the Jews, which they considered to be a sign of devotion and good will toward that people. In 1728, a group of Pietist thinkers headed by Johann Callenberg in the Prussian city of Halle, the hub of German Pietist activity and the home of Pietist educational and missionary centers, founded a mission to the Jews called the *Institutum Judaicum*. They were not the first Protestants who attempted to bring the gospel to the Jews; such efforts began with Martin Luther and his contemporaries. But Pietists were the first to systematize evangelism among the Jews. Their literature and techniques influenced Protestant missions to the Jews for generations, as other Pietist or evangelical missionary groups often copied or emulated their methods. Training its missionaries systematically, the *Institutum Judaicum* offered its evangelists knowledge of Jewish culture, including Jewish languages.[9] The mission set out to publish books intended for the propagation of Christianity among the Jews as well as for disseminating knowledge on Judaism and Jews among Christian supporters and interested laypersons.[10] Missionaries working on behalf of the Institute took tours of Jewish communities, visiting with Jews, engaging in conversations, and encountering their customs and ways.[11] The Pietist and, later on, evangelical methods of evangelism did not always correspond with twenty-first century standards of openness to other people's faiths. Missionaries did not shy away from making provocative statements, engaging Jews in debates on the appropriate manner of reading sacred texts and arguing whether the Messiah had already come.

9. The institute was officially called the *Institutum Judaicum et Mahammedicum*, but its activity among Muslims was secondary and it quickly became known as the *Institutum Judaicum*.
10. *Catalogues* (Halle: Institutum Judaicum, 1739).
11. Christoph Bochinger, "Die Dialoge Zwischen reisenden Studiosi und Juden in religionwissennschaftlicher Perspective," *Jewish History Quarterly* 4 (2006): 509–20.

Evangelical missionary initiatives followed in the footsteps of Pietist missions in their theological perceptions, published literature, and their more appreciative, albeit ambivalent, attitude toward the Jews. However, the scope of evangelical activity and the support it received in the English-speaking world have been much larger than what the Pietists elicited in continental Europe.[12] In a reversal of roles, Pietist missionary groups in Europe in the late twentieth and early twenty-first century, in places such as Scandinavia, Germany, Switzerland, and Holland, began accepting ideas and adopting attitudes and techniques from evangelicals.

The Institute in Halle published a series of books to acquaint Christians with Jewish life, culture, and languages. The instruction manuals demonstrated the systematizing of Jewish missionary efforts and the keen interest in the Jews, their cultures, and the effective means to approach them. Not only did the Institute's people use the books, but other members of the community did so as well as activists of other Pietist and evangelical missionary groups that began proliferating in the early nineteenth century.[13] The Institute also published books dealing with, or intended for, Muslims, but their number was small in comparison to the number of publications relating to Jewish themes. The *Catalogue* for 1748 included a series of books about the Jews and their culture and a larger selection of books intended for Jews in Jewish languages. This included three books in "the Syrian language," that is, Aramaic, "in Hebrew print."[14] This short selection included the Epistle to the Romans and the Epistle to the Hebrews. A selection of no less than forty-seven books awaited Jewish readers in the German Jewish dialect, which eighteenth-

---

12. A. E. Thompson, *A Century of Jewish Missions* (Chicago: Fleming H. Revell, 1902).

13. Johann Heinrich Callenberg and Wilhelm Christian Just Chrysonder, *Schriften Zur Jiddischen Sprache* (Halle: Institutum Judaicum, 1733); facsimile edition: Marburg, N. G. Elwert, 1966.

14. "Catalogues," Halle, 1733, 1736, 1748 in the archive of the Frankische Stiftung Ad 263 (6) i8° ("Lehrer der Christlicher Erkenntnis").

century Jews in Germany still practiced. The list starts with Jewish sacred texts, including *The Five Books of Moses*. The title points to a Christian understanding of the text and its role. Other books often carried non-Christian titles to appeal to Jewish culture and sentiments. *The Book of Zion* and *the Book of Solomon* awakened strong yearnings among Jews, as well as among Pietists and evangelicals. Likewise, the Institute published a compilation of the writings of the prophets Isaiah and Jeremiah, as well as the visions of Ezekiel and Daniel.

These were not arbitrary selections. Pietist missionaries, and the evangelical missionaries who followed in their footsteps, considered the messianic hope to serve as a meeting point between the Pietist Christian faith and Jewish yearnings for the realization of the messianic age. From this mutual point of view, the Pietists set out to convince Jews that the Messiah had come, and was about to return, rather than appear for the first time. They believed that prophetic passages in the Hebrew Bible, such as in Isaiah, would convince Jews that the Pietist messianic interpretation was correct. Pietist and evangelical writers would pursue this line of thought well into the twenty-first century.[15]

Pietists and evangelicals tried to convince the Jews not only of the truth of Christology, but of the idea that Jesus was about to arrive for the second time. As a rule, Pietist and evangelical missions to the Jews would become centers of Christian Zionism, propagating the idea that the Jews were about to return to Palestine and build a commonwealth there in preparation for the apocalyptic times and the messianic kingdom that would be ushered in at their end. Pietist visions of restoration to Zion were theological and theoretical. At this stage, no Pietist group had yet taken action to help bring Jews to

15. Arno C. Gaebelein, *The Prophet Daniel* (New York: Our Hope, 1905).

Palestine, besides trying to convince Jews that it was their historical duty to do so.

As dedicated as the Pietists were to spreading the Christian faith among the Jews and learning the realities of Jewish life, they were not devoid of stereotypical images of Jews. Contemporary historians who examine Pietist opinions on Jews are at times taken aback.[16] For example, the diaries of Johann Callenberg reveal opinions on the Jews that are a far cry from twenty-first century standards of tolerance. Mixed opinions on the Jews were another part of the Pietists' heritage that evangelicals would inherit.

Pietism strongly affected the evangelical movement in English-speaking countries in the late eighteenth and the beginning of the nineteenth century. Like Pietists, evangelical Protestants were not composed of one school of thought or organized under one ecclesiastical roof, yet they shared a number of convictions and assumptions. Like Pietists, evangelicals believed that formal baptism and church affiliation were not enough for people to become true Christians. Like Pietists, evangelical Christians emphasized the truth of the Christian Scriptures and viewed them as the messages of God to humanity, advocating a more literal reading of the Bible and often opposing exegetical options that have questioned the authenticity and accuracy of the biblical texts. Like Pietists, many evangelical Christians adhered to a messianic faith and understood biblical prophecies of the restoration of Israel to its ancestral land as relating to the Jews.[17] Like Pietists, evangelical Christians also shared a deep commitment to the spreading of the Christian gospel and found the

16. Giuseppe Veltri, "Die Diarii des Callenberg-Instituts: eine Quelle zur Juedischen kulturgeschichte in der ersten Haelfte des 18. Jahrhunderts," *Jewish History Quarterly* 4 (2006): 652–61.

17. Timothy P. Weber, *Living in the Shadow of the Second Coming* (Chicago: University of Chicago Press, 1988).

mission an appropriate venue and a convenient institutional structure to express their interest in and involvement with the Jews.

European Pietists and Palestine

Since the nineteenth century, Pietist Christians have related strongly to Palestine. In theory, Pietists and evangelicals do not embrace the concept of holy space, but in the nineteenth century these scripturally oriented Christians began relating to Palestine as a holy land. Continental Pietists, a well as English-speaking evangelicals, explored the country's history, topography, and archeology and established a series of educational and medical institutions there, as well as hospices for pilgrims and missionary posts.

While not as politically influential as their counterparts in English-speaking countries, Pietists also became involved at that time in activities that influenced the future of Palestine and, like their counterparts in Britain and America, labored since the 1830s to expand their work in the Holy Land and among its Jewish, and non-Jewish, populations. At times, they cooperated with the British in joint ventures such as the Protestant bishopric in Jerusalem. Members of German and Scandinavian pietistic groups settled in the country, their religious interests often intermingling with political and economic considerations, including the colonial ambitions of their countries.

Pietist ventures in the Holy Land enjoyed, at times, the financial support of Protestant European governments and church agencies. For example, the Reformed and Pietist-oriented Prussian court was supportive of Pietist ventures in the Holy Land. While Pietist societies were at first motivated mostly by their wish to become involved with the Jews and instruct them about their true role and purpose in Palestine, they often turned their attention to the

Christian population in the country, most of whom were affiliated with Greek Orthodox, Greek Catholic, Armenian, and other Eastern churches. By the eve of World War I, German and Scandinavian Pietist agencies, alongside British, American, and other groups, had made an extensive contribution to the building of educational, medical, and welfare infrastructures in Palestine, as well as contributed to the advancement of the country's agriculture, tourism, arts and crafts, and banking. They offered the country's inhabitants services and opportunities that would have otherwise arrived much later. Some of those ventures were carried out in cooperation with evangelical Christians.

In 1895, a Swedish-American Pietist-evangelical group from Chicago headed by Olof Larson, a former ship captain, decided to join a commune that American evangelicals had established in Jerusalem in 1881. Anna Spafford, the leader of the American Colony in Jerusalem, visited Chicago and met Larson's group, which was impressed with her personality and message.[18] The group believed that Jesus was returning soon and that true Christians would meet him upon his arrival in Jerusalem. Larson and his group, about seventy persons, sold their property and proceeded to "hasten to the Holy City to await the second coming of the Lord and witness the fulfillment of Prophecy."[19] Another group of Larson's followers in Nås, Sweden, which had formed after he conducted a series of revival meetings there in 1889, also decided to join the Americans. They believed that the "approach of the Last Day was imminent and they must hurry to meet their Lord in Jerusalem."[20]

---

18. Paul Elmen, "The American-Swedish Kibbutz," *Swedish Pioneer Historical Quarterly* 32 (1981): 205–18.
19. Edith Larson, *Dalafolk i Heligt Land* (Stockholm: Natur och kultur, 1957), 20–27, 33–34, quoted in Ariel and Kark, "Messianism, Holiness, Charisma, and Community: The American-Swedish Colony in Jerusalem, 1881–1933," *Church History* 65:4 (1996): 641–57. I owe thanks to Ruth Kark, who in 1996 initiated a joint paper on the group and conducted large parts of the research.

The commune, which now numbered more than 150 people, moved to a building on Nablus Road, north of the Old City of Jerusalem. The building was eventually purchased from the Muslim Husseini family and became the center of the American-Swedish colony complex. In the 1890s, the location was not yet fully urban, and the American-Swedish colony could develop both urban commercial enterprises and agricultural ones, including a dairy farm, a bakery, a furniture shop, a guesthouse, a tourist shop, and a photography studio. The Swedish-American group became a major economic and philanthropic enterprise in Jerusalem, leaving its mark on the city's development.[21] English was the language of the community, which celebrated the Fourth of July, and the Swedes gradually Americanized. A number of second-generation Swedes who grew up in the commune left for America and built their lives there. Some commented on the female leadership of the colony, which was not unusual for religious-messianic movements in America at the turn of the twentieth century, but stood against the social norms of European and American societies in general. One favorable Swedish description of the community and its leader was that of the Swedish Nobel Prize laureate Selma Lagerlöf.[22]

For Jewish Zionist settlers, the Pietist agricultural villages, neighborhoods, and economic and civic ventures offered an inspiration and a challenge. Among other forms of assistance, German Pietists taught the Jewish agricultural settlers of the 1870s–80s how to till their land and use more advanced agricultural techniques than were then practiced in Palestine. The German and

20. Helga Dudman and Ruth Kark, *The American Colony: Scenes from a Jerusalem Saga* (Jerusalem: Carta, 1998), 102–27.
21. Dov Gavish, "The American Colony and its Photographers," in *Zev Vilnay's Jubilee Volume*, ed. Ely Schiller (Jerusalem: Ariel, 1984), 127–44.
22. Selma Lagerlöf, *Jerusalem*, two vols. (London, 1913); and Lagerlöf, "Address to the Universal Christian Conference in Stockholm" (Stockholm: n.p., 1925), 1–4.

Swedish settlers also provided models of urban neighborhoods run on European standards of sanitation, medical care, education, and civic activity.

The rise of political Zionism at the end of the nineteenth century enhanced the cooperation between Jewish leaders and Pietist activists. Attempting to establish contacts with European Protestant political leaders, Theodor Herzl sought the advice and cooperation of William Hechler. In his convictions and career, Hechler bridged continental Pietism and English-speaking evangelicalism. A tutor at the court of the Grand Duke of Baden, Hechler befriended Protestant German Pietist aristocrats and royalty. In *The Restoration of the Jews to Palestine*, which he published in 1893, Hechler predicted that a breakthrough in the return of the Jews to Palestine would take place in 1897–98. When Herzl began his attempts to create a world Zionist movement in 1896–97, Hechler looked on it as a prophetic moment. He and Herzl met, were impressed by what they considered to be each other's merits and goodwill, and Hechler became, in effect, Herzl's confidant and adviser in matters of European diplomacy.

Hechler and Herzl hoped that the Reformed and Pietist-leaning Prussian royal family would look favorably on Zionist attempts at settling Palestine. With Hechler's help, Herzl met in April 1896 with the Kaiser's uncle, the Grand Duke of Baden, who expressed sympathy for Herzl's goals. Some of the characteristics of the cooperation between Christian and Jewish Zionists began with that early encounter. Herzl did not take Hechler's messianic faith seriously and considered his Christian friend to be a naïve visionary, but nonetheless trusted him. Hechler, on his part, considered the Zionist project to be a very welcome development, one that had been prophesied and predicted long in advance. However, while he saw Herzl as a decent person, he considered him to lack a good understanding of the true meaning of the unfolding of history in general and of the rise of Zionism in particular. Claude Duvernoy, a French Protestant Zionist theologian and historian, described the two as "the prince and the prophet." Theirs was ultimately a marriage of convenience. While they both liked and appreciated each other, they each saw the other as useful and helpful on the road toward the realization of their individual goals.

At this early stage of political Zionism, Pietist support was encouraging, boosting the Jewish Zionist morale. In its turn, the rise of a Jewish national movement aimed at building a commonwealth in Palestine, the early wave of Jewish immigration to and settlement in Palestine, and the revival of the Hebrew language filled messianically oriented Pietists and evangelicals with self-assurance. They considered those developments to be "signs of the times," indications that the current era was ending and apocalyptic events were about to begin. They were certain that they had read the Bible correctly and history was advancing according to plan.

However, Pietist interest in the Jews did not just manifest itself in promoting Zionist agendas and offering, often indirect, support to the Jewish community in Palestine. Pietists would also have an influence on other developments in the life of the Jewish people.

European Christian Zionism, the Holocaust, and the Rescue of Jews

A major element in the Christian Zionist representation of the Holocaust has been the claim that the evils and horrors of the Nazi regime were committed by non-Christians. True Christians—Pietists or evangelicals—who had undergone genuine conversions and were committed to living truthful Christian lives, would not take part in such regimes and atrocities. Nazi transgressions, Pietists and evangelicals contended, had been carried out by anti-Christians, even if some, or even many, of them were nominally members of churches. This outlook is not based on a historical examination of the involvement of Protestant groups with the Nazi regime. Evangelical writers have often ignored the historical reality that many Protestant leaders and churches in Germany supported the Nazis.[23] They have concentrated instead on the heroism of individual members of Pietist groups and presented the actions of such outstanding persons as normative. Such literary constructions have come to convey the message that true Christians behaved in a manner that demonstrated Christian ideals, going out of their way to protect and hide Jews, risking their own lives along the way. In evangelical narratives, good Christians and Jews stood together with Jesus on one side, and the Nazis on the other.

Published in the early 1970s, *The Hiding Place* has been the most popular book on the Holocaust in Pietist and evangelical circles. [24] *The Hiding Place* tells the story of the ten Booms, a devout Dutch Reformed family, who operated a watch shop in the Dutch city of Haarlem. Two unmarried sisters, Corrie and Betsie, lived with their aging father above the shop. During the Nazi occupation of Holland, when the persecution of Jews and others began, the ten Booms sheltered Jews and non-Jews who were hiding from the Nazis. The book offers a vivid account of the rescue activity. The family had to be wary of informers, and kept their activity secret. Daily life with hidden Jews is described with credibility. For example, it was difficult for the hidden persons to remain in their cramped quarters.

---

23. Carol Rittner, Stephen D. Smith, Irean Steinfeldt, eds., *The Holocaust and the Christian World* (New York: Continuum, 2000); Friedrich Zipfel, *Kirchenkampf in Deutschland 1933–1945* (Berlin: DeGruyter, 1965); Robert P. Ericksen and Susannah Heschel, eds., *Betrayal: German Churches and the Holocaust* (Minneapolis: Fortress Press, 1999); and Richard Steigman-Gall, *The Holy Reich* (Cambridge: Cambridge University Press, 2003).
24. Corrie ten Boom with John and Elizabeth Sherrill, *The Hiding Place* (Washington Depot, CT: Chosen, 1971). The 1975 movie of the same name was directed by James F. Collier.

One Jewish woman who could take it no longer gave herself up by walking out into the street; she was recognized and arrested.

The book implies that true Christian believers, brought up on biblical literalism, were in the forefront of the rescue mission. Indeed, according to Joseph Michman, the percentage of Dutch Protestants with Pietist leanings who rescued Jews during World War II was more than three times their percentage in the Dutch population, making up about 25 percent of those who saved Jews.[25] Ten Boom's memoirs also promote the belief that the Lord guides and protects righteous rescuers. One of the miracles that, according to ten Boom, manifested God's guiding hand took place in the Ravensbrueck concentration camp, where Corrie obtained a copy of the Bible and managed, in defiance of all regulations and inspections, to keep it, read it, and share it with others.[26]

The family, however, paid dearly for disobeying the authorities. "The hiding place" was exposed. Corrie and her sister, father, brother, and nephew were arrested. Only Corrie survived. Theirs is a story of Christian martyrdom. The ten Booms kept their faith and values at all times, and were a source of inspiration to the prisoners around them. Corrie portrays her father and sister as saintly figures, bringing tranquility and hope to the prison cells or concentration camp barracks where they were interned. She herself emerges from the pages of her reminiscences as a remarkable person, highly conscientious, humorous, and humane. Readers are invited to look upon her as an exemplary Christian. Jesus, she informs the readers, was her source of strength during her time of trial, offering her solace and inspiration when confronted with harsh imprisonment and the deaths of those who were so dear to her.[27]

25. Joseph Michman, "Some Reflections on the Dutch Churches and the Jews," in *Judaism and Christianity Under the Impact of National Socialism*, ed. Otto Dov Kulka and Paul Mendes-Flohr (Jerusalem: Zalman Shazar Center, 1987), 349–52.
26. Ibid., 193–94.

Holding to a more literal reading of the Scriptures, ten Boom asserted that the Jews were God's chosen people, destined to regain their role as God's first nation. The German attempt to destroy the Jews was futile and ultimately harmed the perpetrators, who "have touched the apple of God's eyes."[28] A major message of the book is the Christian command of forgiveness and love for one's enemies. The ten Booms felt sorry for the Germans, who were engaged in evil and destruction. After the war ended with German defeat, ten Boom promoted a message of forgiveness and reconciliation. The book's evangelization efforts thus target Germans, too, as potential converts. It carries the message that the truly converted are utterly forgiven, and Christian victims and persecutors of yesteryear are currently situated in the same boat—that of the redeemed.

Similar messages are promoted in other Pietist memoirs of the Nazi regime. They attempt to depict the courage and righteousness of the truly converted. Taken as a whole, such books promote the idea that all people who lived or died under the Nazi regime, Jews and Gentiles alike, were in need of the ameliorating gospel, if they had not held to it earlier, and that once they repented and converted they had all been forgiven and should themselves forgive. Pietist and evangelical narratives were perhaps the first non-German publications to look on the Germans as victims of the war the Nazi state had initiated, even if many of them supported Germany's war efforts. Such narratives portray ex-Nazis as people who for a while had been led astray by the powers of the devil, but were redeemed when they repented and accepted Jesus as their Savior. Amazingly, secular memoirs and novels with similar emphases on German suffering in the last stages of the war became popular only in the 2000s.[29]

27. Ibid., 163, 189, 223.
28. Ibid., 86.
29. For example, Irmgard A. Hunt, *On Hitler's Mountain: Overcoming the Legacy of a Nazi Childhood* (New York: HarperCollins, 2005); Anonymous, *A Woman in Berlin* (New York: Picador, 2006).

Autobiographical memoirs, along Pietist or evangelical lines, of ex-Nazis include those of Maria Anne Hirschmann: *Hansi's New Life* and *Hansi, the Girl Who Loved the Swastika.*[30] The books narrate the political and spiritual journey of a Nazi woman who eventually became a born-again Christian and an evangelist. Hirschmann recounts the suffering of the Germans at the end of the war: the shock of the defeat, the fear of being raped by Soviet soldiers, and the exile to West Germany from the Sudetenland, which again became part of Czechoslovakia. She emphasizes the spiritual transformation she has undergone. "Jesus and I became friends one warm summer night under the stars. . . . I was like Paul, a chief sinner; I had rejected Christ deliberately when I became a Nazi. . . . I despised His name and His life story as unacceptable to German superiority."[31]

Hirschmann complains about the Jews, who in her opinion failed to show forgiveness in the years following the war. Jewish journalists "tortured" her by asking her if she knew about the concentration camps. While Germans bear guilt, she declares, Jews carry hate and prejudices.[32] She asserts that she forgave her own oppressors, including the Soviets who had harassed Germans like her at the end of World War II.[33] Hirschmann's memoirs end with an encounter with Corrie ten Boom. At first, she writes, she was afraid to meet this righteous Dutch Pietist who, she knew, had spent time in a concentration camp. But ten Boom accepted her warmly. She even wrote a preface to Hirschmann's book, in which she expressed the importance of forgiveness. Thus Hansi's Nazi past is forgiven by both Jesus and his followers.

---

30. Maria A. Hirschmann, *Hansi: The Girl Who Loved the Swastika* (Wheaton, IL: Tyndale House, 1970); Maria A. Hirschmann, *Hansi's New Life* (Old Tappan, NJ: Fleming H. Revell, 1980).
31. Hirschmann, *Hansi's New Life*, 106.
32. Ibid., 118.
33. Ibid., 88.

Another narrative offers a different angle on spiritual Pietist journeys through persecution and suffering. Johanna Dobschiner's autobiographical book, *Selected to Live*, gives a special meaning to the conversion of victims of the Nazis.[34] It tells the sad story of a German-Jewish family who fled from Germany to Holland. In 1940, the Nazi occupation caught up with them. The first to be taken to a concentration camp and killed were Dobschiner's two brothers. She hid when her parents were arrested and deported and consequently lived in homes to which the Jewish council assigned her, working as a nurse in hospitals and children's homes. The deportations continued, and the inhabitants of such institutions were also rounded up and sent to death camps. Dobschiner was "chosen" by a clandestine Pietist Dutch network that rescued Jews and placed them in Christian homes. Her first hiding place was in the house of a conservative Dutch Reformed minister who was later executed by the Nazis.

Dobschiner describes her rescuer, "Domie," in terms similar to those generally reserved for Jesus. For her, he symbolized purity, love, protection of the meek, and self-sacrifice. "He died to secure my life in this world, Christ died to secure it in the next," she wrote.[35] In addition to being the religion of her saviors, a Pietist form of Christianity embodied for the young woman hope for a new life, and the adoption of Jesus as a personal Savior helped to overcome the loneliness of the hiding place.[36] Her survival, predetermined by God, opened her eyes to the truth of the Christian faith. Christians, she found out, were kind people. Their behavior, she decided, must result from their faith. "It must be a special religion . . . hence their kindness in taking us in."[37] "I felt protected and loved among them," she concludes.[38] She claims that if Jews only knew what Christianity was

34. Johanna-Ruth Dobschiner, *Selected to Live* (London: Pickering and Inglis, 1976).
35. Ibid., 224.
36. Ibid., 159, 197.
37. Ibid., 163.

really about, they would embrace it wholeheartedly. "The trouble is that our people don't know it, they have to be told," she writes.[39] In keeping with the Pietist and evangelical outlook on the Jewish people, she foresees a hope and future for the Jews in the messianic age. "God would one day send the Messiah. He would deliver Israel and call nations to see true light in God."[40]

Jan Markell's *Angels in the Camp* offers another perspective.[41] Like other books of its kind, its purpose is to educate the Pietist and evangelical communities about the realities of life under the Nazi regime as well as to give evidence about God's mercy and protection. Markell wrote and edited Anita Dittman's testimony, which offers a window into the travails of *Mischlinge* (the term used in Nazi Germany for those who were determined to be of mixed ancestry) and their emotional and spiritual perspectives. Dittman, who was a daughter of a Jewish mother and an "Aryan" father, gravitated toward Christianity, finding solace and meaning in her precarious life.[42] Growing up with her mother and sister, Anita joined a Lutheran congregation whose pastor took special interest in converting Jews. Unlike "full Jews," Dittman was allowed to continue her studies in regular schools well into the war years. However, in the summer of 1944, the Nazis sent her to Barthold, a labor camp for children of mixed marriages, where the young inmates dug ditches. Finding solace in her faith, Dittman was certain that Jesus protected her and attributes her survival to his divine saving graces, as well as the good will of her pastor.

38. Ibid., 213.
39. Ibid., 191.
40. Ibid., 156.
41. Jan Markell, *Angels in the Camp: A Remarkable Story of Peace in the Midst of the Holocaust* (Wheaton: Tyndale House, 1979).
42. Ibid., 9.

Like other evangelical and Pietist books of its kind, *Angels in the Camp* attempts to offer answers to questions that readers might have in relating to the evils that a Christian country inflicted on vulnerable members of its own and other societies. The protagonist-narrator therefore differentiates "true" Christians, who remained loyal to Christian principles, from "nominal" Christians. "But those people [who identified with the regime] aren't Christians; they just give real Christians a bad name," Dittman asserts.[43] This book presents the eventual German defeat as a result of the country's brutal and unethical behavior. Dittman's Pietist pastor also makes the claim that "the Jews are the apple of God's eye. Because Germany has harmed them, she will never be the same."[44] Like all Holocaust memoirs produced by Pietist and evangelical publishing houses, this one, too, has a clear agenda of emphasizing the healing powers and ever-present constructive guidance of Jesus. The book's subtitle, "A Remarkable Story of Peace in the Midst of the Holocaust," offers the message that the harsh times of the Nazi regime enabled a select group of people to discover the truth of the gospel and that true Christians can find peace and reassurance even in the midst of horror. The book confronts the question of how "a loving, all powerful God would allow such horrible things to happen" and offers an answer: "Granted, millions perished, but God also allowed millions to survive."[45]

Pro-Israel Reformed and Pietist Activities and Organizations

While maintaining its own elements, the Pietist European community has become, in recent decades, more strongly attached to evangelicalism. Therefore, it should be no surprise that Pietists have

43. Ibid., 44.
44. Ibid., 64.
45. Ibid., 61.

often collaborated with evangelicals in establishing Christian Zionist advocacy groups. One of the largest and best-known Christian Zionist organizations is the International Christian Embassy Jerusalem (ICEJ), whose leadership is composed mostly of Pietist and Reformed Christians. Its story tells us a great deal about the growing Pietist and evangelical activity in support of Israel in recent decades, and the relationship that has developed between the Pietist and evangelical communities around the globe and the society and government of Israel.[46]

In the 1970s, Pietist and evangelical activists in Jerusalem founded the Almond Tree Branch, which was intended to muster support for Israel around the globe. One of the more dynamic participants was Jan Willem van der Hoeven, a young Dutch minister who served from 1968 to 1975 as the warden of the Garden Tomb, where, according to the belief of a number of Protestant Christians, Jesus had been buried. Van der Hoeven came up with the idea of organizing large annual gatherings of Christian supporters of Israel during Sukkoth, the Jewish harvest festival commemorating the tent sanctuaries, or tabernacles, used during the exodus. His theological rationale was twofold: first, according to the Bible (Zech. 14:16), gentiles were also commanded to gather in Jerusalem during the festival. Second, he pointed out that whereas Christians celebrate two of the "pilgrimage festivals" commanded in the Bible—Easter and Pentecost—there was no general Christian celebration of Sukkoth. So in 1979, the Almond Tree Branch launched its first annual Feast of Tabernacles, a weeklong assembly of mostly Pietist and evangelical supporters of Israel that is highlighted by a march through the streets of Jerusalem.

---

46. Paul C. Merkley, *Christian Attitudes Towards the State of Israel* (Montreal: McGill-Queens, 2001), 170–80; Timothy P. Weber, *On the Road to Armageddon: How Evangelicals Became Israel's Best Friend* (Grand Rapids: Baker Academic, 2004), 213–34.

In 1980, the Israeli Knesset passed the "Jerusalem Law," which declared the whole of the city to be the capital of the State of Israel. In protest, almost all countries with embassies and consulates in Jerusalem moved their diplomatic staffs to Tel Aviv. This evacuation provided a dramatic point at which the Almond Tree activists announced the creation of the ICEJ, presenting it as an act of sympathy and support for Israel on the part of true Christians at a time when even friendly or neutral countries betrayed her.[47] The Embassy chose as its logo two olive branches hovering over a globe with Jerusalem at its center. "This symbolizes the great day when Zechariah's prophecy will be fulfilled, and all nations will come up to Jerusalem to keep the Feast of Tabernacles during Messiah's reign on earth,"[48] the Embassy's leaders announced.

Israeli officials, including the mayor of Jerusalem, Teddy Kollek, noted the propaganda value of the Embassy's creation and welcomed the new organization. It made the point, they believed, that even though many countries had removed their embassies and consulates from Jerusalem due to Arab pressure, the Western Christian world backed Israel. The Embassy chose Johann Luckhoff, who had served as pastor in the Dutch Reformed Church in South Africa, as its administrative director. Van der Hoeven, who emerged as the group's ideologue, held the post of ICEJ spokesperson until the late 1990s. Van der Hoeven and Luckhoff, as well as other workers and participants in the activities of the ICEJ, point to the geographical scope of Protestant interest in the Jews and Israel. While the United States serves as the hub of contemporary Christian Zionism, there are

47. Merkley, *Christian Attitudes Towards the State of Israel*, 176–83; Victoria Clark, *Allies for Armageddon: The Rise of Christian Zionism* (New Haven, CT: Yale University Press, 2007), 201–30.
48. Jan Willem van der Hoeven, "If I Forget Thee O Jerusalem," Sukkoth brochure (Jerusalem: International Christian Embassy, 1984), 4.

large constituencies of Protestants who take interest in Jews and Israel in other countries, mostly in Europe and Latin America.

The Embassy's major aim has been to strengthen interest in Israel among Protestant Christians around the world, mostly Pietists and evangelicals, and to translate that goodwill into concrete agendas, including extensive philanthropic programs in Israel. The Embassy wishes to represent Christianity worldwide and has made great efforts to open branches and gain supporters in as many countries as possible; however, much of the ICEJ's base of support is in Europe. Its branches and representatives can be found in Scandinavia, Holland, Germany, Switzerland, and the United Kingdom. There have also been volunteers for the Embassy in predominantly Catholic countries—Spain, Portugal, France, and Belgium. In recent years, representatives have also worked for the Embassy's interests in Eastern Europe and the former Soviet Union, and also in Australia, New Zealand, and a number of African nations. ICEJ has also received support from Latin America and East Asia, and thousands of Latin Americans participate in annual tours of the Holy Land sponsored or initiated by the Embassy.

The Embassy's international work has increasingly become electronic, although it also distributes journals, brochures, leaflets, DVDs and CDs, and broadcasts radio programs. Embassy representatives also recruit pilgrims for the annual Tabernacles gatherings and collect money for the Embassy's public enterprises in Israel. Much of the day-to-day work of the Embassy is devoted to this international mission, but also to providing welfare services among new immigrants and needy Israelis. Aware that many Jews are suspicious of Christian charitable enterprises, ICEJ has often distributed its parcels through Israeli agencies. The ICEJ has also offered financial support for the absorption of Russian and Ethiopian Jews.[49] Along with the International Fellowship of Christians and

Jews, the ICEJ is among the first Christian institutions to systematically donate money to Jewish Israeli enterprises, setting new norms in the relationship between Christian Zionists and Jews. Most Pietists and evangelicals involved in the fate of the Jews, by contrast, have supported missionary agencies that aim at spreading the Christian message among Jews, although such agencies also serve as pro-Israel lobbies. Likewise, Christian Zionist agencies, including the ICEJ, supported the building and enlarging of homes and infrastructures of Jewish settlements in the West Bank.[50]

Since the late 1970s, the policy of Israel's foreign ministry has been to encourage Christian pro-Israel activity. Israeli officials have met with Pietists and evangelical leaders and groups who come on visits, and have spoken at gatherings such as those organized by the ICEJ. Timothy Weber has observed that "both sides pay a price for the alliance." Among other sacrifices, in order to build ties with Israel the ICEJ has toned down the historical Pietist commitment to evangelize the Jews.[51]

During the 1980s and 1990s, Jan Willem van der Hoeven emerged as a major Christian Zionist speaker on Israel and its role. He expressed a premillennialist vision of Israel as a transitory but necessary stepping-stone on the messianic road.[52] According to that view, Israel is a positive development in the unfolding of history, and it is therefore necessary to protect it against the enemies that struggle to undermine it. Identifying with right-wing Israeli policies, van der Hoeven repudiated Arabs who militate against Israel's existence. Arabs who are "true Christian believers," he claimed, supported the

49. Arlynn Nellhaus, "Go Tell It On the Mountain," *The Jerusalem Post Magazine*, October 9, 1992, 6–7.
50. "US Gives Tax Breaks for Donation to Aid Settlements in the West Bank," *The New York Times*, Tuesday, July 6, 2010, A1, A10–11.
51. Weber, *On the Road to Armageddon*, 230.
52. Jan van der Hoeven, *Babylon or Jerusalem* (Shippensburg, PA: Destiny Image, 1993).

Israeli cause, as did his first wife, Vidad.[53] Van der Hoeven at times expressed negative sentiments toward the Muslim faith, which he saw as making claims on territory that was not its own. Allah, he claimed, was not the Abrahamic God but a pagan deity that emerged in Arabia before the rise of Islam. During the Gulf Wars, he prayed to God to "crash the power of Allah," by which he meant a defeat of the Iraqi forces.[54] The relation of Christian Zionists such as van der Hoeven to Islam cannot be separated from their relation to Jews and Israel.[55]

Outlooks such as van der Hoeven's gained some momentum in the 1990s and 2000s after the fall of the Soviet Union and the transformation of China into a country open to the West. This era created new political realities that attracted Pietist and evangelical attention, including the two Gulf Wars and terrorist acts by radical Muslim groups. Some conservative Protestant activists have interpreted the new developments as indications that Arab Muslim rulers and nations play a role in the events of the end times, mostly that of the evil northern empire that is destined to invade Israel.[56] While some conservative Christian leaders have made an effort to be gracious in relating to Islam, others, such as Franklin Graham, have not disguised their disdain.[57] Likewise, in the wake of September 11, 2001, Hal Lindsey wrote a book that presented Muslims as playing a negative, but central, role in world history.[58] Whereas thinkers such as Lindsey previously tied Israel's place in God's plans for humanity with their rejection and fear of the Soviet Union, now Islam and

---

53. *Le Maan Tzion Lo Echeshe* (in Hebrew) (Jerusalem: International Christian Embassy, 1990), 13.

54. Van Der Hoeven, *Babylon or Jerusalem*, esp. 47–71, 131–46, 169–78.

55. Thomas S. Kidd, *American Christians and Islam: Evangelical Culture from the Colonial Period to the Age of Terrorism* (Princeton, NJ: Princeton University Press, 2009); Stephen Spector, *Evangelicals and Israel: The Story of American Christian Zionism* (New York: Oxford University Press, 2009), 50–110.

56. Elishua Davidson; *Islam, Israel, and the Last Days*, (Eugene, OR: Harvest House, 1991); Randall Price, *Unholy War: America, Israel and Radical Islam*, (Eugene, OR: Harvest House, 2001).

57. Spector, *Evangelicals and Israel*, 76–110.

58. Hal Lindsey, *The Everlasting Hatred: The Roots of Jihad* (Murieta, CA: Oracle, 2002).

Muslim groups have come into the picture. Thus the Christian Zionist relation to the Jews has constantly meshed with other global considerations and related to additional participants on the political and theological map.

While he prefers Jews to Muslims, van der Hoeven's attitude toward the Jews has been complicated. He has dedicated his life to muster support for Israel, firmly believing that the Jews were heirs of biblical Israel and God's chosen people. However, he has also harbored feelings of frustration and disappointment, for example, over the fact that many Israelis have been unwilling to support a firmer national political agenda. In order to be accepted by the world's liberals, he complained, they were willing to compromise their historical aspirations. In so doing, they were betraying their purpose in God's plans for the end of the age.

In a speech delivered during the Embassy's 1989 Tabernacles celebration, he attacked moderate and left-wing Israeli politicians, declaring that giving up the territories Israel had occupied since 1967 would mark the second time the Jews rejected God.[59] For him, "land for peace" would not mean a decision aimed at promoting peace and enhancing the well-being of Israel and its neighbors. Such a move would have disastrous implications, as it would impede the divine plan for human redemption. The Jews are not just another people who can make choices according to ever-changing political needs; they have a duty and purpose in history. For the Jews to refuse to play their role would therefore constitute an unforgivable treachery toward both God and humankind. Van der Hoeven's words convey the frustration many Christian Zionists have felt regarding the Jewish refusal to accept Jesus as a savior as well as look upon historical developments the way they do. In their view, a second

59. Spector, *Evangelicals and Israel,* 150; Michael Krupp, "Falsche Propheten in Jerusalem," an essay sent to the Protestant religious press in Germany, October 3, 1988.

refusal on the part of the Jews to accept Jesus, or to prepare the ground for his arrival, would mean missing their second opportunity for redemption.

Over the years, the ICEJ has become one of the more controversial Christian agencies that work in the Middle East or take an interest in its fate, with the opinion on the group representing attitudes toward Christian Zionism at large. Middle Eastern churches, as a rule, have no contact with the Embassy or with similar Christian Zionist groups, and reject their messages and activities. Middle Eastern Christianity generally holds that the Christian church is the heir of biblical Israel and that Judaism has no further purpose in God's plans for humanity. Most of these churches have Arab constituencies and are sympathetic to the Palestinian demand for national liberation. They see the Embassy as an institution that offers one-sided support for Israel.

Mainline Protestants have also not been enchanted by the ICEJ and its agenda. Mainline churches tend to be committed to political justice worldwide, supporting movements of national liberation and expressing sympathy for the Palestinians' quest for independence from Israeli rule. In their opinion, Israel should be judged like all other countries: on the basis of political justice.

The Middle East Council of Churches (MECC), an institution affiliated with the World Council of Churches, represents Arab and Middle Eastern churches. It takes a very critical view of Israel and has officially opposed the Embassy's Christian Zionist agenda.[60] In its May 1988 meeting in Cyprus, it denounced Christian supporters of Zionism and declared, "The consultation was referring here especially to the western fundamentalist Christian Zionist movement and its political activities conducted through the self-declared

---

60. On the MECC and Israel, see Merkley, *Christian Attitudes Towards the State of Israel*, 184–86.

International Christian Embassy in Jerusalem."[61] It was evident that the very name "International Christian Embassy" aroused anger among members of the MECC.[62]

Although the ICEJ claims to represent all true Christians and is often regarded as the representative of conservative—mostly evangelical and Pietist—Christian supporters of Israel, not all Christian Zionists identify with its methods. Some object to its willingness to refrain from missionizing Jews as a condition for establishing a close relationship with the Israeli government. *Mishkan*, an English-language magazine originally established by Scandinavian Pietists, dedicated a special issue to criticizing the non-missionary policy of the Embassy.[63] This policy obviously has touched a sensitive nerve among many conservative Protestants who, while supporting Israel, have remained firmly committed to evangelizing the Jews. For most pro-Israel organizations, showing political support for Israel has not taken precedence over spreading the gospel among the Jews.

In the early years of the state, Israeli officials took only marginal notice of Pietist and evangelical Christianity, concentrating instead on relationships with the Catholic Church, Orthodox and Middle Eastern Christianity, and mainline Protestantism.[64] Israeli leaders did notice the existence of groups and individuals who supported the country on account of their Christian biblical faith, but could not make sense of their beliefs and motivations.[65] Likewise, they often did

---

61. "Signs of Hope," *1988 Annual Report of the Middle East Council of Churches*, Cyprus, July 1989.

62. *What is Western Fundamentalist Christian Zionism?* (Limosol, Cyprus; The Middle East Council of Churches, April 1988; rev. ed., August 1988). The revised edition is somewhat more moderate than the first.

63. *Mishkan*, no. 12 (1990).

64. Uri Bialer, *Cross on the Star of David* (Bloomington: Indiana University Press, 2005).

65. For example, Michael Pragai's book *Faith and Fulfillment* (London: Valentine Mitchell, 1985). The author, who served as the head of the department for Christian churches and organizations in the Israeli Ministry of Foreign Affairs, demonstrated a complete lack of knowledge of the nature of the evangelical support of Zionism and of the differences between conservative and mainline/liberal churches.

not see the connection between pro-Israel opinions and activities and missionary work. Orthodox Jewish activists occasionally protested against this missionary activity, and some Jews attempted to harass missionaries, but this went against the government's policy and the police were given the task of protecting missionary centers.[66]

In the late 1970s, as the evangelical influence on American political life became more apparent, the Israeli government took more notice of this segment of Christianity and took measures to establish contact with it.[67] Israeli officials began receiving invitations to speak at Christian Zionist conferences or greet groups of pilgrims. Likewise, Israeli leaders began approaching such evangelists directly, requesting support.

Ironically, many of the Israeli friends of groups such as the ICEJ are in the nationalist-religious wing of Jewish society. For example, it seems that there is a greater affinity and a more cordial relationship when the right-wing Likud Party is in power. Evangelical leaders and groups such as the ICEJ have received special privileges and prizes, such as permission to hold gatherings in the courtyard of the Knesset, the Israeli parliament, as part of its Tabernacles celebrations, or the presentation by the speaker of the Knesset of the Israeli Quality of Life Award.[68] In July 1991, the liberal Jerusalem weekly *Kol HaIr* published an article reporting that the ICEJ was conducting welfare activities and distributing money to needy new immigrants in the offices of the Likud and Moledet (a small and now defunct right-wing nationalist party).[69] In 1988 the magazine *Nekuda,* an organ of the Jewish settlements in Judea and Samaria, published a favorable

---

66. Per Østerbye, *The Church in Israel*, (Lund: Gleerup, 1970).

67. "Israel Looks on U. S. Evangelical Christian as Potent Allies," *Washington Post*, March 23, 1981.

68. For a photograph of such a gathering, see Tzipora Luria, "Lelo Tasbichim: Notztim Mechuiavim LeYesha" [Without inhibitions: Christians committed to Judea and Samaria], *Nekuda,* March 17, 1989, 31.

69. Yael Eshkenazi, "*HaKesher HaNotzri Shel Moledet*" [The Christian connection with Moledet], *Kol HaIr,* November 1, 1991, 30.

article on the Embassy entitled "Without Inhibitions: Christians Committed to Judea and Samaria." Emphasizing that the Embassy had no missionary intentions, it described the group as representing pro-Israel Christians who realized that the Bible authorizes the Jews to settle their land.[70]

Conclusion

Christian Zionism is an unusual phenomenon. In no other case in the history of interactions between ethnic, national, and confessional groups has one religious group considered members of another religious and ethnic community to be the chosen people and to play a decisive role in the events that would lead humanity toward redemption. There are therefore at times amazing elements in the theology, perceptions, and activities of Christian Zionists. One of them is their attitude toward Jews, which is not necessarily composed only of admiration. While they departed in meaningful ways from traditional Christian views on Jews and Palestine, early Christian supporters of Zionism also upheld many cultural stereotypes of Jews and for a long time maintained older angers and frustrations over the Jewish refusal to recognize Christian claims and tenets of faith. One can sometimes find echoes of such seemingly contradictory feelings and claims in the writings and speeches of contemporary Christian Zionist activists.

Pietists initially offered evangelical Christians examples and encouragement for constructing their venues of interaction with the Jews, but in a reversal of roles evangelicalism later became a larger and more influential movement than Pietism ever was. In the era following World War II, the borders between Pietism and

70. Luria, "LeLo Tasbichim," 30–34.

evangelicalism began to erode, and many Pietists came to follow more evangelical paradigms and terminology. In the last generation, Pietists and Reformed Europeans who have adopted Christian Zionism have played a secondary role in comparison to their more numerous and influential evangelical counterparts. This, however, should not lead us to overlook the long and rich history of continental Pietist and Reformed Christian Zionism or its contemporary activities.

Moreover, in spite of the predominance of evangelicals in many countries in recent decades, one should not underrate the Pietist role in constructing Christian Zionist ideas, institutions, and initiatives, and in offering continued moral and material support to Jewish Zionist or Israeli endeavors. On its own, Pietism would probably not have made the same impact or played the part it did in shaping the history of Jewish and Christian Zionism, and, by extension, the course of the modern Middle East. However, Pietist European Christian Zionists have influenced both the thought and actions of English-speaking evangelicals and also worked alongside evangelicals. Pietists' major contribution to Zionism centered in offering Jewish Zionists encouragement and support in crucial moments in their history, as well as offering a counterbalance in public debates, in a number of Western countries, to hostile or skeptical Christian opinions on Zionism. Their impact in those realms has been significant.

12

Mischief Making in Palestine

American Protestant Christian Attitudes toward the Holy Land, 1917–1949

Mae Elise Cannon

The history of American Christian engagement in Israel and Palestine is one of the most controversial and influential factors contributing to US involvement in the Middle East. American Christians have been personal friends with Israeli prime ministers.[1] American Protestant missionaries have advocated for justice on behalf of the Arab communities and Palestinian refugees with whom they serve. Christian Zionists have raised millions of dollars in support of the Israeli government and the growing settlement movement. American presidents, motivated by Christian influences, have both supported Israel and criticized her policies. These are just some of

---

1. A version of this chapter was previously published in *Cultural Encounters: A Journal for the Theology of Culture* 7:1 (June 2011): 49–66.

the examples of ways that American Christians have influenced the relationship between the United States and the land of Israel/Palestine. The United States' political engagement with Israel and Palestine is the most distinguishing factor determining the nature of relations and perceptions between the United States and the Arab world. Rashid Khalidi, the Edward Said Chair in Arab Studies at Columbia University, makes this claim: "It was the superimposition of Cold War rivalries on the Arab-Israeli conflict that revolutionized both the conflict and American relations within the region."[2]

Historians, politicians, journalists, and religious editors all write about and debate the dynamic causes and multifaceted complexities of the ongoing violence between Israel, Palestinians, and surrounding Arab nations. The United States' involvement with Israel and the Palestinian conflict has a huge impact on American foreign policy and international relations. American Christians are one of the leading contributors to determining how their nation engages with Israel and the question of Palestine. Thus it is vitally important to understand the relationship of American Christians to Israel and Palestine from a historical perspective. An awareness of this backdrop will assist Christians and others who are vitally interested in the welfare of the Holy Land in their efforts to support thoughtful initiatives on behalf of Middle East peace.

Since the late nineteenth century, different groups of American Christians have shifted their theopolitical perspective toward Jews and Arabs in Palestine based on emerging theological ideologies, political actions, and other considerations. However, contemporary scholarship has vastly oversimplified the historical attitude of American Christians toward the Jewish Zionist movement and the land of Palestine. When considering the relationship between

---

2. Rashid Khalidi, *Resurrecting Empire: Western Footprints and America's Perilous Path in the Middle East* (Boston: Beacon, 2004), 127.

American Christians and Israel, religious historians have incorrectly bifurcated the engagement of American Protestants into two categories: pro-Zionists and anti-Zionists.

Even academics polarize discussions about the topic. In 1979, David Rausch, assistant professor of history at the evangelical Bethel College in St. Paul, MN, wrote: "The more Fundamentalist in theology that one is the more pro-Jewish one becomes; *and* [*sic*] the more Liberal in theology one is, the more there is a chance for anti-Semitism to occur."[3] Rausch represents this polarizing perspective, falsely assuming fundamentalism equals support of Israel and liberalism equals anti-Semitism. This oversimplification neglects to acknowledge the intricacies of American Protestant attitudes toward Palestine, including diverse theological beliefs, multifaceted concerns for Jewish refugees from World War II, commitment to access and maintenance of holy sites in Palestine, treatment of Arabs, and the desire for a peaceful solution to the Palestinian problem.

This chapter looks at the development of American Christian involvement in Palestine and its relationship to the Jewish Zionist agenda from the time of the Balfour Declaration (1917) through the establishment of the State of Israel (1948) and the subsequent Arab/Israeli War. In order to understand the nature of the Israeli/Palestinian conflict in the twenty-first century, historians must not oversimplify the past. If historical complexity is misunderstood or ignored, people will be tempted to oversimplify solutions to the current conflict.

While many people in the twenty-first century believe fundamentalist and conservative Christians have historically provided the most support for Israel, this was not the case prior to the establishment of the state. Contrary to popular belief, liberal

3. David A. Rausch, *Zionism Within Early American Fundamentalism 1878–1918: A Convergence of Two Traditions* (New York: Edwin Mellen, 1979), 342.

American Protestants provided the foundation for American Christian involvement in Palestine and its relationship to the Jewish Zionist agenda from the time of the Balfour Declaration (1917) through the establishment of the State of Israel (1948). Christian Zionists in America played the role of "mischief makers" in Palestine by adopting a one-sided approach in support of the development of a Jewish state at the cost of the indigenous Arabs living in the land. Unlike the actions of Protestant liberals during this time, a just solution to the conflict between Israel and Palestine demands a multifaceted response that demonstrates justice and equitable concern for all parties involved.

The 1948 Arab-Israeli War further complicated American Protestant attitudes toward the Holy Land. Prior to 1948, Protestant liberal Christian Zionists viewed Jewish refugees from the Holocaust as victims in need of justice. These Zionists viewed the settlement of the Jews in the Holy Land and the establishment of the new state as a "just" solution to the Jewish refugee problem. Protestant liberal sympathy toward Jewish refugees continued through 1948 and the creation of the nation of Israel. However, after the Arab-Israeli War, American Christian attitudes shifted drastically.

The remainder of this chapter follows the trajectory of influential American Protestant liberals and the influence of the American Christian Palestine Committee (ACPC) and its leadership exemplified by Carl Hermann Voss through historic events such as the Balfour Declaration, the early Arab revolts, Jewish immigration during World War II, the Partition Plan, and the Arab-Israeli War. Liberal Protestants who had previously supported the Zionist cause now desired justice on behalf of the displaced Arab population who became refugees after the war. After 1948, conservative evangelicals and fundamentalists took up the mantle of Christian Zionism and viewed the restoration of Jews to Israel as fulfillment of biblical prophecy that would eventually lead to the second coming of Christ. This marked the beginning of the prevailing relationship between American conservative Christians and the Jewish State of Israel.

Liberal Protestant Perspectives toward Zionism, 1917–1949

In the early twentieth century, the vast majority of American Protestants advocated Jewish restoration to the Holy Land. Both theologically liberal and conservative American Christians supported Jewish aspirations for a homeland in Palestine. However, as noted above, it was American liberal Protestants and not conservative Christians who were the most influential pro-Zionists in the years preceding the State of Israel. Through organizations such as the American Christian Palestine Committee (ACPC), Protestant clergy organized campaigns for education, awareness, and political advocacy on behalf of Jewish restoration to Palestine. As an expression of the intricate relationship between Protestant liberals and the Christian Zionist movement, magazines like *The Christian Century* published abundant articles about Palestine and the political situation in the Middle East. Liberal Protestants were deeply involved and invested in Jewish settlement in Palestine. Some historians have claimed that the State of Israel would not exist if it were not for the support of American Christian liberal Protestants during this era.[4]

Dean Alfange, chairman of the ACPC of Greater New York, asserted in 1945 that Jewish claims to the land were legitimate and should be supported by any means necessary, even violence. Alfange called on Jews in Palestine "to win their independence the way Americans won theirs in 1776" by resorting to arms, insisting that "bloodshed and rebellion are the answer to the Palestine question."[5]

4. Paul Charles Merkley, *Christian Attitudes towards the State of Israel* (Montreal: McGill-Queen's University Press, 2001), 162.

At the time of Alfange's speech, most American Protestants had great empathy for the suffering of Jewish refugees and thus supported the agenda of Jewish Zionists for settlement of Palestine by the Jews. However, a small number of Protestant clergy began to express concerns and criticisms toward Christian Zionism. By the late 1940s, *The Christian Century* started to get the reputation of being not in full support of the Christian Zionist agenda. For example, in 1946, the magazine's editorial board responded to Alfange's speech and argued that this pursuit of violence would have tragic effects and that there was not "a single mitigating factor in deliberate mischief-making of this kind."[6] According to *The Christian Century*, the ACPC and its constituents led the way in making mischief in Palestine.

The involvement of American Protestants in support of the establishment of the State of Israel in Palestine further convoluted an already complex situation in the Middle East. Christian Zionists supported any means necessary, even violence, in seeing their aspirations for Jewish restoration to the land come to completion. These advocates used parallel ideas of American patriotism and triumph as the ideological framework to justify the creation of a Jewish homeland in Palestine. Such mischief making was not helpful at bringing about a peaceful solution to the Jewish refugee problem in Europe while also respecting the dignity and human rights of the people already living in Palestine.

American Christian Palestine Committee (ACPC)

In 1942, the Christian Council on Palestine (CCP) was founded by American clergy (almost all Protestant liberals) in order to "concentrate on winning clergymen and leaders of Christian

5. Editorial, "More Mischief-Making on Palestine," *The Christian Century*, January 9, 1946, 37.
6. Ibid.

opinion" to the Zionist cause.[7] Zionism, as defined by the first Zionist Congress in 1897, "seeks to recognize a legally secured homeland in Palestine for the Jewish people."[8] During the late nineteenth and early twentieth centuries, Jewish aspirations for a homeland in Palestine increased significantly under the leadership of Theodor Herzl, Chaim Weizmann, David Ben-Gurion, and others. The Jewish Zionist movement emphasized the need for a "Return to Zion" and encouraged Jewish immigration and settlement in the Holy Land. Christians who supported the restoration of the Jews to the Holy Land became known as Christian Zionists. Founding members of CCP offered resounding support for Zionism and included leading liberal Protestants such as Paul Tillich, William F. Albright, Carl Hermann Voss, and Reinhold Niebuhr.[9]

Niebuhr was a Protestant liberal theologian and one of the most significant American religious leaders of the twentieth century. Based on his theology of Israel as God's chosen people, Niebuhr was a staunch advocate of Zionism. In fact, he founded and edited a journal, Christianity and Crisis (1941), in order to be able to express his perspectives on socialism, pacifism, and Zionism with freedom. Niebuhr desired to speak boldly and be a "prophetic voice" on behalf of Zionism within the Christian community. Organizations like the CCP represented a diverse range of denominational affiliations and theological views, but did not extend to evangelicals and fundamentalists. While the support of evangelical and fundamentalist Christian Zionists was welcomed, it was not "celebrated out loud in the company of liberals and not talked about in the pages of official Zionist journals."[10]

---

7. Paul Charles Merkley, *The Politics of Christian Zionism* (New York: Routledge, 1998), 142.

8. Theodore Huebener and Carl Hermann Voss, *This Is Israel: Palestine Yesterday, Today, and Tomorrow* (New York: Philosophical Library, 1956), 50.

9. Stephen Sizer, *Christian Zionism: Road-Map to Armageddon?* (Leicester: Inter-Varsity, 2004), 83.

10. Merkley, *Politics of Christian Zionism*, 136, 142, 116.

The American Palestine Committee began in 1932 as a pro-Zionist political advocacy group and included senators and members of the House of Representatives, in addition to senior officials from President Franklin D. Roosevelt's administration. In 1946, the American Palestine Committee and the Christian Council on Palestine merged to become the American Christian Palestine Committee (ACPC).[11]

The ACPC became one of the leading political advocacy organizations on behalf of Zionism. During this era, official Zionist leaders dealt "publicly at least, only with the theological left," most of whom were involved in leadership with the ACPC.[12] Paul Merkley writes of the influence of the leadership of the ACPC: "In the circumstances of the years immediately following the Second World War, this minority of pro-Zionist liberals was able to nudge a majority of Christians into supporting the politicians who brought about the creation of a Jewish state." The lobbying efforts of the ACPC played a very significant role in shifting American public opinion in the pro-Zionist direction leading up to the 1948 conflict. According to Merkley, unique dynamics around the world contributed to the success and popular support of the Zionist movement among American Christians:

> The Zionists' opportunity to win the hearts of mainstream Protestants was brief, created by extraordinary and unrepeatable circumstances; the uncovering of the Holocaust; the intolerable situation of Europe's surviving "displaced" Jews; and the realization that Jews not admitted to Palestine would have to be admitted in vast numbers to the Western democracies.[13]

11. Dan Cohn-Sherbok, *The Politics of Apocalypse: The History and Influence of Christian Zionism* (Oxford: Oneworld, 2006), 136, 137.
12. Merkley, *Politics of Christian Zionism*, 115.
13. Merkley, *Christian Attitudes*, 162, 44, 162.

Regrettably influenced by anti-Semitism, Western countries, including the United States, did not welcome Jewish immigration. Because of growing anti-Semitism in the United States, Breckinridge Long, of the State Department, had the task of "preventing Jewish refugees from reaching America's shores."[14] Encouraging Jewish settlement in Palestine seemed like a positive solution to many decision makers because it addressed the needs of Jewish immigrants and kept refugees out of the Western world. In large part, the advocacy of American Christian Zionists, mostly liberal Protestants, fostered the success and popular support of Jewish claims in Palestine. Protestant liberal support of Zionism was never as influential as in the decades prior to the 1948 conflict, and was largely encouraged by the work of ACPC and its executive secretary, Carl Hermann Voss.

Carl Hermann Voss

The intimate relationship between American liberal Christians and the emerging State of Israel is well exemplified in the story of Carl Hermann Voss. Voss was a Unitarian clergyman who served as the executive secretary of the Christian Council on Palestine prior to becoming one of the founding members of the American Christian Palestine Committee.[15] In the early twentieth century, Voss, like many other liberal American Christians, endorsed the movement for a Jewish state in Palestine. He supported the establishment of the State of Israel as a homeland for the worldwide Jewish community. During World War II, Voss's work with the ACPC advocated for the land of Palestine to be established as a refuge for the survivors of the Jewish Holocaust and a national state for the Jews. In Voss's

---

14. Michael B. Oren, *Power, Faith, and Fantasy: America in the Middle East, 1776 to the Present* (New York: W. W. Norton, 2007), 430.
15. Merkley, *Politics of Christian Zionism*, 143.

New York Times obituary, he was described as a "vocal campaigner for a secure Jewish state" who supported the partition in Palestine and urged the United States to provide aid to Israel that would assist in the absorption of Jewish refugees: "He took the position that Washington and the world were not doing enough."[16] He wrote prolifically out of his concern about the "misinformation disseminated by those who do not sympathize with the aspirations of the state of Israel."[17] Voss took it upon himself to rectify the situation through writing pamphlets such as *Answers on the Palestine Question*, first published in 1947.[18]

Like other Christian Zionists of this era, Voss's support of the Zionist movement was inspired by his theological belief that the restoration of Jews to Palestine was a part of God's divine plan. Voss, like other Christian Zionists, saw the Jews' return to Palestine as nothing short of miraculous. In reference to the fulfillment of God's covenant with Abraham, Voss believed the entire world was amazed by the accomplishment of the Jews establishing a state in Israel: "Not only Jews stood in awe but non-Jews as well—for the Zionist hope, in this fulfillment, had overtones of the Eternal."[19] Voss's view was representative of Christian Zionists and their belief that the establishment of the Jewish state was an expression of divine providence. Prior to 1948, Protestant Christians placed little emphasis on eschatology. Ideas of Armageddon and the prophetic role of the Holy Land in fulfillment of biblical promises concerned most Christian Zionists little during this period.

16. Wolfgang Saxton, "Carl H. Voss, 84; Minister Advocated Creation of Israel," *The New York Times*, Obituaries, March 18, 1995.
17. Carl Hermann Voss, *The Palestine Problem Today: Israel and its Neighbors* (Boston: Beacon, 1953), xi.
18. Carl Hermann Voss, *Answers on the Palestine Question* (New York: American Christian Palestine Committee, 1947).
19. Voss, *The Palestine Problem Today*, 3.

Complexity and Multifaceted Christian Perspectives

Although American Christians, with liberal Protestants leading the way, were in favor of Zionist goals prior to 1948, questions about Palestine, Jewish immigration, and Arab concerns were still very complex and indicative of the quickly changing circumstances during that time. Christian responses shifted in response to political activity and events from the time of the Balfour Declaration through the Arab-Israeli War in 1948. Responses expressed in editorials and articles in *The Christian Century* tended to shift in response to policy changes and events such as the Balfour Declaration (1917), the Arab revolts and the response to these revolts set forth in the British White Paper (1939),[20] the increased immigration of Jews to Palestine (1940s), and the United Nations Partition Plan (1947). In order to better understand these complexities and multifaceted perspectives, it is helpful to take a closer look at these key events and responses by the American Christian community.

The Balfour Declaration, issued by the British on November 2, 1917, represented one of the first political statements of advocacy for the Zionist movement and its claims for a Jewish state in Palestine. It promised a Jewish homeland in Palestine through the following policy statement:

> His Majesty's government views with favour the establishment in Palestine of a national home for the Jewish people, and will use their best endeavors to facilitate the achievement of this object, it being clearly understood that nothing shall be done which may prejudice the civil and religious rights of existing non-Jewish communities in Palestine, or the rights and political status enjoyed by Jews in any other country.[21]

---

20. Also known as the MacDonald White Paper, named after Malcolm MacDonald, the British Colonial Secretary who presided over its drafting.
21. Huebener and Voss, 69.

Arthur James Balfour, the creator of the policy statement, was shaped by the dispensationalist views of family members in Britain and was sympathetic to the Zionist cause.[22] Christian Zionists lauded the declaration, and like Carl H. Voss believed the statement to be clear and decisive as it "discounted the Arab claim to the exclusive ownership of that country." Others felt the policy ambiguous and undefined. In addition, Voss argued that only the "extremely nationalist Arab faction" was troubled by the Balfour Declaration.[23] *The Christian Century* did not place much emphasis on the Declaration and instead emphasized the British battle against the Turks in Palestine.[24]

The British promise to the Jews of an eventual homeland in Palestine seemed secondary to the Allied victory in the land of the Ottomans. While dispensationalism played a significant role in British involvement in Palestine, it had less influence on American Christian Zionism during this period. In the early twentieth century, fundamentalist Christians in America did not have a strong voice concerning Jewish aspirations in Palestine. Although many of them adhered to theological dispensationalism, following a national trend they in large part adopted a negative view toward the Jewish community, who were viewed as "Christ-killers."[25] It was common for fundamentalists to express anti-Semitic feelings toward Jewish Americans and the global Jewish community, and most were not leading advocates of Christian Zionism in America.[26] This sentiment

22. Sizer, 63.

23. Huebener and Voss, 70.

24. Edgar DeWitt Jones, "Palestine, the Jews and the World War," *The Christian Century*, July 12, 1917, 13.

25. For more about the relationship between fundamentalism and the Zionist movement, see David A. Rausch, *Zionism within Early American Fundamentalism, 1878–1918: A Convergence of Two Traditions* (New York: Edwin Mellen, 1979).

26. Anti-Semitism has a complex history that is beyond the scope of this chapter. An accurate interpretation and understanding of anti-Semitism would be inclusive of all Semitic people—both Arabs and Jews. However, in this context, anti-Semitism refers specifically to the

was echoed by Charles Crane of the King-Crane Commission, which was empowered by the American government during the summer of 1919 to investigate the wishes of the indigenous Arab community in Palestine.[27]

In the decades following the Balfour Declaration, several Arab revolts symbolized discontent and amplified Arab anxiety in response to British rule and increased Jewish immigration. In an attempt to quell Arab frustration, former British Secretary of State for Dominion Affairs Malcolm MacDonald issued an official white paper in 1939 that limited Jewish immigration to a maximum of 74,000 to Palestine over the following five years, at a rate of 10,000 per year. In addition, the white paper also granted entrance to Palestine for 25,000 Jewish refugees per year fleeing from the Nazi regime.[28] The MacDonald White Paper repudiated the Balfour Declaration by not directly supporting the Jewish right to a homeland in Palestine. In addition, the paper limited Jewish immigration and emphasized Arab rights in the land. Voss and other leading Christian Zionists protested: "Thousands of refugees fleeing the Hitler terror were prevented by the British from reaching the haven of Palestine."[29]

On the other hand, the sensitivity of the 1939 White Paper toward Arab concerns was in accordance with the views of Christian fundamentalists, who were declining in intellectual prestige and influence in America. These events provoked a crisis in the Zionist community leading to the resignation and retirement of significant leaders such as Chaim Weizmann.[30] The remaining Jewish leaders in the Zionist movement turned even more significantly to their

---

Jews. While historic anti-Semitism has been directed primarily toward Jewish communities, anti-Arabism is steadily increasing in the twenty-first century.

27. Sizer, 80.
28. Voss, *The Palestine Problem Today,* 18.
29. Huebener and Voss, 87.
30. Ibid., 77.

friends among liberal church leaders "who had greater leverage with the presidency and were more interested in Jewish rights than in converting Jews or fulfilling biblical prophecy."[31]

As World War II progressed and fascist pressure increased in Europe, American Christians expressed growing concern about the Jewish refugee problem. Albert Viton, a writer and political diplomat, wrote in *The Christian Century* about the increased need for Jewish immigration to Palestine, claiming "bitter necessity not merely idealistic and emotional attachment to the Holy Land" would be the compelling force of immigration on behalf of the Zionist movement.[32] Zionists such as Voss despaired about the continual limitations upon Jewish immigration and rejoiced when restrictions were lifted: "When World War II ended in 1945, thousands of Europe's surviving Jews were barred from entering Palestine and were forced to languish in the D. P. camps—homeless, penniless, despairing. Moved by their plight, President Truman urged Britain to allow at least 100,000 to enter Palestine."[33]

The Christian Century acknowledged in several articles the increasing tensions resulting from the needs of Jewish refugees and increased Arab nationalism. Throughout the decade prior to 1948, a sense of hopelessness about the situation became increasingly apparent within the American Christian community. Christians emphasized the need for intervention by the newly established United Nations to work toward an amenable outcome. The overall efficacy of the United Nations was at stake. The American Christian community did not play a productive role in minimizing the unrest in Palestine; rather, Christian Zionists compounded the conflict through their pursuit of a one-sided agenda in favor of a Jewish state

---

31. Sizer, 80.
32. Albert Viton, "Palestine: The Problem," *The Christian Century*, September 30, 1942, 1184.
33. Voss, *The Palestine Problem Today,* 18.

in Palestine without taking into consideration the Arab community that already lived and occupied the land. The United Nations, according to Viton, must "do or die in Palestine."[34]

In early 1947, the United Nations issued an inquiry into Palestine. *The Christian Century* responded by saying that it was too early to be "optimistic," but that the "intervention by the UN holds out greater hope than anything that has happened since Lord Balfour and Sir Henry MacMahon made their mutually contradictory promises to Arabs and Jews during the First World War."[35] This was one of the last positive claims from *The Christian Century* in regard to the situation in Palestine. The Century's response to the subsequent November 29, 1947 partition of Palestine was overwhelmingly negative and placed significant blame on the United States: "*The Christian Century* is frankly dismayed at the moral and military responsibilities which the United States assumed in forcing this vote through an obviously reluctant Assembly."[36] A growing group of liberal Protestants believed that the United States used its political influence to strong-arm the United Nations into passing the partition plan for Palestine.

American Christians expressed significant concern about the partition plan and its implementation. As expressed through the pages of *The Christian Century*, few had any hope that the plan would be successful. One of the greatest concerns expressed was about the lack of clarity in terms of the implementation of the plan. An editorial published on December 3, 1947 said: "But on the vital question of who is going to impose the partition and keep order until the two nations settle into peaceful relations with each other, the document

---

34. Albert Viton, "Palestine: A Test for U. N.," *The Christian Century*, October 22, 1947, 1268–69.
35. Editorial, "United Nations Launches Its Inquiry into Palestine," *The Christian Century*, May 28, 1947, 677.
36. Editorial, "U. N. Assembly Votes for Palestine Partition," *The Christian Century*, December 10, 1947, 1509.

is disappointingly defective."[37] The same editorial posits that perhaps the Security Council set itself up for a failed attempt at peace.

The Christian Century acknowledged how the partition further inclined the land of Palestine toward war: "As this is being written, a few hours after the vote was taken, world Jewry is reported in transports of rejoicing, while Arab threats of bloody resistance are being redoubled."[38] Christian Zionist advocates gave assurances that Arab resistance to the partition were merely idle threats that would not be acted upon, but liberal Protestant leaders Reinhold Niebuhr and S. Ralph Harlow wrote a letter to *The* New York Times expressing concerns and identifying the risk of the partition's implementation amid Arab hostilities.[39] Writing in hindsight, Carl Hermann Voss detailed the events:

> Israel accepted the U. N. partition decision, believing it would guarantee peace, freedom, and self-determination for both the Jews and the Palestinian Arabs. ... But the Arabs rejected it and sent military units into Palestine to harass lines of communication and attack Jewish settlements in an effort to prevent partition.[40]

The Christian Century anticipated the violence and wrote with sensitivity toward Jews seeking refuge in Palestine. The magazine argued that Jews faced the potential for further terrorization with the implementation of the partition:

> No people on earth deserves the refuge of peace as do the Jews who have managed to survive the horrors of their recent experiences in Europe. We are convinced, however, that partition will expose the Jews to dangers as terrible as any they faced from Hitler. Not only

---

37. Editorial, "Palestine Partition Plan Published," *The Christian Century*, December 3, 1947, 1476–77.
38. Editorial, "U. N. Assembly Votes for Palestine Partition," *The Christian Century*, December 10, 1947, 1509.
39. Editorial, "The Partition Gamble," *The Christian Century*, December 17, 1947, 1542.
40. Voss, *The Palestine Problem Today*, 26.

in Palestine and other parts of the Near and Middle East. If partition involves sending an American army to Palestine and drags the United States into war there, the effect on the position of Jews in this country may be tragic. . . . It is too late to turn back now. The die has been cast. But the future is dark, very dark. And there is smell of blood in the air.[41]

Frustrations increased among many supporters of Christian Zionism as the political situation in Palestine unfolded. Christian work in the Middle East suffered because of disruptions after the partition. Beginning in the early nineteenth century, several American Protestant denominations, including the Methodists, Southern Baptists, and Presbyterians, practiced missionary activity in the Middle East. Pliny Fisk and Levi Parsons, two of America's first missionaries to Palestine, represented an integration of piety and patriotism in their deployment to the Middle East.[42] In addition to focusing on the desire for Christian conversion[43] as a "light to the nations," missionaries endorsed patriotic ideas about the promulgation of freedom as an ideological virtue.[44] Fisk and Parsons, like other missionaries who would follow, desired to spread the ideology of freedom and self-governance expressed in the American Revolution. By the late nineteenth century, missionaries continued to emphasize Jewish conversion during the first stages of restorationism, but were ineffective.[45] This resulted in a shift of attention in which American Christian missionaries then focused their efforts on the Arab Muslim population, leading to American Protestant missionaries' support of Arab concerns.

In general, Christian Arabs supported the Grand Mufti of Jerusalem and were in alignment with Muslim Arabs. Thus many American

41. Editorial, "The Partition Gamble," *The Christian Century*, December 17, 1947, 1543.
42. Oren, 87.
43. Francis J. Bloodgood, "Palestine's Christian Remnant," *The Christian Century*, October 19, 1949, 1226.
44. Oren, 87.
45. Merkley, *Politics of Christian Zionism*, 73.

Christian missionaries in Palestine worked closely with the Arab community and subsequently were vocally "pro-Arab."[46] Bayard Dodge, one of the founding members of the American University in Beirut, is one example of an American missionary who exercised Arab loyalty in this way. He was not anti-Semitic toward Jews, but heavily criticized the Zionist movement, viewing it as a "tragedy." Dodge opposed Zionism primarily because the Arabs to whom he ministered opposed it and because he believed "it would harm American interests in the Middle East."[47] As the partition increased political pressure, some liberal Protestants began to voice discontent and express frustration toward the Zionist movement. The partition increased tensions and ultimately led to the abandonment of Palestine by the British. Jewish Zionists almost immediately made a declaration of the new State of Israel. Surrounding Arab states responded, beginning the Arab-Israeli War of 1948.

The 1948 war marked a major shift for many American Protestants in their views of justice toward different populations in Palestine. After World War II and prior to the 1948 war, liberal church leaders in America cried for justice on behalf of Jewish refugees and pursued their increased settlement in Palestine. As Carl Hermann Voss witnessed increased Jewish immigration and settlement in Palestine from Europe, he wrote: "Because I had seen the persecuted and dispossessed in the detention centers in Germany and Austria, it was a memorable experience now to see these same men and women come home at last." This statement bears witness to the marked sympathy toward Jewish refugees from Europe at this time. For Zionists like Voss, God was on the side of the Jews and the establishment of the Jewish state was an expression of divine providence:

---

46. R. W. Murphey, "Fear Permanent Palestine Strife: Observers See Violence Attendant on Partition as Sign that Real Peace," *The Christian Century*, February 11, 1948, 180.
47. Sizer, 81.

Israel's uniqueness lies, therefore, neither in colonization nor in its struggle for freedom, but rather in achieving the seemingly impossible task of restoring the children of Israel, scattered for almost two thousand years over the face of the earth, to their ancient homeland and building there the third Jewish commonwealth.[48]

On May 14, 1948, the day before the British Mandate for Palestine was due to end, David Ben-Gurion, then Chairman of the Provisional State Council of Israel, and future first Prime Minister of Israel (1955–1963), read a declaration of independence, known in Hebrew as Yom Ha'atzmaut, and announced the establishment of the State of Israel.[49] For some Protestant liberals, like Voss and Niebuhr, the establishment of the Jewish State of Israel marked the success of many of their aims. The following day, five member states of the Arab League invaded Palestine and the 1948 Arab-Israeli war officially began. The war continued through the spring of 1949 and ended with armistice agreements between Israel, Egypt, Lebanon, and Jordan. Christian Zionists responded to the success of Israeli nationalism with fervor and celebration. Voss wrote, "The war was over. . . . Israel had finally triumphed over its enemies. Peace which it had sought so long, peace, which it needed so badly for its development was at last more than a promise."[50]

Other American Christians did not share Voss's optimism. Many Protestant Americans began to see the settlement of the Jews in Palestine as an injustice toward the Arab population because of the war and its resulting refugees.

---

48. Voss, *The Palestine Problem Today*, xiv, 2.
49. Walter Laqueur, *A History of Zionism: The First General History of Zionism* (New York: Holt, Rinehart and Winston, 1972), 584.
50. Huebener and Voss, *This Is Israel*, 93.

Arab Refugees

One of the consequences of the 1948 conflict was the expulsion of huge segments of the Arab population from Palestine. The United Nations estimated around 750,000 Arabs were expelled from their homes and towns in the newly established State of Israel. Narrative accounts report that many of the Arabs living in Palestine fled their homes anticipating return in a few days or weeks after the conflict. Today, more than half a century after the conflict, many of these families still hold land titles and the keys for the front doors of their homes. The land and property of the Arab community was redistributed to Jewish residents of the new State of Israel. Historians debate whether this was forced removal at the hands of the Zionists or if the Arab nationalists provoked fear in their community, causing the Arab population to flee.[51] Palestinian Arabs call this event Nakba, which means "catastrophe" in Arabic. In the twenty-first century, the question of how to respond to this issue remains one of the most relevant and problematic ones in solving disputes between Israel and Palestine. Palestinian refugees demand the "right to return." Israel does not acknowledge Palestinian rights in this regard. After the 1948 war, Palestinian refugees were not absorbed into neighboring Arab states. Today, the Palestinian refugee population is the largest in the world, exceeding five million people. In 1948, the displacement of hundreds of thousands of Arab refugees had significant consequences for the perspectives of many American Christians and their support of the Zionist movement.

---

51. See Ilan Pappe, *Ethnic Cleansing of Palestine* (Oxford: Oxford University Press, 2006); and Benny Morris, *The Birth of the Palestinian Refugee Problem Revisited* (New York: Cambridge University Press, 2004).

Shifting Attitudes after the 1948 Arab-Israeli War

The 1948 conflict was the culmination of the shift of American liberal Christians away from the support of Israel and the Zionist movement. After the war, *The Christian Century* displayed this change and emphasized care for Arab refugees while calling for justice on behalf of the displaced population. Many American Christians adopted the belief that the Arab refugees were forced from their homes, making them less sympathetic to the Zionist cause. Special empathy was shown for Arab Christians who had been displaced:

> But the Arab Christians have suffered the same fate that has befallen most of the other Arabs in the Holy Land. They are either a part of that pitiful horde of almost a million refugees who have been driven from homes and livelihood to a bare existence in the refugee camps which now ring Israel, or they have barely managed to stay on in Palestine, reduced to abject poverty and filled with apprehension as to the future . . . without help from outside Palestine their future is grim.[52]

Many American liberal Protestants turned their support against the Zionist movement in response to the resulting Arab refugee problem. Liberal elites writing in *The Christian Century* began to show increasing concern in response to Zionist activity. Representative of this growing sensitivity of liberal Christians toward Arab concerns, Daniel Bliss, an American Christian pastor and missionary who served as the first President of the American University in Beirut, called on the Christian community in the United States to exercise justice on behalf of the Arab residents of Palestine who had been displaced as a result of the war.

Christian Zionists who continued to be supportive of the Zionist cause also had concerns about the Arab refugee population. Voss

---

52. Francis J. Bloodgood, "Palestine's Christian Remnant," *The Christian Century*, October 19, 1949, 1227.

asserted that both the Jewish and Arab refugee problems were important and that "every civilized person should be concerned . . . with the plight of a million and a half homeless men, women, and children of a common Semitic origin." After the 1948 war, Voss empathized with the experience of Arab refugees and asserted that Israelis were similarly concerned. He described life in the Arab refugee camps with vivid imagery and great sensitivity:

> Life in an Arab refugee camp is a shabby existence, debilitating and demoralizing, especially for those who left comfortable homes and established businesses or professions. The diet is far from adequate. Jobs are difficult to find in Jordan, barred by law in Egypt and Lebanon. For most Arab refugees, life in such camps is similar to the dreary existence they knew in the mud huts of squalid villages in Palestine or the existence still known today by many millions of Arabs—indigent villagers or Bedouins—who inhabit this depressed sector of the world.

Voss maintained that Israelis sought peace and desired to respond in helpful ways toward the Arab population. He also placed significant blame on surrounding Arab nation-states and emphasized their responsibility to respond to the needs of Palestinian Arab refugees.[53]

Voss, while remaining ardently pro-Zionist, acknowledged injustices to the Arab community. He affirmed that the 175,000 Arabs who remained in Israel after the war were "unconsciously forced into second class citizenship" and did not receive recognition as true representatives of Israel. Many would argue that second-class conditions for Arab residents of Israel have not changed in the twenty-first century. Arabs were forced to carry specially marked identification cards while they submitted to restricted movements and carried permits even for short distances. Arab areas of Israel remained under military rule. Property was often seized for security reasons, and at times entire villages had been destroyed. Voss wrote

53. Voss, *The Palestine Problem Today*, 1, 34, 39, 36.

of these conditions: "The attitude seems to be that no Arab can be completely trusted." While acknowledging hardships endured by the Arab community, Voss maintained that the Israelis would relax security regulations as quickly as possible. To some degree, he viewed these challenges as unavoidable consequences of Israel being a "young country."[54] While Christian Zionists such as Voss remained loyal, many other American Protestants were less forgiving of the consequences of the 1948 war and subsequently shifted their support away from Israel.

After the Arab-Israeli war, Christian opinion in America diversified and Zionism began to be more heartily supported by evangelicals and fundamentalists and less supported by Protestant liberals. The reason for such growing support among conservative evangelicals and fundamentalists was that they began to see the political success of the nation of Israel as confirmation of the fulfillment of biblical prophecies.[55] This transition marked the beginning of several decades of profound support by American evangelicals and fundamentalists of the State of Israel.

Conclusion

In the second decade of the twenty-first century, one must ask how these historical events help inform and provide perspective on contemporary discussions about peace between the Arab community in Palestine and the State of Israel. As the philosopher George Santayana has been quoted as saying, those who do not understand history tend to repeat it. The history of the conflict is complex and multifaceted. Decades of wars and mistrust have not provided fertile ground for peaceful resolutions that are amenable to the many parties

54. Huebener and Voss, *This Is Israel*, 154, 155.
55. Merkley, *Christian Attitudes*, 6.

involved in the conflict. The shifting trajectory of how American Protestant Christians have perceived justice is helpful in providing historical context.

American Protestant Christians, led by liberals, showed the greatest support toward Christian Zionism in the years preceding Arab-Israeli War. Leading Christian Zionists such as Carl Hermann Voss showed that attitudes toward Israel were not one-sided, but often multifaceted. They simultaneously supported Zionist claims and showed sensitivity toward Arab concerns. After the Arab-Israeli War, American Christian attitudes, particularly of liberal Protestants, shifted away from support of the Zionist movement in favor of justice on behalf of the displaced Arab community. The 1948 war and subsequent success of the Jewish state marked the beginning of prevailing evangelical and fundamentalist support of Israel.

Christians today must not be tempted to bifurcate and oversimplify the issues, but instead must learn from the lessons of history. For a variety of reasons, in the early twentieth century, many liberal Protestants quickly sided with the Zionist cause only to become more circumspect later. History can be a wonderful teacher: it is unwise to take a one-sided approach. Evangelical and fundamentalist Christian Zionists could learn from the mistakes of their liberal counterparts. A multifaceted response that demonstrates judicious and equitable concern for all parties involved in the conflict would today go a long way toward guarding against further mischief making, which only negatively impacts Jews and Arabs alike.

Today, American Christians across the conservative-liberal spectrum exemplify very diverse ideas of what justice should look like in Israel and Palestine. Many conservative evangelicals continue to follow on the heels of certain forms of dispensationalism and advocate unmitigated support of Israel. Other conservative evangelicals adopt a pro-peace agenda, calling for justice, security, and freedom on behalf of both Israelis and Palestinians. Liberal Protestants and Catholics continue to be the prominent voices on behalf of the liberation of the Palestinian Occupied Territories and the establishment of an independent Palestinian state.

In the midst of these diverse perspectives, there continue to be many issues of legitimate concern, which the global Christian community cannot ignore. The State of Israel worries about the safety and security of its borders in the middle of a hostile Arab world. Arab Israelis, Palestinians who remained within the borders of Israel after 1948, continue to experience racism and grievances that make them feel like second-class citizens. Palestinians living in Jerusalem and the Occupied Territories have limited mobility and suffer the consequences of daily living under the pressures of military rule. For Arab Palestinians, other daily realities include home demolitions, security checks, and the building of settlements.

Many Christian Zionists propagate the idea that Israel has the biblical right and obligation to occupy and control the entire "Holy Land," from the Mediterranean to the Euphrates, regardless of the cost and sacrifice of the people residing in the land. American Christians have the opportunity to become informed about the political history of Israel and Palestine and to advocate for peaceful solutions that demonstrate justice for all parties involved. We need to stop making mischief that only furthers instability and hostility and provide measured counsel and support that promotes stability and peace.

Heavily involved and deeply invested from the beginning of the twentieth century to the present, American Christians have often been "mischief makers" in Palestine.

13

Israelis, Israelites, and God's Hand in History

Finnish Christian Attitudes toward the Creation of the State of Israel

Timo R. Stewart

News of the approval of the United Nations Partition Plan for Palestine reached most Finns via radio on Advent Sunday 1947, perhaps after returning from their traditional Lutheran church service in the dark, cold days of early winter. Due to the time difference between New York and Helsinki, the vote came too late to appear in Sunday's papers. On Monday, however, front pages were brimming with news from soon-to-be formerly British Palestine. Many of Finland's numerous Christian papers also covered the event with enthusiasm. There was widespread excitement over the decision to create a Jewish state, yet war in the Holy Land seemed imminent.[1]

When the fighting started in Palestine, it seemed to take place on a rather small scale compared to the cataclysmic struggle that had ended only two and a half years before in Europe. Finland itself was no stranger to the horrors of war. The Winter War of 1939–1940 and the Continuation War of 1941–1944 against the Soviet Union, as well as the Lapland War of 1944–1945 against Nazi Germany, had left almost 100,000 Finns dead, the same number with a permanent disability, nearly half a million refugees from lost territories, massive war reparations, and an exhausted nation with an uncertain future. Despite all this, the fighting in faraway Palestine and the birth of a Jewish state captivated Finnish imaginations and prompted colorful religious speculation.

In the following, I will analyze how Finnish newspapers and especially the Christian press interpreted the news of the creation of Israel and the events immediately preceding and following it in the years 1947–1949. I will show how Christian responses ranged from indifference among traditionalists to bold conclusions about the fulfillment of prophecies among Pentecostals as well as Lutheran Evangelicals. A third group, falling somewhere between the extremes of the first two, is composed of mainstream Lutheran publications that were interested in the creation of Israel but were not as clear in placing it into theological context. Finally, I will address the surprisingly complete lack of contemporary criticism of these Christian Zionist interpretations and present an outline of the Christian Zionist activity that blossomed after 1949.[2]

---

1. *Helsingin Sanomat*, December 1, 1947; *Uusi Suomi*, December 1, 1947; *Ilta-Sanomat*, December 1, 1947; *Hufvudstadsbladet*, December 1, 1947.

2. I define Christian Zionists as *Christians who believe that Zionism is part of God's plan revealed in the Christian Scriptures.* Consequently, they see it as a good development that should be welcomed and supported. While it was also applicable before the creation of Israel, this definition comes close to the one phrased by Stephen Spector: *Christian Zionist* denotes "Christians whose faith, often in concert with other convictions, emotions, and experiences, leads them to support the

Setting the Stage of Popular Opinion:
The pro-Zionist Mainstream Press

The Finnish mainstream secular press followed the undertakings of the Zionists with great sympathy throughout 1947. The UN partition vote and Israel's independence in May 1948 only added to the enthusiasm.[3] The horrors of the Holocaust were still fresh in everyone's minds, and although Finland had refused to persecute its Jewish citizens, eight refugees had been sent to Nazi Germany. The case was of great interest in December 1947, as Arno Anthoni, the wartime head of Finland's intelligence service (the *Valtiollinen poliisi*, or Valpo) was being tried for it at the same time.[4]

It is not immediately apparent why distant Palestine would have been of interest to Finns. Finland's own Jewish population was small—less than two thousand—and Finland had no part in deciding Palestine's fate as it was not yet a member of the United Nations. Besides, there were plenty of other pressing concerns. The Allied Control Commission only left Helsinki in September 1947, Soviet troops were still stationed near the capital, and uncertainties about Soviet influence and the country's future were rife. Finns watched with trepidation as the Soviet occupation forces influenced political life in Eastern Europe and the Cold War set in. The possibility of a communist takeover in Finland could not be discounted. Indeed, Finland's postwar period (1944–1948) has been referred to as "the years of danger."

Nevertheless, the events in Palestine proved riveting both before and especially after the partition resolution. When news of fighting

---

modern state of Israel as the Jewish homeland." Stephen Spector, *Evangelicals and Israel: The Story of American Christian Zionism* (New York: Oxford University Press, 2009), 3.

3. Here, I am consciously echoing conclusions present in unpublished works by both Raimo Lammi and Tiina Kirkas.

4. An account in English can be found in Hannu Rautkallio, *Finland and the Holocaust: The Rescue of Finland's Jews* (New York: Holocaust Library, 1987).

was reported from December 1947 onward, the name recognition of the battle sites must have added immensely to their news value. At the same time, this recognition lent a particular perspective. The context from which all Finns knew the promised land—the Old and New Testaments—described a land populated by Jews. Moreover, after a name was chosen for the new state in May 1948, the Finnish word for biblical Israelites (*israelilaiset*) was the most linguistically natural choice to denote modern Israelis as well.[5] Conversely, the Finnish word often used at the time for Palestine's Arabs (*arabialaiset*) literally translates as "Arabians," which implies a people foreign to Palestine.[6]

Even though the mainstream press generally avoided overtly religious references, the justification of Zionism's claim to Palestine was never explicitly questioned. Finland lacked a colonial history of its own, but it had struggled to gain independence from Tsarist Russia only thirty years before and had recently fought the Soviet Union to retain it. The argument for the Palestinian Arabs—that they were both the clear majority and the indigenous population of a land that was holy also to Muslims and Christians—could have struck a chord. This was all the more so, since many of their rivals for control of the land came from Russia or were socialists. But it did not. Although a few papers briefly mentioned the Arab position,[7] none seemed to take it very seriously.

From the start, the Zionist argument received better coverage in the mainstream media because of well-publicized visits by Zionist officials. The leaders of the Finnish Jewish community were available for comment as well, while there was no corresponding

---

5. This was not inevitable. *Israeliitta*—a word similar in connotations and form to *Israelite*—used to exist in Finnish. It appears, for example, in the 1642 Bible translation that was in use until the eighteenth century and even after that in spoken language.
6. The more neutral term, "Arabs" (*arabit*), was also used and later became universal.
7. Three such examples are from Christian papers: *Herättäjä*, August 8, 1947; *Församlingsbladet*, November 13, 1947; Per Wallendorff, "Arabisk och judisk syn på Palestina," *Församlingsbladet*, September 9, 1948.

representative for Palestinian Arabs. Finns who had traveled to Palestine and knew something of the country had for decades described Zionists in a positive light while denigrating Arabs as cruel, treacherous, and backward.[8] In fact, Finnish accounts of the Orient are remarkably similar to the French and British works analyzed by Edward Said in *Orientalism* (1978). Moreover, the Finnish missionaries who were living or had lived in Palestine worked almost exclusively with Jews and had a very high degree of identification with them.[9]

It seems that these three factors—sympathy for Holocaust victims, the unchallenged assumption of Zionist entitlement to Palestine, and general cultural identification with the Jews compared to the Arabs—strongly influenced the way Finns saw the situation. On this basis, it was easy to frame the conflict as a Jewish—not Arab—struggle for independence. It also appeared to contemporaries that the Zionists, through resourcefulness and hard work, just might succeed in making a living in a tough environment and besting their many enemies as well.

The pioneering underdog aspect of Zionism resonated deeply in Finland, which celebrated its thirtieth independence day a week after the partition resolution and had recently survived two wars against its far larger eastern neighbor. The way the Zionists portrayed themselves—as a hardworking people in a poor land opposed by numerically superior oriental enemies—was strikingly similar to

8. For example K. Aug. Hildén, *Palestiinassa—Matkamuistelmia* [In Palestine—travel memoirs] (Helsinki: J. C. Frenckell ja Poika, 1891), 108, 179; A. A. Granfelt, *Pyhä maa—Kuvia ja kuvaelmia* [Holy Land: pictures and descriptions] (Helsinki: Kansanvalistusseura, 1913), 28; Hilja Haahti, *Pyhillä poluilla* [On holy trails], second ed. (Helsinki: Otava, 1924), 204; Aapeli Saarisalo, *Galilean rauniomailta* [From the land of ruins in Galilee] (Porvoo: WSOY, 1927), 46–49.

9. This is true of Ester Juvelius (1876–1962), Aapeli Saarisalo (1896–1986), Aili Havas (1903–1988), Rauha Moisio (1909–1999), and Kaarlo Syväntö (1909–1998), but not exclusively of Elna Stenius (1875–1949).

Finnish self-perception. Finns also saw themselves as a bastion of the West against the East, a sentiment aptly captured in the first lines of a popular wartime poem:

The border opens like an abyss.

Before me Asia, the East.

Behind the West and Europe;

as a guardsman, I protect it.[10]

Adding a Biblical Layer:
Three Kinds of Christian Papers

Many Christian papers—both weeklies and monthlies—went even further. "Literal fulfillment of the Bible"[11] was the headline used to describe this "sign of the times"[12] by *Sana* (*The Word*), a popular weekly published by a new evangelical revival movement inside the Lutheran church. The more traditionally Lutheran biweekly *Kotimaa* (*Homeland*) was more specific and claimed the prophet Jeremiah had foretold the creation of the Jewish state.[13] "The Arabians [*sic*] will find it completely futile to try and fight this tide," the paper wrote later in its editorial. "The creation of the Jewish state . . . is based on God's clearly revealed promise, which seems to have reached its time of fulfillment."[14]

Editorials, articles, and news items in Christian papers provide an interesting perspective on how Finnish Christians reacted to Israel's creation in 1947–1949. Not all the Christian papers caught the same

---

10. The poem, *Rajalla* [On the border]by Uuno Kailas, appeared in Uuno Kailas, *Uni ja kuolema* [Dream and death] (Porvoo: WSOY, 1931). Unless otherwise noted, English translations of Finnish-language works throughout this chapter are by the author.

11. *Sana*, December 12, 1947.

12. "Tilin avaus," *Sana*, January 3, 1948.

13. *Kotimaa*, December 2, 1947.

14. "Kulunut vuosi," *Kotimaa*, December 30, 1947.

enthusiasm. The texts can be divided, very roughly, into three categories depending on the frequency and boldness of their interpretations concerning Israel.

First, there are the traditionalist papers, belonging to old revival movements inside the Lutheran Church. They give the event very little or no attention and make even fewer speculations. Second are the newly emerging evangelical revivalists inside the Lutheran Church and the Pentecostal movement outside of it who write about Israel very often and make bold theological claims as to the significance of Middle Eastern political events. Third are mainstream Lutherans, not affiliated with revival movements, who are interested in Israel and sometimes see biblical significance in Israel's creation but leave the theme almost completely theologically undeveloped.

The first group—the traditionalists—includes papers published by the four old revival movements inside the Lutheran Church of Finland.[15] The vast majority of Finns, 95 percent at the time,[16] were members of the Lutheran Church. A significant number of at least the more active church members were affiliated to some extent with one of the four revival movements, although no exact figures are available. By the 1940s, the revivalist fervor of these movements had long since cooled and they had come to be seen as active and

---

15. The movements are known as *rukoilevaisuus* (the Prayerful), a movement that started in the eighteenth century originally with an emphasis on sanctification, prayer, and healing; *herännäisyys* (the Awakened), originating in eastern Finland in the late eighteenth century and early nineteenth century and emphasizing the insufficiency of deeds and trust in atonement; *Laestadianism* (named after its founder Lars Levi Laestadius, 1800–1861), which spread in Swedish, Norwegian, and Finnish Lapland and is known for stressing the difference between believers and nonbelievers; and finally *evankelisuus* (to avoid confusion with evangelicals, I shall designate them the Pietists), who split from the Awakened in the nineteenth century, differentiated by an emphasis on joy in the certainty of salvation. Their main papers are, respectively, *Länsi-Suomen Herännäislehti* (published by the Prayerful), *Herättäjä* and *Hengellinen Kuukauslehti* (published by the Awakened), *Siionin Lähetyslehti* (published by the Laestadians), and *Sanansaattaja* (published by the Pietists).

16. Finland's total population was just over four million in 1950. "Population structure," Statistics Finland, http://www.stat.fi/tup/suoluk/suoluk_vaesto_en.html (accessed April 29, 2013).

distinctive, yet undisruptive, movements firmly in the fold of the Lutheran Church.

The revivalist papers, as well as the more highbrow Lutheran theological publications,[17] display a near-complete absence of essays or even chance comments on the biblical significance of Zionism or the new State of Israel. There is very little mention of Zionism or Israel in any of these papers, although a few of them include individual articles (but no editorials) that make vague reference to the principle of God bringing his people back to the promised land near the end of days.[18]

The likely reason for this lack of interest is the force of Lutheran tradition. On this issue, it had long held similar views to the Catholics and the Orthodox,[19] whose publications during 1947–1949 also make no connection between the political events in Palestine and their faith.[20] Martin Luther had said as much in his *New Preface to the Prophet Ezekiel* (1541), which was included in a well-known Finnish Bible edition from 1878: "Over against the blindness of the Jews, it should be known especially that all the prophecies which say that Israel and Judah shall return to their lands and possess them in a physical way forever, have been long since fulfilled, so that the hopes of the Jews are utterly vain and lost."[21]

17. *Teologinen Aikakauskirja* and *Vartija*.
18. The two articles making reference to God's plan to repatriate the Jews to Palestine were Eino Rimpiläinen, "Etsikonajoista," *Siionin Lähetyslehti* 6/1948; *Länsi-Suomen Herännäislehti* 9/1949, pseudonym Tunto: "Sanan vaihto." Additionally *Herättäjä* paid some attention to events in Palestine without giving them spiritual significance.
19. By 1950, the Orthodox Church had almost seventy thousand members, amounting to 1.7 percent of the total population. There were very few Catholics in Finland in the 1940s. "Population structure," Statistics Finland, http://www.stat.fi/tup/suoluk/suoluk_vaesto_en.html.
20. *Aamun Koitto* (the Orthodox Church of Finland) and *Kellojen kutsu* (the Catholic Church in Finland).
21. Citation from Brooks Schramm and Kirsi I. Stjerna, *Martin Luther, The Bible, and the Jewish People: A Reader* (Minneapolis: Fortress Press, 2012), 157. Printed in Finnish in Gustaf Dahlberg, *Pyhä Raamattu, tarpeellisilla selityksillä varustettu—Vanha testamentti. 4 osa* [The Holy Bible with necessary explanations—part 4 the Old Testament] (Turku: Wilén, 1878), 1815.

Antti J. Pietilä, professor of theology at the University of Helsinki, was very firm on this principle in his work on Lutheran doctrine from 1932: "Under no circumstance can one use biblical prophecies to support the many dreams of Israel's return to Palestine and its national re-establishment and unification." However, he then immediately proceeds to muddy the waters by adding, "before it acknowledges Christ and starts preaching him to the nations." But this, of course, had not happened. According to Pietilä, "Christianity has abolished Israel's special position as a religious people."[22]

The second group of papers is smaller and includes relative newcomers on the Finnish Christian scene. These are the publications of the small but quickly growing Finnish Pentecostal movement and the still-disparate groups that would eventually come to be seen as the popular and dynamic fifth Lutheran revival movement, the Finnish Lutheran Evangelicals.[23] Unlike the older revival movements, the Pentecostals and the Lutheran Evangelicals were influenced by ideals from the United States and Britain, often mediated by Swedes and especially Norwegians.[24] Although the fifth revival movement also remained inside the Finnish Lutheran Church, its theology was characterized by a more literal hermeneutic as well as some Calvinist leanings.

The interpretations put forward in *Ristin Voitto* (*Victory of the Cross*), the main Pentecostal paper, and *Sana* (*The Word*), published by the Finnish Bible Society (*Kansan Raamattuseura*, or KRS)—a major

22. Antti J. Pietilä, *Kristillinen dogmatiikka III* [Christian Dogmatics III] (Helsinki: Valistus, 1932), 496–97.

23. The terminology can become confusing, as the word *evangelical* also appears in the name of the Evangelical Lutheran Church of Finland. When speaking of evangelicals in the North American and British sense, I will refer to Lutheran Evangelicals. Incidentally, Finnish has derived two different words from the same root to avoid this confusion: *evankelinen* and *evankelikaalinen*.

24. For the Pentecostals, see Lauri K. Ahonen, *Suomen helluntaiherätyksen historia* [History of the Finnish Pentecostal movement] (Hämeenlinna: Päivä, 1994), 32–60.

Lutheran Evangelical organization—have much in common. Writers in both seem to take it for granted that God cursed the Jews after they rejected Jesus and that their woes throughout history are a result of this. They also claim that the Jews still have significance in God's plan and particularly that Zionism is at least a partial fulfillment of that divine plan. They look forward to the unfolding of even more dramatic events in Palestine, culminating in mass conversion. "Based on the Bible, we are in no doubt about what this aims at. In the land of their fathers, they [the Jews] will see clearly that the Messiah is not coming in the future, but has already come. They will understand who Christ is."[25]

The Christian Zionism expressed in these articles does not necessarily mean they are free of anti-Semitic stereotypes or particularly warm toward Jewish Zionists: "Did the Jews feel any desire for the land of their fathers just a few decades ago? No! Their only desire was for business, getting rich. . . . But today there is movement in the dead bones. (Ezek. 37)"[26] While the Jewish state is portrayed as clearly prophesied in the Bible, it was considered necessary to reaffirm the orthodoxy and normativity of such a belief. "The understanding that things concerning the Jews are the timepiece of world events is widely held," claimed *Sana*.[27] "Every child of God knows that we are living in a time of great biblical prophecies," echoed a writer in *Ristin Voitto*.[28] But prophetic certainty comes easier with hindsight. Perhaps unsurprisingly, both papers started publishing more on the topic and become increasingly confident only after the partition plan was approved by the United Nations and Israel declared its independence.[29]

25. *Sana*, December 2, 1948.
26. Kauko Olander, "Juutalaiset ja Palestiina," *Ristin Voitto* 10/1947.
27. *Sana*, May 28, 1948.
28. Esko Vanhala, "Elämme suurta, raamatullisten ennustusten täyttymisen aikaa," *Ristin Voitto* 6/1948.

However, there are fewer specific clarifications on how the authors reached their conclusions beyond vague references to fulfilled prophecies and "signs of the times." The authors must have assumed their audiences were familiar with their way of interpreting the relevant prophecies, or they had no clear system for doing it themselves. For example, recurring references are made to Zionism or Israel as a fig tree, alluding to a verse from the Gospels: "From the fig tree learn its lesson: as soon as its branch becomes tender and puts forth its leaves, you know that summer is near" (Matt. 24:32). Usually, the actual verse is not cited in full or even part, and no reference is made to where it could be found in any of the three Synoptic Gospels.[30]

Another verse that is frequently, and this time straightforwardly, - cited is Luke 21:24: "Jerusalem will be trampled on by the Gentiles, until the times of the Gentiles are fulfilled." Often this is found in conjunction with the observation that the United Nations had not granted Jerusalem to the Jewish state, and later that Israel did not actually hold the Old City of Jerusalem. This is interpreted to mean that the "times of the Gentiles" are drawing to a close but have not yet ended. Many then connected this to their expectation of a mass conversion of Jews as a nation, with some citing Rom. 11:25-26: "a hardening has come upon part of Israel, until the full number of the Gentiles has come in. And so all Israel will be saved."

Although the same verses and generally similar interpretations regularly appear in numerous articles by varied writers, no unifying system is clearly discernible. Due to the vague way in which Israel is presented as the fulfillment of prophecy, it is difficult to trace the source of these beliefs, but they could have been inspired by

---

29. The primary articles, editorials, and news items used for this section are found in *Ristin Voitto* and *Sana* throughout 1947, 1948, and 1949.

30. In addition to Matt. 24:32, the story is found in Mark 13:28 and Luke 21:29-30.

dispensationalism or other premillennial prophetic scenarios, of which many had been translated or even written in Finnish.[31]

In such premillennial prophetic systems, the role of Israel, even when central, is usually part of an overall picture that often incorporates, for example, the outlook for world evangelization, the significance and sometimes the identity of the antichrist, and other "signs of the times." In the Finnish context, such themes were not usually developed very far. At least in the religious papers, Israel is plugged in as prophecy "lite." Rather than using the success of Zionism and Israel as proof of a preexisting and developed eschatology, most writers only make the point that Jesus is coming soon and then use this sense of immediacy for calls to convert.

The third group of papers consists of the aforementioned mainstream Lutheran *Kotimaa* (*Homeland*) and its Swedish-language[32] counterpart, *Församlingsbladet* (*Congregation Paper*). For the years 1947–1949, the group can also be seen to include a Lutheran Evangelical revivalist paper, *Herää Valvomaan* (*Awake and Watch*), which was affiliated with the Finnish Bible Institute (*Suomen Raamattuopisto*, or SRO) and would eventually take up Israel as a core theme. However, in the years 1947–1949, the views on Israel promoted by all these papers fall somewhere between the two groups described above.[33]

Especially the first two papers include plenty of news items about recent events in Palestine. Their obvious interest in the issue sets

31. Two early examples of premillennialist literature are translations from Swedish and English, respectively: Fredrik Franson, *Taiwaan kello eli Profeetallinen sana* [The heavenly countdown] (Wiipuri: A. Skutnabb, 1898); H. Grattan Guinness, *Light for the Last Days—A Study in Chronological Prophecy* [Lopun aika—Historiallisia ja profeetallisia tutkistelemuksia] (Jyväskylä: Gummerus, 1898).

32. Finland has two national languages, Finnish and Swedish. In 1950, Swedish was the first language of 8.6 percent of the population. "Statistics Finland—Population structure," http://www.stat.fi/tup/suoluk/suoluk_vaesto_en.html#structure

33. The primary articles, editorials and news items used for this section are drawn from *Församlingsbladet*, *Kotimaa*, and *Herää Valvomaan* throughout 1947, 1948, and 1949.

them apart from the first, more traditionalist group. Additionally, all three feature some individual articles attributing a degree of religious significance to the creation of Israel. However, compared to the second group, the Israel theme achieves less prominence, and the few existing interpretations are generally more cautious and can be attributed to a relatively small group of individuals. Direct Bible citations are also even less common than in the second group.

Nevertheless, some of the themes that made their way into *Sana* and *Ristin Voitto* are also in evidence in these more established papers, often through interviews with Finns who had been to Palestine or in news items about the Christian Zionist Karmel Association, which was established in Finland in late 1949. They also make reference to the vision of the valley of the dry bones in Ezekiel 37, which is interpreted as foretelling Israel's rebirth. The "times of the Gentiles" are also mentioned, as is the hope that the Jews would be converted en masse.

The important role of Christian Zionist individuals is apparent. The most active interviewee by far was Professor Aapeli Saarisalo, a former missionary and very effective propagator of Christian Zionist interpretations of Israel's significance.[34] Saarisalo's fundamentalist views on scriptural authority kept him out of the University of Helsinki's Faculty of Theology, but he eventually succeeded in becoming Professor of Oriental Literature in 1935. Saarisalo saw himself first and foremost as a biblical archaeologist, but his main impact in Finland was as a popularizer of research on Jewish and Christian connections with the Holy Land's past.

Saarisalo's credentials as university professor and his past as a missionary and archaeologist in Palestine enabled him to seize the position of preeminent commentator on the events of 1947–1949,

34. His views are presented in, for example, *Kotimaa*, June 4, 1948; Aapeli Saarisalo, "Kuivat luut kolisevat—Raamattu valaisee siionismin ja Palestiinan kysymystä," *Kotimaa*, July 6, 1948.

even though he had not visited Palestine for fifteen years. He often dropped into the offices of Christian and other papers to offer his views, which were invariably spiced with references to prophecy, biblical covenants, and positive recollections of Zionists in the 1920s and early 1930s.

Professor Yrjö J. E. Alanen, the editor of *Kotimaa* until the end of 1947 and an occasional writer after that, also appears as an influential voice in portraying the creation of Israel as the fulfillment of prophecy and a milestone on the road to the conversion of all Jews. As Professor of Systematic Theology at the University of Helsinki, Alanen's views carried weight. He found an outlet for them in *Kotimaa*, which was seen as the main Lutheran paper, although not officially associated with the church. Already in late May 1948—before the first truce of the Palestine War—Alanen was certain that "the historical chain of events that has now begun cannot have any other ending than the people of God permanently gaining their old home."[35]

While too much should not be read into the editorial choices of these papers in covering speeches and interviewing Christian Zionists, it is interesting that no balancing viewpoint is offered. The absence is so complete that even a few interviews with Christian Zionists, with an occasional article espousing such viewpoints, creates the impression that seeing Zionism as the fulfillment of prophecy was the only interpretation available.

35. Yrjö J. E. Alanen, "Toteutuva ennustus," *Kotimaa,* May 21, 1948.

Silence as an Enabler:
The Dearth of Challenges to Christian Zionism

As we have seen, bold interpretations of the theological meaning of faraway political events were not the exclusive playground of Pentecostals and Lutheran Evangelicals. Christian Zionist messages were also put forward in mainstream Lutheran papers, and on rare occasions also among traditional revivalists. Later, this trend would be greatly strengthened in these very same groups due to the success of Christian Zionist and other pro-Israel organizations, authors, and preachers, as well as mass tourism to Israel and voluntary work on kibbutzim.

The best indication of the growth potential for Christian Zionist beliefs in Finland may be the utter lack of criticism of Christian Zionist interpretations during 1947–1949, or even later. Some secular critics did express hesitations in the popular press about certain aspects of the Zionist movement or the Palestine War of 1947–1949. One prominent Finnish academic even made the following harsh statement in 1950: "The demands by the Zionists for political rights and economic privileges in Palestine do not have, when it comes to historical facts, any kind of substantive base in reality."[36] A Danish priest, Axel Torm, later the president of the Danish Israel Mission, was also quoted elaborating some of the secular objections put forth by Palestinian Arabs to giving up their land to foreign immigrants.[37] However, these are the exceptions, and even such limited reservations were not offered from a specifically Christian point of view even in Christian papers.

Why did nobody explicitly question the practice of equating biblical promises with modern-day political events? It can hardly

---

36. Armas Salonen, *Allahin kansat—Islamilaisten kansojen historia vuoteen 1950* [The people of Allah—the history of the Islamic nations until 1950](Porvoo: WSOY, 1950), 630–31.
37. Per Wallendorff, "Arabisk och judisk syn på Palestina," *Församlingsbladet*, September 9, 1948.

be attributed to a general Finnish cultural antipathy to public controversy. Rancorous and highly publicized theological debates were held, at least in print, both before and after this period. They involved, among other things, infant baptism, the role of the Lutheran Church in society, social justice, born-again experiences, and a number of ethical questions. Christian Zionist interpretations had been in evidence in Finland previously, but they were hardly a sine qua non for Lutheran theology. Christian Zionist interpretations were clearly within the realm of debate. It just never surfaced.

Perhaps the silence is indicative of the sheer wonder with which the creation of Israel was received, particularly given the positive slant the secular press put on it. The problems inherent in the solutions of 1947–1949 were not evident to the vast majority of Finns. For example, the roughly 700,000 Palestinian refugees were hardly mentioned.

Furthermore, while Lutherans were not accustomed to thinking of eschatology in general and had traditionally not reserved any particular role for the Jews, some may have felt this to be an oversight. The near absence of eschatological teaching left a vacuum that was easily filled by preachers of varying quality. Israel was exciting and unexpected. Who would dare say it was just a political event devoid of theological meaning? In the end, nobody did.

The Karmel Association, founded in 1949, would eventually give some practical outlets for funneling Christian enthusiasm for Israel (see below). However, at this early stage in 1947–1949, nobody in Finland called on Christians to actually do anything in support of the State of Israel other than pray and perhaps work on evangelization. Instead, the many who viewed Israel with religious interest tried to use it as a tool for domestic evangelization by making the connection between the creation of the Jewish state and the imminent return of Jesus.

On a more personal level, believers interpreted Israel as a clear and very tangible sign of God's existence through his work in history. If one read the Bible to say that Israel was prophesied, the creation of Israel "proved" the Bible. It is a circular argument, but the thrill of seeing God's hand in history was hard to resist. Later, it would have political consequences of its own.

The Blossoming of Finnish Christian Zionism

The enthusiastic reaction to the creation of the State of Israel in 1948 resulted in the founding of the Karmel Association the very next year. Taking its inspiration from Norway, and including the ubiquitous Professor Aapeli Saarisalo among its founders, the Karmel Association would work hard to spread the good news of Israel to a receptive Christian audience. Eventually, it was to boost pilgrimage to the Holy Land, which started with overland trips but gained momentum in tandem with more affordable air traffic.

By the early1960s, Finns sent by the Karmel Association would make up the first Christian groups to volunteer on Israeli kibbutzim. Their arrival was greeted with surprise in Israel, but volunteering soon became an international trend, especially after the Six-Day War in 1967. In the 1970s, Finns founded their own *moshav* near Jerusalem to commemorate the eight refugees handed over to Nazi Germany during World War II. In the 1990s, Finland and its numerous Christian Zionist organizations and churches would play an active role in facilitating the immigration to Israel of Jews from the former Soviet Union.

Although Finland's political and economic ties with Israel were never particularly close, relatively large amounts of Christian Israel literature, ranging from travel accounts and picture books to prophetic treatises, were published. Christian Zionist organizations focused on facilitating travel to Israel, and after the political mood had turned more critical in the late 1960s, on organizing demonstrations and petitions on behalf of the Jewish state.

It was not until long after secular critics had called the solid, although mainly symbolic, Christian support for Israel into question that some theologians hesitantly followed suit. The foundations of strong support for Israel—based on specifically theological but also perceived cultural and historical connections—have proved to be very strong. Although Finnish Christian Zionism reached its height in the 1980s, it continues to draw supporters from within the very same groups—both Lutheran and Pentecostal—whose papers were quick to offer biblical explanations for the events of 1947–1949.

14

The Rise of Hitler, Zion, and the Tribulation

Between Christian Zionism and Orthodox Judaism

Gershon Greenberg

While Nazi persecution expanded into the Holocaust (1933–1940), a central concern for both Orthodox Jews and Christians was the Holy Land. Zionist Christians and Jewish religious thinkers shared many common themes. Both linked suffering to sin, and sin to salvation.[1] Together, they viewed dispersion as the result of sin. Both interpreted empirical, historical events in concert with higher, mythical processes directed by God. They shared the conviction that Israel was unique

---

1. An earlier version of this chapter was presented at a plenary session of the 2009 World Congress of Jewish Studies (available on the Congress web site). I am indebted to William David Faupel (Wesley Theological Seminary, Washington, DC) and Yaakov Ariel (University of North Carolina, Chapel Hill) for enlightening discussions, and to the staffs of Fuller Seminary Library in Pasadena, CA, and the Flower Pentecostal Heritage Center archives for their gracious assistance.

and superior. They also brought the cataclysmic events onto an apocalyptic stage; they understood that the persecution was unprecedented and believed that redemption was imminent. But they approached these themes from totally different perspectives, as two sides to a coin. Christian Zionists believed that Orthodox Jews were participating in a Christian drama that they were currently unaware of. Orthodox Jews were not concerned with the Christian drama. They had their own drama, and would have found the notion that they were headed for a Christian end irrelevant.

The Christian Perspective

Christian thinkers who subscribed to dispensationalist metahistory identified Hitler's rise to power and Israel's return to the Land of Israel as part of the events of the apocalypse. Specifically, these events indicated the transition from the Age of the Church (under the ministry of the Spirit), through the rapture into the tribulation ("Jacob's trouble"), which would culminate in the battle of Armageddon and the return of Christ.[2] Jewish expulsion from Germany, and then other parts of Europe, correlated with entry into Palestine. Entry into Palestine correlated with the tribulation and recognition of Jesus the Messiah.[3] The trifold dynamic, delineated mythically above and enacted historically below, included Jewish conversion to Christianity. Christian Zionists believed that,

2. My references to the sequence of apocalyptic events are based on Hart R. Armstrong, *Even So Come* (Springfield, MO: Gospel, 1950), 20. The Age of the Church (under the ministry of the Spirit), when Israel is cast off, is bordered by the ascent of Christ and descent of the Holy Spirit before, and the first resurrection (descent of Christ, ingathering) and the rapture of the saints after. This is followed by the millennium (the reign of the saints, the exaltation of Jews, and the chaining of Satan). This ends with Satan's last revolt and final doom, followed by eternity in the new heavens and new earth.

3. I have capitalized Messiah when referring to Jesus and used the lowercase when referring to the messiah of Judaism.

knowingly or unknowingly, Jews were participating in the process. By returning to the land, the Jew was participating implicitly in the Christian myth. Ultimately, the true Jews would explicitly recognize Jesus as the Messiah.

Hitler's Rise to Power through Kristallnacht

The Stone Church in Chicago, founded in 1906, was a station for traveling Pentecostal evangelists in the Midwest. It was identified with the Assemblies of God and published *The Latter Rain Evangel*. In summer 1933, Pastor Niels P. Thomsen told his congregation that God was stirring up the West (Deut. 32:11-12) to make it impossible for Jews to live anywhere but in Palestine, the land he promised to them. In particular, Jews in Germany, numbering 600,000, had become comfortably settled and were not inclined to go to Palestine to till the land as pioneers and be taken into conflicts with the Arab population. To fulfill his promise, God was now forcing them out. For their part, the Jews, who were cursed to be troublemakers because they rejected the true Messiah, instigated trouble and incited Germans to expel them. Thomsen drew from Keith Leroy Brooks, the founding president of the American Prophetic League. The League was devoted to tying world events to prophecy, exposing subversive forces within Christianity, assisting missionaries, and promoting Bible study in anticipation of the end of days: "In these days, rushing so fiercely toward the consummation, a great fellowship should be built up among those who love the prophetic Scriptures and wait for the coming of the Lord."[4] He also served on the board of

---

4. The American Prophetic League's directors were Dr. Keith L. Brooks (President), Rev. Britton Ross (Vice President) and Laura W. Brooks. Its council was composed of Dr. Arthur I. Brown, P. Lyon, Dr. Harry W. Vom Bruch (associated with Billy Sunday), Dr. E. L. McCreery, Dr. Jacob Hyman (a Hebrew Christian), Prof. Howard W. Kellogg (author of *The Coming Kingdom and the Re-Canopied Earth* [Los Angeles: American Prophetic League, 1936]),

directors of the American Board of Missions to the Jews, headed by Joseph Hoffman Cohn. Brooks believed that Hitler's project would produce a major exodus of Jews and that Palestine would provide the only door open to them. Indeed, thousands of Jews were already fleeing Germany and were on their way back to Palestine. God was opening Palestine for them, for these were the last days, when the prophecies of Scripture were to be fulfilled. In Palestine, they would enter into the period of the tribulation and Armageddon. Thomsen anticipated that the Jews would endure a period of misery when a covenant would be struck between the Jews and the antichrist. The present suffering of Israel was building toward that terrible punishment. Then, Israel would learn of God's judgment and the people would have to accept or reject Christ as the Messiah.[5]

Charles S. Peter of Jerusalem also elaborated on Israel's role in *The Latter Rain Evangel*. According to Peter, the coincidence between Hitler's rise to power and increased immigration to Palestine had to be an act of God: "God knew how to make the Jews go back to Palestine, and how to make Moslems willing to receive them—a veritable miracle."[6] J. H. Hoover, a Baptist preacher in Santa Cruz who became a Pentecostal known for targeting evolution and

Dr. Harry H. MacArthur, Rev. John F. MacArthur, Dr. Walter A. Pegg (author of *Historic Baptist Distinctives* [Wheaton, IL: Conservative Baptist Foreign Mission Society, 1952]), and Rev. Roy L. Lavrin (author of *Life Begins: A Devotional Exposition of the Exposition of the Epistle to the Romans* [Chicago: Van Kampen, 1948]). See Britton Ross, "Concerning the American Prophetic League, Inc.," in Keith L. Brooks, ed., *Prophetic Questions Answered: Questions that Have Been Submitted to the American Prophetic League, Inc., and Answered by its President* (Grand Rapids: Zondervan, 1941), i–ii.

5. Niels P. Thomsen, "The Present Jewish Crisis: The Bride of Christ Escapes Tribulation," *The Latter Rain Evangel* 25:9 (1933): 14–16. Like Thomsen, Perry Franklin Haines, a Methodist minister in Pennsylvania, thought God had Satan use Hitler to separate Jews from their wealth, forcing them to return to his promised land. Haines, *The End from the Beginning: The Significance of Jewish Persecution and Looking into the Future Through God's Ancient Newspaper, Including the Outcome of the Present War* (Grand Rapids: Zondervan, 1942), cited by Paul Boyer, *When Time Shall Be No More* (Cambridge, MA: Harvard University Press, 1992), 218.

6. Charles S. Peter, "Late News from Palestine: Getting Ready for the Final Drama of the Ages," *The Latter Rain Evangel* 26:1 (1933), 7–10, 21.

communism, interpreted the coincidence between Jewish persecution under Hitler and the rush to Palestine as a fulfillment of prophecy about Christ's return, to be followed by the destruction of evil powers in the tribulation, Armageddon, and the millennial kingdom. As promised by Ezekiel, Jews were now gathering from the countries—thousands from sixty lands, according to Hoover—into their own land (Ezek. 28:25). Having been cast off during the Age of the Church, they would suffer during the tribulation and be exalted during the millennium. For Hoover, Jews were simultaneously the worst and the best of humankind. By their iniquity of refusing to obey God's laws and rejecting their Savior, they brought misfortune down upon themselves. But Jews were also "perhaps the most distinguished, progressive . . . people in the world today." They would outlast Nazism. Hitler's declaration in *Mein Kampf* that "I now believe I must act in the sense of the Almighty Creator. By fighting against the Jews I am doing the Lord's work" was an absurdity. He could no more destroy God's people than brush the sun out of the sky. German Jews existed before Hitler and would exist after he was gone. That is, Hitler's persecution belonged to the apocalyptic drama, which excluded total destruction of the people of Israel.[7]

Leonard Sale-Harrison of Sydney, Australia drew the Balfour Declaration into the picture. In *Israel's Regathering: The Return of the Jews*, he wrote that anyone who was not blind would see that the regathering of Jews into the land of their fathers was underway. God let World War I happen in order to deliver the land from the

7. J. H. Hoover, "Hitler and the Indigestible Jew: An Address Given at Enid, Oklahoma," *The Pentecostal Evangel* 1037 (1934): 2–3. On Hoover, see Gerald W. King, "Streams of Convergence: The Pentecostal Fundamentalist Response to Modernism," *Pentecostal Studies* 7:2 (2008): 64–84.

tyrannical Turks. The British mandate signaled the beginning of the return of the Jew.[8]

Keith L. Brooks drew from "Hitler's chief organ," the *Völkischer Beobachter* of Julius Streicher. In an early edition (June, 27, 1920), Benno Imendörfler had written that Zionists were seeking to establish an independent power base in Palestine from which to direct the Jewish conspiracy, but the effort stalled. They did not succeed in having *Ostjuden* flee their homes in the East and move to Germany as a stage for going to Palestine. Palestine turned out to be too small, so Jews were staying in Germany.[9] In May 1935, Brooks cited *Völkischer Beobachter* for the financial side to Germany's pressuring Jews to leave for Palestine. A three-part article from "B. B." described the obstacles to Jewish emigration: Jews had little desire for strenuous field work and the Arab population opposed increased Jewish immigration. From the German side, there was both the issue of the flight of capital and the prospect of Jews' returning to Germany because they were unable to establish themselves abroad. To help overcome the obstacles, in early 1935 the German state established that while emigrants could remove no cash amount from Germany, they could take the equivalent of five thousand dollars if they were going to Palestine. "B. B." saw the larger picture positively: Should the territory under the British Mandate develop as the Zionists wished, over the next decade it could easily absorb a million Jews—meaning a substantial reduction of the Jewish population in Germany. There was also enough land for cultivation in Samaria and

8. L. Sale-Harrison, *Israel's Regathering: The Return of the Jew* (Harrisburg, PA: L. Sale-Harrison, 1934).
9. Benno Imendörfler, "Die wahre Gesicht des Zionismus," *Völkischer Beobachter* 34:59 (1920): 1–2; Francis R. Nicosia, *Zionism and Anti-Semitism in Nazi Germany* (Cambridge: Cambridge University Press, 2008), 71; Keith L. Brooks, "The Nazis Start Boosting Zionism," *Prophecy Monthly: Current Events in the Light of Scripture* 7:8 (1935): 9; Keith L. Brooks, "Israel Coming Out of Egypt Again," *Prophecy Monthly* 17:8 (1935): 14–15.

the like for a large contingent of farmers. To Brooks, the German mindset fit the higher program.[10]

In 1937, Brooks described the inevitability of the emigration-return process, which enacted and affirmed the dispensationalist's divine plan. On the historical plane, while anti-Semitism made it clear that the only refuge was the Holy Land, persecution revived Israel's racial and national identity—inducing the people to restore it. World War I opened the way for the Jews to return, while Hitler's actions were bringing the process to a head: the hatred behind his actions was immeasurable; he was an inveterate Jew-hater, the modern Haman. The American Christian leaders who thought his "Aryo-mania" was only to save the German nation from "Jewish communism" were naïve. One had to read *Mein Kampf* in the unexpurgated German edition, which he refused to allow to be published abroad, to understand the depth of his contempt for the Jew.[11] On the plane of myth, the land awaited the people of Israel for the end times and the onset of Jacob's trouble (Jer. 30:27). Invoking the themes of the *had gadya* ("one goat") of the Passover seder liturgy, Brooks identified the angel of death who killed the butcher with Crusaders and Turks. The Holy One who killed the angel of death was Jehovah, taking vengeance against the Turks. Then the Jews would be restored in their land in anticipation of the Messiah's rule. The process could not be stopped. The Zionist movement would succeed, for it was God who opened the doors of Palestine, and the door opened by God could not be closed by man: "Hear the word of the Lord, O ye nations, and declare it in the isles afar off and say, he that scattereth Israel will gather him and keep him as a shepherd does his sheep" (Jer. 31:10 KJV). Further evidence could be found among

---

10. B. B., "Die Liquidation der deutschen Judenfrage," *Völkischer Beobachter* 48:131 (1935): 2; 48:133 (1935): 2.
11. Keith L. Brooks, *The Jews and the Passion for Palestine in the Light of Prophecy* (Grand Rapids: Zondervan, 1937), 24.

Orthodox Jews. They awaited their messiah, even though he tarried. Ultimately, they would discover that their messiah was Christ: "What will be the purpose of the Jews, when at the end of the time of 'Jacob's trouble' they look upon their messiah to find that He will bear the marks of Calvary's wounds in His hands?"[12]

Louis Bauman, a minister influenced by the premillennialist Isaac D. Bowman, was a supporter of the dispensationalist Bible Institute of Los Angeles (Biola). He considered the Jews to be the world's spiritual light (Matt. 5:14; John 1:9) such that when Israel was present in a nation that nation became successful, and when Israel sinned the nation descended into "spiritual midnight." Jews were persecuted at the behest of God for their sins. His servants included Pharaoh, Haman, Antiochus Epiphanes—and Hitler, who tortured slowly and killed by inches, the worst and last of all persecutors. The sole refuge for the people was the Land of Israel. For it, they suffered—but they were destined to have it by unbreakable covenant with God (Obad. 1:17). Hitler's anti-Semitism would also trigger the tribulation and the second coming. During the time of Jacob's trouble there would be Jews in the restored land who would defy the antichrist (whom Baumann associated with Mussolini), and they would be protected by God: "All who ate of it were held guilty; disaster came upon them, says the Lord" (Jer. 2:3). During the tribulation, as tyrants splattered their blood on the garments of the Messiah, they would encounter Christ—their Savior, who they themselves provided ("Salvation is from the Jews," John 4:22). Jews would ask about the wounds in his

---

12. Ibid., preface, 17–18, 23–28, 31–34. The expulsion-return correlation lasted for many years. In 1960, Louis Hauff of the San Bernardino Assemblies of God church wrote that "Hitler's determination to destroy the Jews caused many Jews to return to Palestine." While during World War I the Zionists "fished" for Jews to return them to the land, during World War II Hitler's torturers "hunted" Jews down for this (see Jer. 16:10)—destroying a third of their number. Louis H. Hauff, "Israel and the Budding of the Fig Tree," *The Pentecostal Evangel* 2409 (1960): 4–5, 19. This motif surfaced again in John Hagee, *Jerusalem Countdown: A Warning to the World* (Lake Mary, FL: FrontLine, 2006), 32.

hands, and he would respond that he was wounded in the house of his friends (Zech. 13:8). With this, Israel would burst out of bondage, as a child born following the pains of birth (Isa. 66:8), and come to Christ.

Bauman included Hitler's assault against the Jews in a larger, cosmic battle. Judaism and Christianity were victims together: "To utterly destroy freedom you must destroy Christianity. To destroy Christianity you must first destroy its foundation—even the Jew. The foes of the Jew are inevitably the foes of the Christian." Hitler's campaign against the German churches and the Jews were branches of the same tree, rooted in Nazi loathing for God and Bible. Beyond the battle between Aryan and non-Aryan, there was a titanic struggle between conflicting philosophies of totalitarianism and freedom, regimentation and self-determination, demagoguery and democracy, mobocracy and constitutionalism, brute force and humanitarianism, pantheism and monotheism, neo-paganism and Christianity, between a God on earth and a God in heaven.[13]

Not all those associated with Christian Zionism aligned Nazi persecution with the suffering they brought upon themselves by their act of deicide. Joseph Hoffman Cohn rejected the connection categorically in *The Chosen People*, published by the American Board of Missions to the Jews. Speaking in May 1938 of the calamities befalling Jews in Austria, Germany, Romania and Poland, he declared:

---

13. Louis Bauman, *"The Time of Jacob's Trouble": An Answer to the Question of a little Jewish Girl: "Tell Me, Father, What Makes Folks Hate Us So?"* (Long Beach, FL: self-published, 1938), esp. 7, 15, 17, 21, 27, 32–33, 36, 55, 68, 117, 132. See Matthew Bowman, "Persecution, Prophecy and the Fundamentalist Reconstruction of Germany, 1933–1940," in *American Religious Responses to Kristallnacht*, ed. Maria Mazzenga (New York: Berghahn, 2009), 183–204; Louis Bauman, "Light from Bible Prophecy on the European War and Its Results," *Sunday School Times*, December 2, 1939, 868; Bauman, *Light from Biblical Prophecy as Related to the Current Crisis* (New York: Fleming H. Revell, 1940), 32, 45, 51; Bauman, "The Nation's Call to Prayer," *Prophecy Monthly* 13:1 (1941): 5–8.

It will not do to fall back on the specious sophistry as some do, that the Jew is getting what he deserves, and that this comes to him because he rejected the Lord Jesus Christ. What a libel and what a terrible slander against God! Do not Christian Jews suffer side by side with unbelieving Jews, in Germany, in Austria, in Poland, in Romania? Is God punishing the Christian Jews too? What a shameful and wretched thing it is when a man is down and out, and suffering to hell agony, for the Pharisee to stand by, and tell him, "I told you so." Shame upon any professing Christian who can be so brutal and heartless as to adopt such a position. "Vengeance is mine, saith the Lord, I will repay." God never appointed a follower of Christ to be His whipping lash.[14]

In the Wake of Kristallnacht

The triadic correlation of the historically enacted myth continued through the war as the persecution expanded into mass murder. Following *Kristallnacht*, in February 1939 the Toronto minister Ian S. Bain, echoing Charles S. Peter from October 1933, wrote that the coincidence between Nazi oppression and Jews' returning to Palestine could only come from God. There, they would accept the Messiah who died for them. He asked his fellow Christians to pray for the Jews as they moved toward that point. He expressed both philosemitic and anti-Semitic views, as had Hoover in February 1934. The Jews were the "greatest living miracle of the contemporary world." They were a supernatural people with a supernatural book, unequaled in religion, culture, spirit, and ethnicity in all of history. However, they rejected Christ's offer to lead them back to God as well as their responsibility for his blood (Matt. 27:25). Because of this, they became an irritant to the nations (Ezek. 5:15). Bain cited the anti-Semitic *Jews Must Live* (1934), by the self-hating Jew Samuel Roth, to the effect that Jewish history was as tragic for the Jews as it was for those nations that suffered them: "Our major vice of old, as

14. Joseph Hoffman Cohn, "Getting What He Deserves?" *The Chosen People* 43:8 (1938): 5.

of today, is parasitism. We are a people of vultures living on the labor and the good nature of the rest of the world."[15]

In 1940, Brooks brought his view of history enacting the myth of the apocalypse forward. The "signs of the times" indicated the end of the Age of the Church and the beginning of the tribulation. The passage was focused on the Land of Israel's cultivation and the revival of the Hebrew language. He discounted the idea that the land—by which he meant the territory extending "from the river of Egypt to the great river, the river Euphrates," (Gen. 15:18)—could not accommodate the number of living Jews, let alone any increased amount. Brooks anticipated that Russia and Germany would plunder the land's riches (Ezek. 38:39) and that an antichrist would appear as a dictator who would overthrow many nations (i.e., Hitler).[16]

The well-known creationist Henry Rimmer, who studied at Whittier College and Biola and served as a Quaker pastor and Presbyterian minister, added new ingredients to the apocalyptic drama in 1940: Jews had to return to Palestine to be present for the judgment following Armageddon.[17] Following the tribulation,

15. Samuel Roth, *Jews Must Live: An Account of the Persecution of the World by Israel on All Frontiers of Civilization* (New York: The Golden Hind, 1934). Roth (Orthodox Jew, poet, pornographer) dedicated the book to "The first generation of Jews that will learn to pronounce my name softly." It addressed Jewish hatred contained in Genesis and as a national instinct, the Jew in business, Judaism as a misfortune, and Jews and the woman market. The appendix was entitled "Do Jews emit a peculiar odor?" Ian S. Bain, "The Jew in the Present Dilemma," *The Latter Rain Evangel* 3:4 (1939); 12–13; Bain, "Did Prophets Speak of Germany?" *The Pentecostal Testimony* (published by the Pentecostal Assemblies of God in Toronto), June 1938, as cited in Alan T. Davies and Marilyn F. Nefsky, *How Silent Were the Churches? Canadian Protestantism and the Jewish Plight During the Nazi Era* (Waterloo, Canada: Wilfred Laurier University Press, 1977), 163, n. 60.

16. Keith L. Brooks, "Is the Land of Promise Large Enough?" in *Prophetic Questions Answered* (Wheaton, IL: Van Kampen, 1951), 9; Brooks, "Review of *The Jews and Armageddon* by Milton B. Lindberg," *Prophecy Monthly* 12:3 (1940): 14–16.

17. An earlier view tied the desire to return directly to deicide. In 1910, the Pentecostal minister W. H. Cossum, a dispensationalist, wrote: "God . . . is keeping their hearts turned over to Palestine and the land of Abraham and the prophets, of Moses and the Temple; yea the land of their terrible mistake in crucifying their Messiah. Back they must come like the murderer to the scene of his crime and like the wandering child to his home." W. H. Cossum, "Mountain Peaks

when Christ would be revealed in his brightness, those who did not renounce their crime and convert would be subjected to fiery judgment. The suffering of the Jews over history, beginning with Pharaoh and Haman and culminating with Hitler, was required to dissolve their guilt for rejecting the son of God, trampling upon him and despising the blood they shed. Hitler drove the people back to the land for judgment. Rimmer recognized the irony: "By driving the preserved people back into the preserved land Hitler, who does not believe in the Bible and who sneers at the Word of God, is helping to fulfill its most outstanding prophecy! Thus does the wrath of men sometimes serve the purpose of God." In other words, God's good purpose could somehow be carried out by an evil instrument. Rimmer renewed a point made by Hoover in February 1934: Hitler persecuted the people but failed in his purpose to destroy all of Israel. An instrument of the apocalyptic drama, Hitler brought the people to judgment. For that, Jews had to live. Rimmer predicted that the tribulation would be far worse than the "mass murder" that was underway. The sadism of the present war would be dwarfed by the assaults of the coming day, when "bestial license would be utterly unrestrained."[18] In his review of Rimmer's *Palestine: The Coming Storm Center*, Brooks revisited the matter of Arab opposition brought up by Brooks in May 1935. He refuted the Christian writers who held that the Jews had no real claim on Palestine, and argued that by entering the land they deprived the Arabs of their property and rights. In fact, the Arabs had not possessed the land for some six centuries. Nor did Jews crowd out Arabs; for every Jew who returned to Palestine, six Arabs emigrated from Syria, Iraq, Trans-Jordania and Arabia into the land—whether to take

of Prophecy and Sacred History: The Land of Israel—Its Past, Present and Future," *The Latter Rain Evangel* 3 (1910): 17.

18. Henry Rimmer, *The Shadow of Coming Events* (Grand Rapids: Eerdmans, 1946), 12–13, 69–132.

advantage of the new prosperity created by the Jews or to carry on their tradition of pillage.[19]

Norman Olson, founding president of the Laymen's Bible Study League, Bible teacher at Trinity Methodist Church in Los Angeles, and author of *Short Course of Bible Study: Tracing the Progressive Revelation of God*, added the ingredient of retribution against Israel's enemies, including Hitler. The return of the Jews to their land was set from on high. It was induced below by anti-Semitism. The very instruments of their dispersion and suffering on account of their rejection of Christ, making them the greatest social outcasts in the world, were the catalyst of their return. Suffering and return were both functions of Israel's relation to Christ: one the result of rejection, the other serving to undo rejection through presence in the land for judgment and conversion. Nevertheless, the instruments, those who persecuted the "harmless and helpless" Jews, would be subjected to God's judgment. Israel would continue to exist (conversion at the end times was an absolute, and Jews had to be alive to convert), while the persecutors would be reduced to ruins.

19. Keith L. Brooks, "Dr. Rimmer's Thrilling New Book on Palestine," *Prophecy Monthly* 12:11 (1940): 22–24. The Methodist preacher Arthur Edward Bloomfield (1895–1980) drew a comparison between the Holocaust and the tribulation. With the Holocaust, Hitler turned the Jews toward Palestine. It would take a greater Hitler, the antichrist, to turn them to God. While Hitler used gas chambers to get rid of six million Jews, the antichrist would aim to do away with all Jews. Since there were too many for gas chambers, they would be driven into the Egyptian deserts, where their bones would not clutter up good ground. Arthur Edward Bloomfield, *Before the Last Battle: Armageddon* (Minneapolis: Bethany House, 1971), 69, cited by Boyer, *When Time Shall Be No More*, 216. See also Bloomfield, *How to Recognize the Anti-Christ* (Minneapolis: Bethany Fellowship, 1975), and *Where is the Ark of the Covenant?* (Minneapolis: Bethany Fellowship, 1976). In this vein, see also Charles H. Stevens, according to whom the destruction of six million Jews was a prelude to the tribulation. Stevens, "Israel in the Tribulation," in *Focus on Prophecy*, ed. Charles Feinberg (Westwood, NJ: Fleming H. Revell, 1963), 33–44. Feinberg, a missionary with the American Board of Missions, taught at Dallas Theological Seminary and was dean of Talbot Seminary. According to John Walvoord, the bloodbath of the tribulation would be worse than Hitler's. Walvoord, *Israel in Prophecy* (Grand Rapids: Zondervan, 1970), 107, 113–14, cited by Timothy P. Weber, *On the Road to Armageddon: How Evangelicals Became Israel's Best Friend* (Grand Rapids: Baker Academic, 2004), 150–51.

During the Age of the Church, when Israelites were denied the right to the land and had no communication with God (Lev. 26:14–39; Hosea 3:4), Christ gathered a church of believing Israelites and gentiles. Following return and the rapture, Israelites would reinherit their land and rebuild their temple (Lev. 26:40–46; Ezek. 39:28–29; Jer. 23:7–8). During the tribulation, God's wrath would be poured out on unbelieving gentiles, apostate Israelites, and apostate Christian churches (Revelation 17). Satan would be cast down (Rev. 12:9) and represented by the antichrist. Many would suffer martyrdom for their faith in Christ, while others would be preserved and enter the millennial kingdom. Many Israelites would become convinced that Jesus was their Messiah. They would repent of their rejection of him, convert, and become missionaries for Christ. Finally, they would inherit the kingdom, when earth and heaven will be completely renovated.[20]

The Deeper Beliefs of Orthodox Jews about the End of Time

Through 1940, Christian Zionists believed that a process was underway that was at once mythic and historic. It manifested a triadic dynamic that correlated expulsion, return, and ultimate conversion. It was inevitable that some Jews would accept Jesus as their Messiah and repent of their earlier rejection. The objective truth of Christ and Israel's conversion to him awaited the overcoming of subjective blindness. Different ingredients were involved in the advance: Nazism forced Jews out, while the only refuge for them (it was believed) was Palestine. This did not mean that Nazism was any

---

20. Norman Olson, *Short Course of Bible Study: Tracing the Progressive Revelation of God* (Grand Rapids: Zondervan, 1959) 175; Olson, *The Restoration of Israel* (Los Angeles: Laymen's Bible Study League, 1940), 6–7, 15–16, 34–37.

less evil or that its goal of genocide would be reached. On the psychological level, Christian missionaries were indispensable. Through their prayer and active efforts, the Jews would become aware of what they truly believed but failed to acknowledge. As the Nazis were evil vessels, in the apocalyptic drama, the missionary was the good vessel.

Christian Zionists believed that the inevitable recognition of Christ was already starting to take place. In 1933 in *The Latter Rain Evangel*, Thomsen reported an incident in Złoczew, Poland. A certain Pinhas Blokh, who had been fasting, was found crouching on the synagogue steps, chanting psalms, clutching his beard and praying to God to send the messiah. He was joined by the Jews of Złoczew. This went on for thirteen days, when the weakened Blokh was taken to a hospital. He escaped his confinement, staggered through the dark streets, and returned to the steps. The next morning he was found dead.

For Thomsen, the incident belonged to the process of yearning unconsciously for the true Messiah, which would culminate in open recognition and conversion. He was convinced that a large company of Jews would be present in Palestine by the time of the rapture. At the present time, they were returning in unbelief, not in the name of the Lord. "That day will come, and yet before it can come some things must take place. And let me say right here, that we ought to pray very definitely that the Lord will hasten that day."[21]

In 1932, Brooks spoke of "a note of terror that indicates a growing fear on the part of the Jews that their people face a climax of the world's wrath"—namely the tribulation. He quoted a statement in *Rosh Hashanah Magazine* by Solomon N. Neches, a Jerusalem-born rabbi serving in Los Angeles:

21. Thomsen, "The Present Jewish Crisis: The Bride of Christ Escapes the Tribulation," *The Latter Rain Evangel* 25:9 (1933): 14.

The more one examines the chaos rampant in Jewish communities, the more perplexed he becomes. He can see no way out of this morass. It seems all hope is lost for the Jewish people. Yet despite all this, we have not forgotten our task as Jews. We know that Israel does not suffer in vain. Yes, we are indeed facing a time of trouble unto Jacob, but says the prophet, out of it we shall be saved. The Jew will emerge stronger, more conscious of himself, more willing to do his duty as a Jew, with increased vigor and strength for the rebirth of his people in the holy land.

Brooks also cited a report about the great rabbinical leader Israel Meir Kagan (Kohen) of Raduń (the "Chofets Chayim," 1838–1933). Kagan's eyes filled with tears when he was told of the fearful plight of Jews around Europe, and then he grasped the hand of the one who told him and thanked God that everything moved according to prophecy: "And does not the Talmud say that before the messiah comes great trouble will befall the Jews? How could we have more troubles than at present? Is it not a sign that the feet of him that bringeth good tidings are approaching?" In Brooks's mind, the Chofets Chayim was foretelling the advent of the Christian apocalypse and Messiah—unaware though he was.[22]

That the objective reality was coming to expression subjectively was evidenced by the coincidence between suffering and conversion. At the root of the coincidence was the deep, if unconscious, acceptance of the Messiah. In April 1938, Joseph Hoffman Cohn, head of the American Board of Mission to the Jews (and son of the Baptist minister and former rabbi Leopold Cohn),[23] attacked

22. Keith L. Brooks, "The Time of Trouble Unto Jacob," *Prophecy Monthly* 9:1 (1937), 22–24. See also Solomon N. Neches, *Israel's Message to Mankind: A Rosh Hashanah Message* (Los Angeles: Western Jewish Institute, 1949). I could not identify *Rosh Hashanah Magazine*.

23. Leopold Cohn was born in 1862 in Berezna, Hungary and died in 1937 in New York. According to his autobiography, he studied under the Hasidic rabbi Zalman Layb Taytlboym, at the Hatam Sofer yeshiva in Bratislava and became a practicing rabbi before conversion. Leopold Cohn, *To An Ancient People* (Charlotte, N. C.: Chosen People Ministries, 1996). See Ya'akov Ariel, *Evangelizing the Chosen People: Missions to the Jews in America* (Chapel Hill: University of North Carolina Press, 2000), 28–34, 101–3.

Christians in Nazi Germany who, in the name of Jesus the Messiah who brought peace to Jew and Gentile alike, were shedding blood without pity. In Romania, the Primate of the Greek Orthodox Church, invoking the name of Christ, led the country's Jew-exterminating propaganda efforts. Meanwhile, correspondents in Germany "report to us many conversions of Jews, in spite of Nazi hate. And the Jewish relief committees in their frenzied bewilderment refuse to give money to such converts!"[24]

In December 1939, Will H. Houghton, president of Moody Bible Institute in Chicago and editor of its *Monthly*, cited Efrayim Kaplan's article "The War of Gog and Magog Which Must End All Conflicts: Messianic Feelings in the Current War. The Results of Hatred Towards Jews. The World Must Make Peace With Jews," in *Der morgn zshurnal* (September 3, 1939). Kaplan hoped the war would not last long, that the bloody nightmare that loomed over civilization would end, and that the Allies would triumph and dictate the peace. Surely Hitler would be finished and a humanistic German government put in place. A true peace would require peace with the Jewish people and an end to the tragic "Jewish problem." This meant the creation of a Jewish state in the Land of Israel and the end of suffering in the Diaspora. The conflict would then be seen, rightly, as the "War of Gog and Magog," followed by the messianic reality.[25]

Houghton translated this to mean that in the wake of the war Jews would find their way to the Land of Israel to undergo the seven years of tribulation, the battle of Armageddon, the judgment, and the millennium. Meanwhile, Jews had increased receptivity to the Word of Christ: "Workers among the Jews of America, Europe, Palestine

24. Joseph Hoffman Cohn, "Something Must Be Done . . . The Morning Cometh!," *The Chosen People* 43:7 (1938), 4, 7.
25. Efrayim Kaplan, "Di milhomoh fun 'gog un'magog' vos muz endigen ale konflikten. Dos mashiahishe vos fihlt zikh in der itstigen milhamah," *Der morgn zshurnal* 39:11, 548 (1939), 5, 8.

and other lands agree that the hearts of the chosen people are more open and receptive to the Word of God and the gospel message today than ever before." Once they understood the relationship between their alienating themselves from Christ and their suffering, they would certainly convert. Intensified anti-Semitism softened Jewish hearts and made Jews long for security; that is, awaken to the inner, absolute truth.

Given this opening, Houghton proposed the creation of an army of consecrated Christians to place God's words in the hands of the Jews, optimistic that large numbers would "speedily be born again into the kingdom of God." He also called for a dispensationalist-sponsored International Day of Prayer for the Jews (December 1, 1939) to produce "a mighty volume of believing prayer" toward this purpose.[26] In July 1940, he cited a cable from Warsaw, sent just before September 1939 and published in *Der morgn zshurnal*, saying that the spread of Christianity among the Jewish school youth in Warsaw was assuming proportions of a mass movement.[27]

In July 1940, Houghton cited the *Admo"r* of Lubavitch, Joseph Isaac Schneersohn, who had been quoted by Lazar Kahan in *The Jewish Daily Forward*. Schneersohn arrived in America in March 1940, and during the war wrote that Jews were exiled in order to suffer. Suffering was intended to induce penitent return (*Teshuvah*), and this would allow for redemption. The people of Israel were faced with a choice: *Teshuvah* (penitent return) or death. *Teshuvah* to some

26. Will H. Houghton, "A Day of Prayer for Israel," *Moody Bible Institute Monthly* 40 (1939): 175. Besides Houghton, the call for the Day of Prayer was signed by Harry A. Ironside (Canadian American Bible teacher), Charles E. Fuller (Founder of Fuller Theological Seminary), Louis T. Talbot (President of Biola), Charles G. Trumbull (author of *Victory in Christ*), Donald G. Barnhouse (author of *How to Live a Holy Life*), George C. Davis (Practical Bible Training School, NY) and Leonard Sale-Harrison.

27. Houghton, "Jewish Pangs," *Moody Bible Institute Monthly* 40 (1940): 592. On evangelical conversions during the Holocaust see Yaakov Ariel, "Jewish Suffering and Christian Salvation: The Evangelical-Fundamentalist Memoirs," *Holocaust and Genocide Studies* 6:1 (1991): 63–78. On Moody Bible Institute, see Yaakov Ariel, *Evangelizing the Chosen People*, 93–101.

extent was inevitable—redemption awaited Israel, and it required *Teshuvah*. Accordingly, the sufferings constituted the birth pangs of the messiah. God, Schneersohn wrote, placed Israel in a great concentration camp, and it was abandoned by the world. The only escape was *Teshuvah*, and those who did escape would be swept up in a movement to the land. He was alarmed at the obliviousness of Jews to the crisis, and he was convinced that he was mandated from on high to shatter the indifference.[28]

In his article, Kahan reported Schneersohn's proclamation that the present way would end the exile and usher in the messiah. The worse the afflictions the better, in the sense of filling the measure of the birth pangs of the redeemed. For Houghton, these messianic expressions were about Christ: "The movement [spreading within Judaism] differs from all before it, in that at other times there has been a strong leader who has offered himself as the messiah. This time there is the demand without a false messiah presenting himself." The path to the true Messiah was opening for the Jew.[29]

Schneersohn's messianism was also on the mind of Joseph Hoffman Cohn, as cited by Brooks in October 1941. He compared the Lubavitcher Rebbe's words to the Jews to those of a papal encyclical. Schneersohn, according to Cohn, called for repentance—presumably a reference to his May 1941 article in *Der morgn zshurnal* in which he said that each Jew was facing a life or death choice between awakening to the apocalyptic drama underway and repenting, or dying as the universe became swept up in redemption:

28. See Gershon Greenberg, "Redemption After Holocaust According to Mahaneh-Yisrael Lubavitch, 1940–1945," *Modern Judaism* 12 (1992): 61–84.

29. Lazar Kahan, "Tsvishn di poylishe iden farshprayt zikh itst ah mashiah-bavegung," *The Jewish Daily Forward* April 11, 1940; Houghton, "Jewish Pangs," *Moody Bible Institute Monthly* 40 (1940): 592. Kahan also cited Elhanan Wasserman's *Ma'amar Ikveta di'meshiha* (New York: self-published, 1938). See Gershon Greenberg, "Elhanan Wasserman's Response to the Growing Catastrophe in Europe," *Journal of Jewish Thought and Philosophy* 10 (2000): 171–204

Immediate redemption is ... the call of our time. It consoles the despaired and is good news about the coming salvation (Isaiah 56:1). We must prepare ourselves in heart and soul to welcome the righteous redeemer. Be ready for redemption soon. It is approaching rapidly even if we do not see it.[30]

Brooks felt that Schneersohn's "clarion to Israel to repent and turn to God quickly and, knowing prophecy ... had Dispensational significance." He quoted Cohn:

Those appealed to, remain deaf. But this deafness is a result of the failure of the spiritual leaders to resound the call of our [rabbinic] sages, blessed be their memory: "When punishments come into the world, look for the feet (approach) of the Messiah" [Source uncertain; see Genesis Rabbah, parashah 42, siman 4]. They have neglected to tell the Jewish masses about one foundation of Judaism which is: "I believe in the coming of the Messiah and that before the Messiah comes we must expect just such tribulations as we are passing through now." To all appearances it may be that those are the birth throes of the Messiah before the Salvation of Jewry comes. . . . Among our Jews in this country there is confusion of thought, just as our sages have foretold: "The Messiah, the Son of David, will come amidst confusion of thought, entirely unexpected" [Source uncertain; see Sanhedrin 97a/b].

In Brooks's mind, Schneersohn's declaration that "the perfect salvation is just behind our backs" (cited by Cohn) was really meant in a Christian sense (unknowingly). Cohn associated Schneersohn with John the Baptist ("Prepare the way of the Lord"; Matt. 3:3), saying, "Who knows but that this rabbi is summoning in these last desperate hours of crisis, to meet the Messiah?" At this historical juncture, Brooks concluded, the work of the Christian missionary was crucial: "And if this has the least earmarks of the closing hour of Israel's desolations and captivities, then what a privilege has been

---

30. Joseph Isaac Schneersohn, "Kol kore fun'm lubavitsher rabbin—le'alter li'geulah," Der morgn zshurnal 40:12, 034 (1941), 8.

ours as workers together, that we have been able to bring the last-call witness to an Israel in bondage!"[31]

For his part, Schneersohn was dismayed at the success of Christian missionaries in New York, with their explanation that Jewish blood was being poured out because they had rejected the Christian Messiah. While Jews remained deaf to his own apocalyptic message, they were drawn to the words of the missionaries.[32]

From the Jewish Perspective

There were many lines of thought shared by Christian Zionists and Orthodox Jews during this period: that the end was nigh, that the Jews suffered exile because of sin and exile distanced them from God, that the suffering dispensed from above was a response to sin, that suffering would cease upon a radical change of heart and mind, that the tyrants of the world served a higher process, that reality was composed of history and myth (metahistory) together, and that a remnant of Israel would remain through eternity. Christian Zionists and Orthodox Jews also shared the belief that history descended and darkened as a prelude to ascent and illumination, that the flowering of the land in the interwar period was a sign of redemption, that the Land of Israel was the sole refuge, and that the Holocaust could be repeated again—and be even worse.

For example, Yissakhar Taykhtahl of Munkacz, writing in Budapest in 1943, paired the fact that the current tragedy was unprecedented—insofar as the Jews had no refuge other than the Land of Israel—with the fact that the land had begun to flourish,

31. Keith L. Brooks, "Noted Rabbi Summons Israel to Prepare," *Prophecy Monthly* 13:10 (1941): 19–20. Brooks cited *The Chosen People* monthly; I have been unable to verify.
32. Schneersohn, "Der emes . . . ," *Ha'keriyah veha'kedushah* 1:9 (1941): 2; Ish Yehudi, "Bakent zikh," *Ha'keriyah veha'kedushah* 3:31 (1943): 6.

as prophesied, in the interwar years ("But you, O mountains of Israel, shall shoot out your branches, and yield your fruit to my people Israel; for they shall soon come home"; Ezek. 36:8), and concluded that the people of Israel were under a divine imperative to initiate the end of exile and settlement in the land as the path to redemption.[33] Taykhtahl's thought would resurface following the 1967 war in Israel.

Tsevi Yehudah Kook, head of the Merkaz Ha'rav yeshivah in Jerusalem, identified the interwar period as the moment of resurrection of the "dry bones" (Ezek. 37:1-14). Diaspora Jews, however, did not seize the divinely set opportunity. The metahistorical process advanced, nevertheless. From above, God "surgically" removed the profane portions of Israel's body in exile to enable return to the land—this was the Holocaust. From below, Hitler, driven mad at the prospect of Israel's redemption and with it his own demise, sought to destroy God's people and thereby sabotage the process.[34] According to Kook's disciple Uri Sharki, by failing to join the metahistorical advance set off by the interwar developments, the people invited disaster. When the temple was destroyed, higher gates out of which blessings descended to the people of Israel were shut, leaving only the lower gates open for enough blessings for Israel's survival in the Diaspora to get through. With the initial breakthrough of redemption during the interwar years, the lower gates shut in anticipation of the gates opening above—and the transition meant chaos and destruction.[35]

33. Yissakhar Taykhtahl, *Em ha'banim semehah* (Budapest: M. Kattsburg, 1943).
34. Gershon Greenberg, "Ultra-Orthodox Jewish Thought about the Holocaust since World War II: The Radicalized Aspect," in *The Impact of the Holocaust on Jewish Theology*, ed. Steven T. Katz (New York: New York University Press, 2005), 132–66.
35. Uri Sharki also drew from Mordekhai Atiyah; see Gershon Greenberg, "Ultra-Orthodox Jewish Thought About the Holocaust Since World War II."

In 1947, Hayim Yisrael Tsimerman of Tel Aviv, a leader of the Sokolover line of Hasidism, correlated the flowering of the land in the interwar period to the Holocaust in another way. Citing the medieval biblical commentator Abraham Ibn Ezra (*ad Exodus* 14:13), he explained that as God destroyed in the desert the older generation of Israelites that had internalized the slavish mindset of Egypt and was incapable of taking the land of Canaan, so God destroyed the generation of Israel that did not respond to the interwar signs of flowering: "On account of this trespass alone, that of not ascending to the Land of Israel, the people of Israel suffered the calamitous annihilation of one third of their number."[36] In the work of the kabbalist Mordekhai Atiyah (Mexico City, Jerusalem) following World War II, the idea of a second Holocaust emerged in the context of correlating Holocaust and Zion. The failure of Israel to ascend to the land, thereby sifting the holy sparks of God's presence that became buried in the darkness of exile, provoked God to destroy whatever held the people in the Diaspora. When pious Jews remained in exile even after the war, largely for materialist reasons, continuing to suppress the holy sparks, a process was set in motion whereby another disaster would be inevitable. The tension between divine illumined presence and the darkness of the world would inevitably explode.[37]

Orthodox Jews, however, shared none of the Christian content. From their side of the coin, nothing on the other side existed. As there was little contact with Christian literature of the time (not to mention that the developing Holocaust enveloped their world of thought), there was no incentive to respond. As to how they might

---

36. Gershon Greenberg, "*Tamim Pa'alo* (1947): Tsimerman's Absolutistic Explanation of the Holocaust," in *In God's Name*, ed. Omer Bartov and Phyllis Mack (New York: Berghahn, 2001), 316–41.

37. Gershon Greenberg, "Mordekhai Yehoshua Atiyah's Kabbalistic Response to the Holocaust," *Iggud* 2 (2008): 72–99.

have responded, one may look at what was said much earlier—and also only recently.

In May 1891, Wolf Schur, the editor and publisher in Baltimore of the Hebrew periodical *Ha'pisgah*, responded to the Christian Zionism of William Blackstone, whom Brooks often quoted.[38] He viewed the matter pragmatically. Blackstone was not out to bring Jews under the wings of Christianity now, but in the world to come. That would be after Jews inherited the land of Israel and prospered in it. Accordingly, "Let the Christians do everything in their power to do what is good for us when it comes to the *Yishuv* (settlement). Let the matter of faith rest, until Elijah comes. Then we will see whether or not their dream will be realized."[39]

Shelomoh Aviner, born in 1943 in German-occupied Lyon, France, studied at Merkaz Ha'rav yeshivah in Jerusalem under Tsevi Yehudah Kook, son of Ha'rav Avraham Yitshak Ha'kohen Kook, and was the head of Yeshivat Ateret Yerushalayim (formerly known as Ateret Kohanim) in the Old City of Jerusalem. In December 1999, he stated:

> There is confusion in Christian theory. They wish that the [Jewish] state will collapse. But, thank God, it is not collapsing. If so, the Christians' thought will help it collapse, will cause instability. This is the Catholic school of thought. As over against this the Protestants say: no need to rush. First let them return to the land to build a state for themselves, even build their temple, and when they finish their work, all of them will convert. Indeed, it will be more respected. (But in the meantime, they say it is possible to Christianize the Jews. It is, to be sure, impossible to kill Jews; they have an army. Impossible to oppress them; they have a state. What remains, is to Christianize them. And this is what the Christian missionaries are doing around the world and especially in the

---

38. For example, Brooks referenced Blackstone in Brooks's *The Jews and the Passion for Palestine in the Light of Prophecy*, 16–17 and in "The Christian Forerunner of Herzl," *Prophecy Monthly* 13:5 (1941): 5–17; Keith L. Brooks, "A Place Prepared," *Prophecy Monthly* 12: 4 (1940), 41–42.

39. Wolf Schur, "Shivat tsiyon: Tikvatenu ve'tikvat ha'notsrim ha'temimim," *Ha'pisgah* 3:1 (1891): 1–3.

Land of Israel. The missionary budget in the Land of Israel is a hundred million dollars. Twice as much as in the entire budget for all the world.[40]

True, Aviner acknowledged, Christian Zionists supported Jewish settlement in Judea and Samaria as a fulfillment of biblical prophecy. But this support was bound up with the Christian apocalyptic end. The Christians who were now contributing to building the country would in the future carry the scent of the burnt flesh of thousands of Jews killed in the tribulation. One must not be indifferent about receiving Christian money. In ancient Rome, people had to pay to use the public toilet. The senators were appalled. When they protested to the evil Caesar Vespasian, he responded, "Money has no scent." To the contrary, Aviner said, "The money of the Christians does have a scent. That of the burning of tens of thousands of bodies and tens of thousands of souls" of Jews killed over the centuries by Christians, and of those to be killed during the great tribulation.

According to the rabbinic sages, accepting charity from a gentile in public desecrated God's name: "Those who accept charity from gentiles are incompetent as witnesses; provided, however, that they accept it publically" (*Sanhedrin* 26b). Doing so glorified adherents of the Christian church, who bragged about their support for Israel. It also made it easier for them to carry out their missionary work in youth camps in Judea and Samaria. In this connection, he cited the position taken by the Land of Israel's most prominent rabbi of the twentieth century, Rav Kook, who held that Jews had to avoid going to Christian hospitals, for they were being used to hunt Jewish souls.[41]

40. Shelomoh Aviner, "Yisrael veha'notsrim," *Be'ahavah uve'emunah* 230 (1999): 4.
41. Rav Kook, *Igrot hare'iyah* 4 (Jerusalem: Mossad ha'rav Kook, 1989): 74–76; Shelomoh Aviner, "Ha'oyev ha'notsri," *Be'ahavah uve'emunah* 728, July 31, 2009, 7–8; Shelomoh Aviner, "Notsrim ohavei yisrael? (Be'ikvot bikuro shel ha'apifior be'artsenu)," http://www.kipa.co.il, 1 Tammuz 5763; Shelomoh Aviner, "Al timkor neshamot be'kesef notsri," http://www.kimizion.org, July 26, 2003; Shelomoh Aviner, "She'elah: Eini mevin lamah ha'rabanim asru," http://www.machonmeir.org.il. For non-Orthodox Jewish responses, see Stephen Spector,

Conclusion

Christian Zionism up to and following *Kristallnacht* subscribed to the belief that history was being subsumed in the apocalyptic events that followed the Age of the Church. The pressure to leave Germany and the efforts to return to the land were prelude to the great tribulation, conversion to Christ, and the millennium. The statements by Orthodox Jews about the messiah, to the Christian Zionist mind, were unintended articulations of the process that was underway. In the end, the Jews, at once precious and holy and deeply sinful, would undergo the tribulation, and a number would come to Christ and serve as missionaries for Christianity. Their suffering in Europe was a necessary guide toward this stage. While Hitler served this purpose, he remained evil; there was ambivalence as to whether the Jews' sin against Christ brought Nazi terror upon them. In the end, the Land of Israel for Christian Zionism was a station in the final destruction of Judaism, as Orthodox Jews understood it.[42]

"Criticisms of Christian Zionism," in *Evangelicals and Israel: The Story of American Christian Zionism* (Oxford: Oxford University Press, 2009), 111–41.

42. On February 11, 2010, a conference was held at the *Beit Ha'keneset Ha'dati* in Har Nof, Jerusalem on the impact of evangelical Christianity in Israel. Participants included: Rami Lieber (CEO of the Jewish Israel organization); Itshak Minerbi, Hebrew University; Dr. Jeffrey Wolf, Bar Ilan University; Mina Fanton, founder of Lema'an Haramat Keren Yisrael; Yehonatan Beles, rabbi of the Yishuv of Naveh Tsof; Gideon Perel, rabbi of Elon Shevut; Shalom Gold, rabbinical advisor to Jewish Israel; Elhanan Ben Nun, rabbi of Shilo; and Elyakim Levanon of Elon Moreh. Minerbi, the prominent authority on the Vatican's relationship to the State of Israel, emailed me on February 20, 2010:

> In my short presentation I was mainly making the point that all the Christian denominations are similar. The Catholic Church wants to hamper the State of Israel while claiming to be friend [*sic*] with the Jews (probably American Jews) and trying to confuse the borders between Jews and Catholics. The Evangelists [*sic*] have a more intelligent approach. They distribute a lot of dollars inside Israel, they reach important positions, they praise Israel, but at the end of the day they try to convert Jews in Israel NOW. / My one man [*sic*] struggle is difficult in the first case (Catholics) but it is almost impossible in the second one (Evangelists) [*sic*]. Most of the Jews, including *Rabbanim*, do not read Christian literature. If they do they do not understand it, and I remain *Kol kore ba'midbar* (a voice calling in the desert). Nevertheless I go on.

15

Inverting the Eagle to Embrace
the Star of David

The Nationalist Roots of German Christian Zionism

George Faithful

It is no secret that Christian Zionism in the United States has long been paired with American patriotism.[1] Since at least as far back as William Blackstone's 1891 "Memorial," American Christian Zionists have proclaimed that their support of a Jewish homeland bolstered their own country's privileged relationship with God.[2] Less obvious is the link between German nationalism and Christian Zionism in that country in the period following the Third Reich. Whereas American Christian Zionism has been marked by militarism and triumphalism,

---

1. Most of this chapter constitutes a reframing of material in the author's *Mothering the Fatherland: A Protestant Sisterhood Repents for the Holocaust* (New York: Oxford University Press, 2014).
2. Yaakov Ariel, *On Behalf of Israel: American Fundamentalist Attitudes toward Jews, Judaism, and Zionism, 1865–1945* (Brooklyn: Carlson, 1991), 51, 72, 89, 91, 92, 94, 100.

the German variant has been understandably penitential in the aftermath of the Holocaust. Nonetheless, this chapter will demonstrate that German nationalism provided a foundation for Christian Zionism in Germany in the mid-twentieth century. In that context, Christian Zionism was a spiritual commitment in the process of becoming an ideology, in which Christians promoted the welfare of the Jewish people as a means for advancing God's purposes on earth.

The Ecumenical Sisterhood of Mary exemplified this nascent ideology. The Protestant religious order was originally led by Klara Schlink, also known as Mother Basilea. Schlink's belief in collective national guilt and collective national destiny shaped the sisterhood's vision. While there were Christian Zionists in Germany prior to the Holocaust, these were isolated individuals who tended to perpetuate negative stereotypes about Jews and to be more concerned with their conversion to Christianity than with the establishment of a Jewish state. The Ecumenical Sisters of Mary, on the other hand, promoted the establishment of the State of Israel as a necessity and rejected all negative stereotypes about Jews. In the late 1960s, the sisters alienated themselves from the mainstream of German Protestant church life with their protests against the sexual revolution.[3] This period coincided with the changing of the group's name to the Evangelical

---

3. Dagmar Herzog, "Between Coitus and Commodification: Young West German Women and the Impact of the Pill," in Axel Schildt and Detlef Siegfried, eds., *Between Marx and Coca-Cola: Youth Cultures in Changing European Societies, 1960–1980* (New York: Berghahn, 2006), 272; Dagmar Herzog, "'Sexy Sixties?' Die sexuelle Liberalisierung der Bundesrepublik zwischen Säkularisierung und Vergangenheitsbewältigung," in Christina von Hodenberg and Detlef Siegfried, eds., *Wo "1968" liegt: Reform und Revolte in der Geschichte der Bundesrepublik* (Göttingen: Vandenhoeck & Ruprecht, 2006), 97; Dagmar Herzog, *Sex after Fascism: Memory and Morality in Twentieth-Century Germany* (Princeton, NJ: Princeton University Press, 2005), 148, 150; Sybille Steinbacher, *Wie der Sex nach Deutschland kam: Der Kampf um Sittlichkeit und Anstand in der frühen Bundesrepublik* (Munich: Siedler, 2011), 290; Hermann Ringeling, *Theologie und Sexualität: Das private Verhalten als Thema der Sozialethik* (Gütersloh: Gütersloher Verlagshaus, 1969), 189; Martin Greschat, *Der Protestantismus in der Bundesrepublik Deutschland (1945–2005)* (Leipzig: Evangelische Verlagsanstalt, 2010), 113–15.

Sisterhood of Mary. Until that point, their call for national repentance yielded a significant number of followers and supporters, perhaps the earliest instance of anything constituting a Christian Zionist movement in Germany.

Basilea Schlink crafted a distinctive form of Christian Zionism on the basis of her sorrow for the Holocaust and her reading of the Hebrew Bible, both of which shaped her understanding of the German *Volk* (people).[4] Schlink sought to repent for her nation's immediate past and to overturn anti-Semitism; in so doing, she crafted an anti-German nationalism, a counter-ideology to the main currents of Nazism. Rather than develop a worldview free from nations and nationalism, she deferred to the national interests of Israel and the Jewish people. In short, Schlink and the Ecumenical Sisters of Mary were repentant gentile Germans who supported the Jewish nation, driven by the idea that Germans were collectively guilty for the Holocaust.

The Preceding Generation of Christian Zionists in Germany

There were Christian Zionists in Germany prior to the Holocaust. These individuals tended to perpetuate anti-Semitic stereotypes, though one should note that this was consistent with Christian Zionism elsewhere during that era. Among these few examples are some of Schlink's mentors.

The *Bibelhaus Malche* was a small women's Bible college for prospective missionaries near Berlin where Schlink was a student and then taught in the 1920s. Some in the faculty were influenced by Anglo-American dispensationalism, mixed with the indigenous millennialism circulating in post–World War I Europe. Among

4. Frequently in this chapter, the English word "people" is treated as grammatically singular as a translation of the German *Volk*.

them, Jeanne Wasserzug was herself of Jewish heritage and from a family with the utmost dedication to the missionary expansion of the church, especially in the Middle East. She taught that the Jewish people would play a special role in salvation history.[5]

Also on the faculty of the *Bibelhaus Malche*, Gertrud Traeder translated the *Scofield Reference Bible* into German.[6] In the English-speaking world, Scofield's work popularized dispensationalism by advancing a literal and apocalyptic approach to Scripture, emphasizing the promises that God had yet to fulfill for the Jewish people and advocating a premillennial eschatology, which looks to the peaceful reign of Christ on earth for one thousand years prior to the last judgment.[7]

As Schlink would later insist, Gertrud Traeder taught that the Jews were God's chosen people and that his promises for them in the Hebrew Bible were still valid. She married Jeanne Wasserzug's brother Saturnin, who had served as a missionary in the Middle East and with whom she later founded a Bible school in Switzerland.[8] In 1934, Wasserzug-Traeder published a slender volume in which she proclaimed that "the people of Israel is the greatest miracle in world history" and that only the Bible could explain why it was so different from all other peoples.[9] For Wasserzug-Traeder, as for Schlink, the Jewish people was distinct and miraculous. Wasserzug-

5. M. Basilea Schlink, *Wie ich Gott erlebte: Sein Weg mit mir durch sieben Jahrzehnte* (Darmstadt-Eberstadt, Germany: Evangelische Marienschwesternschaft, 1993), 115–19.

6. Ibid; *Biographisch-Bibliographisches Kirchenlexikon*, s.v. "Wasserzug, Gertrud Margarete Elisabeth, geb. Traeder," http://www.bautz.de/bbkl/w/wasserzug_g_m_e.shtml (accessed May 3, 2011); Gertrud Wasserzug-Traeder, *Gottes Wort ist Gottes Wort: Ein Zeugnis zur Inspiration der Bibel* (Beatenberg, Switzerland: Bibelschule Beatenberg, [c. 1934]), 58–9; Gertrud Wasserzug-Traeder, *Deutsche Evangelische Frauenmissionsarbeit: Ein Blick in ihr Werden und Wirken* (Munich: Chr. Kaiser, 1927), 1, 20–1.

7. Ariel, *On Behalf of Israel*, 48–50.

8. *Biographisch-Bibliographisches Kirchenlexikon*, s.v. "Wasserzug, Gertrud Margarete Elisabeth, geb. Traeder."

9. Gertrud Wasserzug-Traeder, *Warum? Eine Antwort an das jüdische Volk* (Beatenberg, Switzerland: Bibelschule Beatenberg, c. 1934), 3.

Traeder lamented that Jews would want to call themselves "Englishmen, Germans, and Americans first, and then Jews."[10] She asserted that God's promise of the land of Israel-Palestine was an eternal promise for the Jewish people and that the Jews would soon return there so that Christ could return and reign in Jerusalem for a millennium. One of the strongest indications of Wasserzug-Traeder's commitment to an American-style vision of evangelical evangelism was her Swiss Bible school's hosting in 1948 of the international conference of Youth for Christ, an American missions organization, with Billy Graham and Bob Jones Jr. among its featured speakers.[11]

Whatever their similarities, Schlink and Wasserzug-Traeder had unambiguous differences. Like Schlink, Wasserzug-Traeder described God's relationship with the people of Israel as one of enduring love. However, in distinction to Schlink, Wasserzug-Traeder emphasized the ways that God would cause Jews to suffer in order to correct them. Writing in a period of waxing anti-Semitism, Wasserzug-Traeder insisted that before the Jews repented and turned to Christ, they would align themselves with the antichrist, he would betray them, and then they would suffer greatly.[12] The pre-Holocaust context of the above statements provides some explanation for how Wasserzug-Traeder could both love and malign the Jewish people. This remains a marked difference from Schlink, whose estimation of the Jews was always positive, although for both Wasserzug-Traeder and Schlink "the Jews" were an ideological construct.

The spiritual father of Schlink's sisterhood, Methodist pastor Paul Riedinger, also had a well-developed premillennial theology. In 1916, he published a book that purported to reveal the true

10. Ibid., 28.
11. This was part of the vision the Wasserzugs shared with the American evangelists for the re-evangelization of Europe in the postwar period. *Biographisch-Bibliographisches Kirchenlexikon*, s.v. "Wasserzug, Gertrud Margarete Elisabeth, geb. Traeder."
12. Wasserzug-Traeder, *Warum?* 35.

relationship between World War I and the Jewish people. He proclaimed that Jews were the most blessed and the only chosen nation. World War I had revealed their desperate needs; now was time for the people of Israel, the people on which the glory of God on earth depended, to shine.[13] Like Schlink, Riedinger preferred to refer to the Jews as "the people of Israel" (*das Volk Israel*). Like other Christian Zionists, he proclaimed the promises that Israel had been given: land, blessing, and salvation for itself and, through it, for the other nations.[14]

Riedinger insisted that the Jewish people needed to recognize its guilt before it could receive the fullness of God's blessings, including the possession of the Promised Land. In particular, he accused the Jews of greed and of exerting a corrupting influence on the press, illustrating how he perpetuated anti-Semitic stereotypes.[15] The history of Israel showed both that God was faithful and that those who turned away from God would suffer. Whatever might befall the Jews at God's hand was what God had decided they deserved as commensurate with their sins. In his apocalyptic vision of the Jewish people, Riedinger expected a spiritual revival to precede Israel's political revival as a nation.[16]

Schlink's Biblical Literalism

Though isolated in their Christian Zionism, Wasserzug, Wasserzug-Traeder, and Riedinger were all mentors to Klara Schlink. Born in 1904, Schlink studied under Wasserzug and Wasserzug-Trader in the late 1920s, then served alongside them when she joined the faculty of the *Bibelhaus Malche* shortly thereafter.[17] Schlink cofounded

13. Paul Riedinger, *Der Weltkrieg und die Judenfrage in Lichte der Bibel* (Vienna: S. Strauss, 1916), 6.
14. Ibid., 9, 15.
15. Ibid., 49.
16. Ibid., 30–31, 42–43, 49, 52–53, 61.
17. Schlink, *Wie ich Gott erlebte*, 71–73, 115–19.

the Ecumenical Sisterhood of Mary in 1947. Riedinger served as a spiritual father of the nascent sisterhood from 1944 until his death in 1949.[18] Schlink expanded on the vision of her mentors and purged it of any vestiges of anti-Semitism, inverting rather than wholly rejecting German nationalism in the process.

In the aftermath of the Third Reich, Schlink embraced the idea of collective German guilt, echoing some of her contemporaries, such as the signers of the 1945 Stuttgart Confession of Guilt and the 1947 Darmstadt Statement, although both of these documents concerned Germans' guilt in World War II and made no reference to Jews or to the Holocaust.[19] Schlink's explicit reason for embracing collective guilt was her reading of the Hebrew Bible. Her interpretation affirmed the collective identity of each people. She looked to prophets who preached that a particular people had sinned and that the people collectively needed to repent.

According to Schlink, each nation was called to follow the one true God. Any given nation could be righteous and faithful to God. Alternatively, it could sin and accrue deep guilt, in which case it needed to repent lest it face God's judgment, as in the case of the biblical people of Israel. For gentiles, the city of Nineveh provided a paradigm. The prophet Jonah called its people to repent or suffer the wrath of God; they complied and received God's blessing. Other

18. Ibid., 183–85, 205, 213.
19. Wolfgang Gerlach, *Als die Zeugen schwiegen: Bekennende Kirche und die Juden* (Berlin: Institut Kirche und Judentum, 1987), 7–20; Martin Greschat, ed., *Im Zeichen der Schuld: 40 Jahre Stuttgarter Schuldbekenntnis, eine Dokumentation* (Neukirchen-Vluyn: Neukirchener Verlag, 1985), 116, 118; Martin Greschat, *Die evangelische Christenheit und die Deutsche Geschichte nach 1945: Weichenstellungen in der Nachkriegszeit* (Stuttgart: W. Kohlhammer, 2002), 140–49; Hans Prolingheuer, *Wir sind in die Irre gegangen: Die Schuld der Kirche unterm Hakenkreuz, nach dem Bekenntnis des "Darmstädter Wortes" von 1947* (Cologne: Pahl-Rugenstein, 1987), 117, 194. The 1963–1965 "Frankfurt Auschwitz Trials" were some of the first opportunities for the West German public of the postwar generation to confront the details of what had occurred in the concentration camps. Georg Wamhof, ed. *Das Gericht als Tribunal, oder: Wie der NS-Vergangenheit der Prozess gemacht wurde* (Göttingen: Wallstein, 2009), 101.

nations could likewise risk God's wrath should they stray from him and fail to repent. At least since 1945, in the prelude to their order's founding, the future members of the Ecumenical Sisterhood of Mary prayed for their people to repent like the people of Nineveh. In 1949, Schlink began to publicize the idea that Germany faced God's judgment. God was involved in human history. Each nation had a spiritual responsibility to follow God and could be morally culpable.[20]

Nations were moral agents. The Ten Commandments, God's ethical covenant with the Israelites at Sinai, formed his ethical standards for all peoples.[21] In her earliest substantial published work on the Jews in 1956, Schlink affirmed that "according to scripture, the sin of one's people is also one's personal sin," citing as an example the prophet Daniel, who lamented in Babylon over the fate of his people.[22] She applied this principle to the German people in her insistence that they had collectively violated the Ten Commandments.

Schlink's Nationalism

Schlink did not oppose nationalism, provided that it was pro-Jewish. Just as Jewish Zionists in Germany in the early and mid-twentieth century reappropriated elements of German nationalist ideology in

20. Oekumenische Marienschwesternschaft, *Das tat Gott unter Deutscher Jugend 1944–1951: Werden und Wachsen der Oekumenischen Marienschwesternschaft* (Darmstadt-Eberstadt, Germany: Oekumenischen Marienschwesternschaft, 1953), 17, 35; M. Basilea Schlink, *Das königliche Priestertum: Berufung zum Dienst Gottes nach neutestamentlichem Verständnis* (Darmstadt-Eberstadt, Germany: Evangelische Marienschwesternschaft, 1973), 16.
21. M. Basilea Schlink, *Busse–Glückseliges Leben* (Darmstadt-Eberstadt, Germany: Evangelische Marienschwesternschaft, 1998), 38–39; M. Basilea Schlink, *Realitäten: Gottes Wirken heute erlebt* (Darmstadt-Eberstadt, Germany: Evangelische Marienschwesternschaft, 2007), 205; M. Basilea Schlink, *For Jerusalems Sake I Will Not Rest* (Basingstoke, England: Marshall Pickering, 1986), 27, 31, 68.
22. M. Basilea Schlink, *Israel: Gottes Frage an uns* (Darmstadt-Eberstadt, Germany: Oekumenische Marienschwesternschaft, 1956), 21.

their understanding of themselves, so, too, Schlink incorporated material from German nationalism into her Christian Zionist vision.[23]

Potential traces of wartime nationalism are discernible in Schlink's writings well after World War II. In 1949, she likened the spiritual victory of individuals to the military victories of nations.[24] In 1956, invoking military vocabulary (*Krieg, Sieg, Kampf,* etc.), she spoke of the importance of individual soldiers' self-sacrifice on behalf of the *Volk* and for the sake of the Fatherland as an analogy for personal spiritual sacrifice.[25] Each believer was a soldier of faith, fighting personal battles against sin and for salvation, just as each people fought for victory, demanding the self-sacrifice of its troops to that end. Schlink presented these principles as self-evident.

It was not merely her occasional rhetoric but the substance of Schlink's arguments that demonstrates the influence of nationalism. She was convinced that each national *Volk* was united by a common historical and spiritual destiny. She stopped short of ascribing to it a *Volksgeist*, but otherwise stressed that each people possessed a common bond and cohesive collective identity, a tradition dating at least as far back as Johann Gottfried von Herder in the late eighteenth century.[26] German historian Harmut Lehmann has discerned clear Old Testament themes and allusions in nineteenth-century German nationalist rhetoric.[27] This cross-pollination simply strengthens the

23. Sharon Gillerman, *Germans into Jews: Remaking the Jewish Social Body in the Weimar Republic* (Stanford, CA: Stanford University Press, 2009), 2–5; Stephen M. Poppel, *Zionism in Germany, 1897–1933: The Shaping of a Jewish Identity* (Philadelphia: The Jewish Publication Society, 1976), xv, 16, 106, 120–1; Lynn Rapaport, *Jews in Germany after the Holocaust* (Cambridge: Cambridge University Press, 1997), 137.

24. M. Basilea Schlink, *Dem Überwinder die Krone* (Darmstadt-Eberstadt, Germany: Evangelische Marienschwesternschaft, 1996), 7.

25. M. Basilea Schlink, *Lass mein Lieben dich begleiten: Die Passion Jesu–Kurze Betrachtungen* (Darmstadt-Eberstadt, Germany: Evangelische Marienschwesternschaft, 2007), 105.

26. Bernd Schönemann in Otto Brunner, Werner Conze, and Reinhart Koselleck, eds., *Geschichtliche Grundbegriffe* (Stuttgart: Klett-Cotta, 1979, 1992), 7:281–83.

present argument: Old Testament and German nationalist themes intermingled and reinforced the national consciousness of many modern Germans, including Schlink, who incorporated German nationalist themes into her Christian Zionism.

Schlink's Germans

Even though Germany had only been a nation-state since 1871, concepts of Germans as a people had been circulating at least since the Reformation and especially since the Romantic era.[28] Because Germans had lacked a single country to call their own, poets and philosophers defined the German *Volk* as possessing a common language, spirit, destiny, and moral responsibility.[29] The Nazis exploited and adapted these long-established concepts.[30] Schlink herself spoke of the guilt of the German *Volk* and the chosen nature of the Jewish people, which she contrasted with the false message she believed Hitler had preached about Germans being the true chosen people.[31]

According to Schlink, Germany was a nation on the brink of destruction spiritually and existentially, not merely politically and materially, as many believed in the immediate postwar years. Germans as a people had purported themselves to be a Christian nation, but had murdered God's chosen people; as a result, they stood under the threat of God's wrath. They and the other so-

27. Hartmut Lehmann, "The Germans as a Chosen People: Old Testament Themes in German Nationalism," *German Studies Review* 14, no. 2 (1991): 261–73.

28. Karl Ferdinand Werner in *Geschichtliche Grundbegriffe*, 7:171–86, 193–95, 214–15.

29. Horst Zillessen, ed., *Volk—Nation—Vaterland: Der deutsche Protestantismus und der Nationalismus* (Gütersloh: Gütersloher Verlagshaus Gerd Mohn, 1970), 13–47.

30. Brunner et al., eds., *Geschichtliche Grundbegriffe*, 7:420–30; Victor Klemperer, *LTI: Lingua Tertii Imperii, Sprache Des Dritten Reichs: Notizbuch Eines Philologen* (Leipzig: Reclam, 1990), 2.

31. Schlink cited Rauschning as her source, now seen as dubious by many. M. Basilea Schlink, *Israel mein Volk* (Darmstadt-Eberstadt, Germany: Evangelische Marienschwesternschaft, 2001), 13.

called Christian nations were to blame for the plight of the Jews and for all of the traditional stereotypes against them. In 1958, Schlink wrote: "We were the ones who forced the Jews to become usurers and junk dealers and locked them into Ghettoes like tombs. . . . We, the 'Christian peoples,' were the ones who thus deprived the Jews of their rights."[32] To be a German was to be a member of a people with a unified identity, however divided politically between East and West after 1949. Schlink was clear that German identity had a strong moral and spiritual component and that it was not fundamentally political. However, she remained silent as to whether and to what degree it might have been cultural, ethnic, linguistic, or racial. Schlink implicitly taught that to be German was to be a gentile and a Christian, at least in name; the Christian peoples were synonymous with the Western nations.[33]

Schlink taught that God loved Germany. God had always worked in history to spiritually benefit the German people, regardless of how much they understood themselves to be suffering in the present. In 1949, Schlink insisted that God knew his marvelous design, which appeared messy and incoherent for those in the midst of it.[34] God would continue working on behalf of Germans, as he always had, regardless of whether they perceived it or appreciated it. Yet the form of God's work on their behalf could take the form of judgment.

Schlink insisted that God had made Germans, just as he had made all peoples, and that he longed for them to return to him. God had not simply made Germans as individuals, as God made all humans, but God had made the German people as a people.[35] By extension,

32. Ibid., 16–17.
33. Schlink, Israel: Gottes Frage an uns, 13.
34. Schlink, Dem Überwinder die Krone, 28–29.
35. M. Basilea Schlink, Gebetsleben: Anleitung und Gebete (Darmstadt-Eberstadt, Germany: Evangelische Marienschwesternschaft, 1995), 161. Cf. Marienschwesternschaft, Das tat Gott unter Deutschen Jugend, 58.

Schlink taught that God was the creator of each people and had laid the foundation for its identity. That God made all peoples as peoples was a common notion across the spectrum of nationalist thought in the preceding century, as exemplified by Joseph de Maistre, Giuseppe Mazzini, and W. E. B. DuBois.[36]

If God had made the German people as a people, then its identity had been transmitted since its inception through some form of heredity. While Schlink at no point resorted to scientific or pseudo-scientific language of genetics or race, she nonetheless conveyed the idea that each people had an inherited identity of divine origin; the German people was not a mere human construct but was created by God. Schlink's description of the *Volk* was *völkisch* (that is, German nationalist) in its style, though adamantly pro-Jewish and ultimately self-deprecating in its meaning. Though influenced by German nationalism, Schlink embraced service to God and the Jewish people as her first priorities; it was the task of the German people to support God and God's work on behalf of the Jewish people. Germans were foolish if they expected other nations to help them or to treat them as special.[37]

Schlink and the Ecumenical Sisters of Mary were keenly aware of the plight of their fellow Germans. They prayed for the repentance of their nation, which Schlink likened to the nations opposed to God and to God's people in the Old Testament. Still in the rubble, Schlink compared Germans in 1949 to the people of Nineveh, faced with the decision to repent or be destroyed. The German people was suffering and would continue to suffer because God was just and it deserved such treatment; indeed, it needed such treatment in order to correct its path.[38]

---

36. Vincent P. Pecora, ed., *Nations and Identities: Classic Readings* (Malden, MA: Blackwell, 2001), 109, 161, 191.
37. Schlink, *Busse*, 33–44.

Despite their initial material poverty and intense suffering, Germans after World War II lived in a time of God's unmerited favor, a respite before the looming apocalypse in which they faced certain doom should they not repent. That was Schlink's proclamation. Fueled by the tensions between the Cold War powers, Schlink's apocalyptic fervor did not dim during her lifetime—as it has arguably not dimmed in the sisterhood since her death in 2001.[39]

Schlink perceived that the spiritual condition of the German people after the Third Reich was one of deep need. Should the German people as a whole repent, the ensuing revival might reach the other peoples of the world and bring glory to God. Should Germans continue in their spiritual stubbornness to seek worldly things, and to ignore God and the gravity of their sins against the Jews, they would risk annihilation.[40] Schlink encouraged her fellow Germans to pray to God and ask for mercy and forgiveness. For the time being, God the Father, Son, and Holy Spirit mourned for Germany, as they mourned for all peoples who, as a whole, had rejected them; Germans had rejected the Jews, God's people, and to reject God's people was to reject God.[41]

Schlink's Jews

According to Schlink, God had made the Jewish people, just as he had made the German people and all others. Nonetheless, unlike the Germans, the Jewish people had been uniquely chosen as the object of God's love to a greater degree than other peoples.[42] Like

---

38. Marienschwesternschaft, *Das tat Gott unter Deutscher Jugend*, 17–18; M. Basilea Schlink, *Oekumenische Marienschwesternschaft: Weg und Auftrag* (Darmstadt-Eberstadt, Germany: Oekumenische Marienschwesternschaft, 1955), 12; Schlink, *Das königliche Priestertum*, 16.
39. This observation is based on the sisterhood's subsequent publications, especially those authored by Schlink in the 1960s and '70s, and the author's visit to the sisterhood's motherhouse in 2010.
40. Schlink, *Gebetsleben*,155–57.
41. Schlink, *Lass mein Lieben dich begleiten*, 83. Cf. Schlink, *Wie ich Gott erlebte*, 615.

all other peoples, the Jewish people was imperfect and guilty; but now, after centuries of suffering, the guilt of the Jews had been paid for. While Schlink rejected the stereotypes traditionally attributed to them, she noted other, positive general characteristics of the Jews: respectability, nobility of character, professional competence, holiness, uniqueness, and persistence.[43] By virtue of their comportment, the Jews had revealed the falsehoods told against them as such. Theirs was no inferior people. The Jewish people had demonstrated itself to remain the people of God (*Gottesvolk*) and the people of the covenant (*Bundesvolk*), a contract first made between God and Abraham, then perpetuated and expanded by Isaac, Jacob, Moses, David, and Jesus, all Jews par excellence.[44]

Schlink conflated the Old Testament Israelites and the Jewish people of the modern era with Israelis. While embracing Israelis as Israelites has been a normative Christian Zionist trope in the Anglo-American evangelical sphere, Schlink's radically pro-Israeli position was more anomalous in Germany. Martin Greschat notes that by the 1960s many Germans assumed that they could distinguish Zionism from the policies of the State of Israel, supporting the former in principle while often criticizing the latter in favor of the plight of the Palestinians.[45] Schlink made no such distinctions; she was unwavering in her support of Zionism broadly and of the State of Israel as a Jewish, God-ordained reality.[46]

Schlink portrayed Jesus as the Jewish Messiah. Jesus should have been crowned by the Jews as their King, for they were his people and he had come to save them as his first priority; yet he was not the kind of king that his people had expected, for he brought a kingdom

42. Schlink, *Gebetsleben*, 162.
43. Schlink, *Israel mein Volk*, 16, 25.
44. Schlink, *Israel: Gottes Frage an uns*, 7; Schlink, *Israel mein Volk*, 36.
45. Greschat, *Der Protestantismus in der Bundesrepublik Deutschland*, 107.
46. Schlink, *Israel mein Volk*, 15.

of love instead of a kingdom of power. Rather than embrace him, they rejected him and condemned him to death.[47] On this point, Schlink rejected the traditional interpretation of the Jews' inherited culpability as "Christ killers," declaring that Christ's blood was indeed on them, but as the blood of redemption, not the blood of guilt.[48]

Schlink proclaimed that Jesus ached for the Jews to turn to him. He was as pained now as he had been at his first coming when the Jews first rejected him. Because the Jewish people never converted as a people, it remained an object of distress for all three persons of the Trinity. For this reason, Schlink asked God the Son to raise up prophets in Israel to prepare his people for him.[49]

Schlink looked at the establishment of the State of Israel as one of the greatest miracles in history, a tangible sign of God's existence. Schlink did not perceive the new political existence of the Jewish state as a sharp break with the past, but rather part of God's long love relationship with the people of Israel.[50] Schlink's most urgent concern for Jews was their spiritual health. She interpreted Ezekiel 37, the passage about the valley of dry bones, as prophesying a two-phase conversion of the Jews to Christianity. First, the scattered bones would be drawn back together into cohesive bodily forms; this had already occurred with the return of the Jewish people to the land of Israel-Palestine. Second, the bones would return to life; this was the imminent return of Jews to God. Schlink looked to other Scripture passages for confirmation of her certainty that the Jewish people would soon return to God in his fullness, revealed to the nations in the person of Christ.[51] The Jewish people's persistence in existing, against all odds, demonstrated that God existed and kept his promises,

47. Schlink, *Lass mein Lieben dich begleiten*, 53, 149; Schlink, *Israel: Gottes Frage an uns*, 25.
48. Schlink, *Lass mein Lieben dich begleiten*, 107.
49. Ibid., 123, 127, 204.
50. Schlink, *Israel mein Volk*, 77–78.
51. Ibid., 79–80.

and God's promises to the Jews would be complete when they had embraced Jesus as their Messiah.[52]

Schlink remained vague in writing about the specifics of Jewish conversion. She did not specify whether they needed to become Christians in name, but she was clear that they needed Jesus. She did not evangelize Jews, but not for lack of desire; her reason for refraining was that the guilt of Christians, especially Germans, deprived evangelism toward Jews of its credibility. She still believed that Jews needed to convert to the person of Christ as their Messiah. Rather than approach evangelism directly, Schlink encouraged her fellow Christians to pray for the Jewish people and to remind Jews of God's promises in Scripture for them.[53] Schlink's position, although conciliatory and apologetic in tone, did not diverge from traditional Christian exclusivism regarding salvation.

According to Schlink, whether they were Christians or not, Jews pointed to Christ by virtue of his human lineage. Although God could seem distant from a human perspective and individual Jews might feel far from God, they had a close relationship with him because of his unique love for them. As a result, all Christians had a duty to love the Jews. Because the Jews collectively embodied the suffering of Christ, they offered a tangible means for Christians hoping to draw closer to God in the person of Christ. To serve him, all Christians had to do was serve the Jews.[54] Fittingly, Schlink's interpretation of Isaiah 53, which saw the Jewish people as a reminder of Christ as the Suffering Servant, is not far removed from one of the standard Jewish interpretations of the passage.[55] For Schlink, in its suffering, the Jewish people represented Christ.

52. Schlink, *Israel: Gottes Frage an uns*, 9.
53. Ibid., 31–32; Schlink, *Israel, mein Volk*, 142.
54. Ibid., 39–40.
55. Bernd Janowski and Peter Stuhlmacher, *The Suffering Servant: Isaiah 53 in Jewish and Christian Sources* (Grand Rapids: Eerdmans, 2004), 431.

As God's uniquely chosen people, the Jews were God's representatives. As far as Schlink was concerned, those who truly loved God would love the Jews, for they were his people. Those who hated the Jews were the enemies of God, regardless of whatever lip service they paid to God. To cause harm to the Jewish people was to cause God pain; such was the deep compassion that God felt for them.[56] Christians, too, were the friends of God, and true Christians would honor God's longstanding and special relationship with the Jewish people. For this reason, Schlink called the Jewish people "our older brother," emphasizing the identity of Jews and Christians' common heavenly father, the God of Jesus.[57]

The Role of Gender in Schlink's Christian Zionism

Without her saying so explicitly, gender played a significant role in Basilea Schlink's thought and religious practice, with implications for her Christian Zionism. The history of Schlink and the Ecumenical Sisters of Mary as independent women has provided the most tangible basis for this claim. They were as free to pursue heterodox ideology as they were to pursue heterodox praxis. Therefore, once they committed themselves to vowed religious life (an anomaly in Protestantism), and once they had rejected male authority (an anomaly in Christianity), adopting an ideology as anomalous as Christian Zionism in Germany became increasingly possible for their community. One may acquire a certain freedom in the transcending of norms; once one has rejected one tradition, other traditions are likely to follow. Because they lived on the margins of society, both by virtue of their gender and their religious praxis, the sisters may have been more disposed to identify and empathize with those also living

56. Schlink, *Israel: Gottes Frage an uns*, 32.
57. Ibid., 16; cf. ibid., 14, 19.

on the margins, as has been the case for Jews living in the modern era.

The place of gender in Schlink's theology was consistent with that of her female mentors, Jeanne Wasserzug and Gertrud Wasserzug-Traeder. Like Schlink, they were the products of the middle-class women's movement begun in the preceding century. They affirmed traditional *bürgerlich* social values while celebrating the increasing opportunities for ministry afforded to women.[58] Like Teresa of Ávila, Marie de l'Incarnation, and other women leaders of the church before them, they adopted "covert strategies of empowerment," couching in humility and self-professed feminine frailty a vision for challenging the male-centered status quo, especially in the realm of personal spirituality.[59] All of the students and staff of the *Bibelhause Malche* were concerned with women's missionary outreach to all of the unreached peoples of the world, Jews included. They were less concerned with theoretical theologies than with the urgent practical need they perceived, of which Christian Zionism was simply an extension. Because of the gendered precedents provided to them by their own tradition, Schlink and her mentors, Wasserzug-Traeder and Wasserzug, may have been predisposed to identify with the victims in their midst, the Jews. Jewish victimhood became even more palpable in the aftermath of the Holocaust.

58. In that era *bürgerlich* denoted the university-educated at least nominally churchgoing upper-middle class. Wasserzug-Traeder, *Deutsche Evangelische Frauenmissionsarbeit*, 1–6; Rosemarie Nave-Herz, *Die Geschichte der Frauenbewegung in Deutschland* (Hannover: Niedersächsiche Landeszentrale für politische Bildung, 1993), 38–46.
59. Alison Weber, *Teresa of Avila and the Rhetoric of Femininity* (Princeton, NJ: Princeton University Press, 1990), 15. Cf. Mary T. Malone, *Women and Christianity* (Maryknoll, NY: Orbis, 2003), 3, 82, 134; Natalie Zemon Davis, *Women on the Margins: Three Seventeenth-Century Lives* (Cambridge, MA: Harvard University Press, 1995), 105, 206.

Lacunae

Schlink's version of what constituted the Jewish people is as revealing in what she omitted as in what she affirmed. Schlink relegated Jewish guilt to the past, both individually and collectively. Now, every Jew was a victim. She labeled as Jewish even those who assimilated or denied their heritage, as well as those of partial Jewish ancestry. In Schlink's mind, every potential Jew was a member of the Jewish people, even those whose self-understandings ran counter to such claims.

Equally absent from Schlink's written work was a recognition of the significance of Jewish Christians, though some were members of her community. She made no mention in her writings of Jewish Christians, either in her own time or in the history of the church, though *Judenchristentum* had been a staple in mainstream German theological and biblical scholarship since the mid-nineteenth century.[60] Interpreting Jesus, Mary, and the first Christians as Jews formed a significant trend in scholarship during Schlink's lifetime.[61] Her failure to address the Jewishness of the central figures of her spirituality speaks as much to her intellectual isolation as to her failure to integrate the various strands of her thought.

60. Hella Lemke, *Judenchristentum: Zwischen Ausgrenzung und Integration* (Münster: LIT, 2001), 12–16, 257–67.
61. Matt Jackson-McCabe, "What's in a Name? The Problem of 'Jewish Christianity,'" in Matt Jackson-McCabe, ed., *Jewish Christianity Reconsidered* (Minneapolis: Fortress Press, 2007), 7–37; Markus Barth, *Jesus the Jew, Israel and the Palestinians* (Atlanta: John Knox, 1978), 16–18; Gottfried Schille, *Das vorsynoptische Judenchristentum* (Stuttgart: Calwer, 1970), 7–12; Hans-Joachim Schoeps, *Jewish Christianity: Factional Disputes in the Early Church* (Philadelphia: Fortress Press, 1969), 1–8.

Repentance and Service:
Living in Light of Schlink's Vision

The German people had sinned against the Jewish people and needed to repent; otherwise, Germans could be sure that God would destroy them in judgment. In 1949, Schlink published a work explaining that Germany's suffering in the war was the result of God's judgment. Germany's postwar struggles were but a foretaste of God's wrath. Christians who were especially devoted to God could come before God in prayer, interceding on behalf of their nation in repentance in hopes of forestalling God's judgment.[62]

In 1955, Schlink began using the phrase "our German guilt" regarding the Holocaust.[63] This significantly predates mainstream appraisals of the Holocaust in German public life, which did not begin until the 1960s and did not reach maturity until the 1980s.[64] In 1955, Schlink traveled to Israel in order to seek forgiveness and reconciliation with Jews as a German and as a Christian. The next year, she published the first of several books addressing Christians' failures to love and honor the Jews, particularly noting the guilt of the German people against Jews and against God in the Holocaust.[65] In 1959, she established a nursing home in Jerusalem to care for Holocaust survivors.[66] In the subsequent years, she established another contingent of sisters in Jerusalem to minister to tourists throughout the Holy Land by distributing tracts and by marking important sites with plaques. These were inscribed with Bible verses and words of Mother Basilea explaining the significance of the places

---

62. Schlink, *Das königliche Priestertum*, 7, 16, 19, 22, 32.
63. Schlink, *Wie ich Gott erlebte*, 343.
64. Gerlach, *Als die Zeugen schwiegen*, 7–20.
65. Schlink, *Wie ich Gott erlebte*, 344–48.
66. Ibid., 350, 352, 354–55.

they marked, whether in the story of the people of Israel or in the life of Christ.[67]

Repentance was the only legitimate response of faith to realizing one's guilt, Schlink argued.[68] This was true for individuals and for entire peoples, but in order for a whole people to repent, a select few had to lead the way.[69] Schlink and the members of her sisterhood considered themselves to be in this elite. They repented for their own sins and constantly rebuked each other for sins they perceived. Any time anything went wrong in the life of the sisterhood, such as during their numerous building projects in the 1950s and '60s, they assumed that someone among them was guilty of unconfessed sin and they repented.[70] Because they had spiritually purified themselves before God, they could offer acceptable prayers and repentance as Germans on behalf of the German people.[71]

Every day the sisters spend their morning coffee break standing in silence, in memory of the morning call to attention Jewish victims endured in concentration camps.[72] Like Christians worldwide, the sisters celebrate Christ's resurrection on Sunday morning. In addition to this, every Friday at three o'clock, the traditional hour of Christ's death, they mourn and repent of their guilt toward him. Every Friday

---

67. Schlink, *Wie ich Gott erlebte*, 336, 352–54; Evangelische Marienschwesternschaft, *Gottes Treue durch 50 Jahre Evangelische Marienschwesternschaft, 1947–1997* (Darmstadt-Eberstadt, Germany: Evangelische Marienschwesternschaft, 1997), 116–17; Evangelical Sisters of Mary, *This Is Our God: As We Have Experienced Him for 25 Years* (Darmstadt-Eberstadt, West Germany: Evangelische Marienschwesternschaft, 1973), 89; M. Basilea Schlink, *Heiliges Land—Heute: Stätten des Lebens und Leidens Jesu* (Darmstadt-Eberstadt, Germany: Evangelische Marienschwesternschaft, 1992), 10.

68. M. Basilea Schlink, *Mirror of Conscience* (Minneapolis: Bethany Fellowship, 1972); Schlink, *Wie ich Gott erlebte*, 272, 303–4; Schlink, *Busse*, 15, 21, 18, 11.

69. Schlink, *Das königliche Priestertum*, 7, 22, 32; cf. Riedinger, *Von der Hütte Gottes—Dem irdischen und himmlischen Tempel: Wesen und Dienst des neutestamentlichen Priestertums* (Lüdenscheid: Edel, 1991); Riedinger, *Gedanken über das Priestertum des Christus Jesus* (Stuttgart: Bauer, 1946).

70. Marienschwesternschaft, *Das tat Gott unter Deutscher Jugend*, 47–48; Schlink, *Oekumenische Marienschwesternschaft*, 47; Schlink, *Realitäten*, 23, 39–42.

71. Marienschwesternschaft, *Das tat Gott unter Deutscher Jugend*, 22.

72. M. Basilea Schlink, "Kommunität aus der Busse," *Quatember* 20 (1956): 162–64.

at sundown, the beginning of the Jewish Sabbath, the sisters pray for the Jewish people and repent for Christians' sins against them.[73]

The Sisterhood of Mary has continued to develop and grow. With branches on all six populated continents, the sisters spread their message of penitential Christian Zionism. Nearly two hundred in number, most of the sisters are now based at the motherhouse and many are consumed with caring for their most elderly members. Younger sisters tend to be recruits from the overseas branches. Since the Arab-Israeli conflicts of the late 1960s and early 1970s, the sisters' message has been less specifically German, more broadly Christian, and more urgently apocalyptic. The sisterhood has demonstrated a willingness to align itself with Anglo-American evangelicalism, disseminating its translated works through evangelical publishers in the United States and United Kingdom. A further sign of this alliance is that when the sisters changed their name from the *ökumenische* to the *evangelische Marienschwestern* in 1964, they chose to slightly mistranslate their name in English as the Evangelical Sisterhood of Mary.[74] The sisters are now more concerned with Christians' sins against Jews in the present than in the past, either others' or their own, and with the fulfillment of God's promises for the Jews in the future.

The Ecumenical Sisterhood of Mary provides one cogent example of how postwar German Christians' attitudes toward Jews were shaped by their own recent experiences of German nationalism. German Christian Zionism in the generation after the Holocaust was

---

73. Schlink, *Oekumenische Marienschwesternschaft*, 63; Schlink, *Israel: Gottes Frage an uns*, 29.

74. Strictly speaking, *evangelisch* means "Protestant," not "evangelical." For the latter, *evangelikal* is more apt. In the German-speaking world, the sisterhood became keen on both distancing itself from the ecumenical movement, which they no longer held to be orthodox, and on clarifying that they were not, in fact, Catholic, one of the more persistent protests against them. M. Basilea Schlink, *Und keiner wollte es glauben: Positionslicht im Nebel der Zeit* (Darmstadt-Eberstadt, Germany: Evangelische Marienschwesternschaft, 1964), 41, 49, 51, 61, 73; Schlink, *Wie ich Gott erlebte*, 335.

radically different from the German nationalism that preceded it, but the two ideologies shared similar structures and similar contents, with the caveat that the former turned the latter upside-down, inverting its priorities. Pro-Jewish, anti-German nationalism is still nationalism. The better we can understand such instances of Christian Zionism and the reasons for their development, the better we can analyze the broader phenomenon of Christian Zionism beyond the Anglo-American sphere.

16

The Quest to Comprehend
Christian Zionism

Robert O. Smith

Christian Zionism is an old phenomenon. Interest in the subject has intensified since the 2006 founding of Christians United for Israel, when it became an important topic of media speculation and religious debate. Because the subject sits at the intersection of religion and politics, Christian Zionism engenders controversy and broad interest. The subject is a locus of rich intra-Christian conversation since it touches on a variety of topics, including biblical interpretation, fundamentalism, and evangelicalism.

In addition to popular interest, Christian Zionism is an important topic for academic investigation. Specifically, Christian Zionism provides opportunities for reflecting on the intersections of religion with history, popular culture, domestic political movements, foreign policy analysis, and interreligious engagement, among other topics. My colleague Göran Gunner and I hope that readers have found the academic reflections contained in this book helpful in reflecting further on this phenomenon.

As was noted in the introduction, we proposed the seminar on Christian Zionism in Comparative Perspective with the intention of strengthening specifically academic reflection on Christian Zionism. Indeed, several books and other media have focused on the topic. Most often, however, either apologetic defense or invective polemic has inflected these discussions. This is to be expected with a topic so closely related to the contemporary intersection of religion and politics that is the Israeli-Palestinian conflict. Along with many other aspects, the Israeli-Palestinian conflict produces a field within which theologians take an interest in politics and politicians see their interests supported or threatened in theology. While there is certainly room within academic writing and investigation for one to hold and express opinions, we hoped the seminar would provide space for various academic methodologies to encounter Christian Zionism, analyzing the movement with the academic rigor we think it deserves. The chapters in this book show, we think, that Christian Zionism continues to deserve serious academic attention.

While Christian Zionism is often understood as an American or Anglo-American phenomenon, this collection breaks new ground in exploring the implications of Christian Zionism for international contexts. The authors include Finns, Australians, Swedes, Palestinians, and Israelis, in addition to British and American scholars. This strongly international group complements the breadth of academic and methodological approaches presented here and makes the book an important research tool for emerging scholars of religion and politics.

Christian Zionism has in recent years become a more prominent aspect of Christian public expression in the United States and around the world. This seminar has hosted remarkable conversations about how the phenomenon can be studied and observed, through ethnographic, theological, political, and historical analysis. Since the beginning of our collaboration—from the wildcard session in 2009 throughout the seminar ending in 2014—Dr. Gunner and I have sought to construct the panels in ways that represent multiple perspectives. As the diversity in this book shows in part, Israelis, Palestinians, mainline Christians, evangelical Christians, and, yes, Christian Zionists have participated in these conversations. Audience participants in the seminar have often remarked that they attended expecting to find controversy and were pleased to find the high level of discourse. We expect that some readers may approach this book in the same way and, in the end, will share the same observation.

Working toward a Definition

One thing on which seminar participants have not been able to agree fully is how to best define Christian Zionism. We have agreed that Christian Zionism comes in many different shapes, sizes, and countries of origin. We know that Christian Zionists can come from Honduras and Finland just as easily as they might come from the United States. But just what are we talking about here?

I have studied this phenomenon now for about ten years. Most treatments of Christian Zionism I have read offer no definition at all but instead rely on an extended description. A definition can be falsely limiting, but it can also assist in staking out the field of inquiry, parceling out the corner of human experience we are seeking to comprehend. Many popular definitions of Christian Zionism, most of which are concerned primarily with the vagaries of contemporary politics, define it as Christian support for the State of Israel or, more problematically, Christian support for Zionism. These definitions prove less than helpful, however, when one considers that Christian Zionism can be clearly identified prior to the founding of the State of Israel in 1948 or even the emergence of Jewish political Zionism. Several writers assume that many contemporary Christian Zionists are also committed to elements of dispensational premillennialism. But as the studies collected in this book show, theological commitments are rarely the sole or primary driving force behind Christian Zionist activity even today.

Through the years of the seminar, we have offered a working definition of Christian Zionism as a jumping-off point for continuing conversation. Although the community of scholars that has participated in the seminar has never reached unanimity on the definition, it hasn't been fully debunked. And so I again offer, at the conclusion of this book, my favored definition of Christian Zionism: it is political action, informed by specifically Christian commitments, to promote or preserve Jewish control over the geographic area now comprising Israel and Palestine.

This definition has a few implications. First, Christian Zionism is not based on particular configurations of doctrinal adherence (that is, if you believe in Jesus, rapture, and millennium, you are most certainly a Christian Zionist). A second implication is that Christian Zionism is equal parts theological and political; it is theopolitical. Third, the definition allows for the possibilities that a) Christian Zionism has no historical dependence on Jewish political Zionism, and b) despite John Hagee's flag-draped rhetoric, it can emerge from liberal or conservative political leanings.[1]

---

1. Stephen R. Haynes has identified forms of what he calls "liberal Christian Zionism." See "Christian Holocaust Theology: A Critical Reassessment," *Journal of the American Academy of Religion* 62:2 (1994): 562.

Historically speaking, the definition's focus on political engagement means that any assumption that John Nelson Darby is the father of contemporary Christian Zionism is deeply suspect. "We do not mix in politics," Darby said. "We are not of the world: we do not vote."[2] For contemporary American Christian Zionism, the paternity test for Chicago's own William Blackstone is far more likely to come back positive.[3]

But the story doesn't begin in the nineteenth century. By this definition, the first example of Christian Zionism I have been able to locate is a petition to the English War Council in January 1649, suggesting that "this Nation of England . . . shall be the first and readiest to transport Izraells Sons & Daughters in their Ships to the Land promised to their fore-Fathers, Abraham, Isaac, and Jacob, for an everlasting Inheritance" so that God's wrath will be appeased.[4]

As I have worked with this subject over the years, it has become apparent that Christian Zionism is not just a phenomenon but a meme. As Richard Dawkins defines it, a meme is a "unit of cultural transmission, or a unit of imitation."[5] It is an idea, behavior, or style that spreads from person to person within a culture—a unit for carrying cultural ideas, symbols, or practices.

2. John Nelson Darby to the editor of *The Français*, 1878, *Letters of J. N. D.*, 3 vols. (London: G. Morrish, 1914–1915), 2:431, 439.

3. For important studies of William Blackstone, see Yaakov Ariel, *On Behalf of Israel: American Fundamentalist Attitudes Toward Jews, Judaism, and Zionism, 1865–1945* (Brooklyn: Carlson, 1991) and Carl F. Ehle Jr., "Prolegomena to Christian Zionism in America: The Views of Increase Mather and William E. Blackstone Concerning the Doctrine of the Restoration of Israel" (PhD diss., Institute of Hebrew Studies, New York University, October 1977).

4. Johanna and Ebenezer Cartwright, *The Petition of the Jewes For the Repealing of the Act of Parliament for their banishment out of England, Presented to his Excellency and the generall Councell of Officers on Fryday Jan. 5, 1648, With their favourable acceptance thereof* (London: George Roberts, 1649). Dating the petition is complicated by the "old style" and "new style" dating. Until 1752, England's civic year began on March 25. Thus the petition, presented on January 5, fell within the year 1648 (Old Style) but would be understood in contemporary terms as 1649 (New Style).

5. Richard Dawkins, *The Selfish Gene*, second ed. (New York: Oxford University Press, 1989), 192.

Christian Zionism is a meme. This awareness takes us back to the origins of the Cartwright petition and beyond, to the foundations of the ideas Darby passed off as his own, and into the depths of Protestant Western identity. This identity was formed in the crucible of what Nabil Matar has called the "Turko-Catholic threat,"[6] an element of culture that continues to inform how Anglo-American Christians view Arabs—both Muslims and Christians—today.

Development of a Judeo-Centric Tradition

The Protestant Reformations in mainland Europe produced, in part, an English Protestant tradition of Judeo-centric interpretation of prophecy that has shaped Christian Zionism from the seventeenth century to the present. Signaling the new importance of prophecy interpretation, the Turko-Catholic threat led both Luther and Calvin to identify the Pope and the Turk as the two heads of the antichrist. While prophecy provided "strong comfort and comforting strength"[7] for Lutherans and Calvinists, the resulting political theologies were nationalized when they reached Queen Elizabeth's Protestant England.

The book of Revelation took on new significance, especially among English Protestants. That trend began with John Bale, whose *The Image of Both Churches*, first published in 1545, provided the first full-length English-language commentary. In addition to focusing on the apocalypse, Bale read the book to foretell the national conversion of Jews to Protestant faith as part of God's cosmic plan in human history. Thus in Bale we see the first entwining of a special vocation for Jews with English Protestant hope. These ideas

---

6. Nabil Matar, "The Idea of the Restoration of the Jews in English Protestant Thought: From the Reformation until 1660," *The Durham University Journal* 78 (1985): 25.

7. Martin Luther, "Preface to the Prophets" (1532/1545), in *LW* 35:265–66.

took hold such that by 1596, Thomas Morton could suggest that "we cannot doubte but that the glory of God shall be wonderfully enlarged by the conversion of the Iewes, and therefore it may be more desired then our owne salvation."[8]

The next major step in the development of the Anglo-American tradition of Judeo-centric prophecy interpretation came with Thomas Brightman's *Apocalypsis apocalypseos*, another full-length commentary on Revelation, first published in 1609. Brightman's *Apocalypsis* presented a realized and realizable eschatological vision that called Puritans to be heavily involved in manifesting their millennial hopes; at the same time, he assigned a central role for Jews in defeating the Turko-Catholic threat. Brightman's interpretation of Rev. 16:12 ("The sixth angel poured his bowl on the great river Euphrates, and its water was dried up in order to prepare the way for the kings from the east") interprets those kings to be Jews, converted as a nation to Protestant faith: "But what need there a way to be prepared for them? Shal they returne agayn to Ierusalem? There is nothing more sure: the Prophets playnly confirme it, and beat often upon it."[9] This national conversion is not for its own purposes alone. Elsewhere, Brightman taught that, through their conversion, Jews will be conscripted into a Puritan army central to the realization of Protestant eschatological hopes: "after the Conversion . . . *Gog* and *Magog*, that is the Turke and the Tartar with all the wicked *Mahumetanes* shall utterly perish by the sword of the Converted and returned *Iewes*."[10]

---

8. Thomas Morton of Berwick, *A Treatise of the Threefolde State of Man* (London: R. Robinson for Robert Dexter and Raph Jackson, 1596), 336.

9. Thomas Brightman, *Apocalypsis apocalypseos* (Amsterdam: Iudocus Hondius & Hendrick Laurenss, 1611), 440–41.

10. Thomas Brightman, *A commentary on the Canticles or the Song of Salomon* (London: John Field for Henry Overton, 1644), 1055.

In 1611, biblical interpreter Andrew Willet pronounced that "many famous Churches of the Gentiles under the Turke are now quite fallen away and cut off." Reflecting on God's "iustice and severitie," he notes that "these nations . . . are for their unthankfulnes now deprived of the Gospel of Christ: for where the Gospel was sometime preached and professed, now the Turkish Alcaron is taught."[11] Willet dismisses eastern Christians, whose failure to defend their lands against Muslim civil rule has left them deserving of their minority status. For Willet and other English Protestants, theopolitical hegemony was a sign of God's favor; living as a minority, especially in a world that included Muslims, could not be understood as anything but a curse. Proto-Puritan Jews, the Kings of the East, would glorify God by organizing militarily against Muslims and Catholics to extend Protestant hegemony on a global scale.

In *Clavis apocalyptica* (1627 and 1638), Joseph Mede's study of the structure of Revelation led to a premillennial eschatological system. Just as the papal antichrist remains the primary internal enemy in the West, *Clavis apocalyptica* constructs the Turk as the primary external enemy from the East. These enemies are proper to each component of the future composite church of Gentiles and Jews: the two parts of

> the Church of Christ, as it was about to become double by the conversion of Israel . . . appears to have, at that time, its own peculiar enemy; the former the Roman beast, with its uncircumcised origin; the latter, the Mohammedan empire, over a circumcised people, and of an Ismaelitish origin, ominous to the descendants of Isaac.

Mede is certain of the coming "extermination of both . . . to be accomplished at the coming of Christ."[12]

---

11. Andrew Willet, *Hexapla: that is, A Six-Fold Commentarie upon the most Divine Epistle of the holy Apostle S. Paul to the Romanes* (Cambridge: Cantrell Legge, 1611), 508, 704.
12. Joseph Mede, *A Translation of Mede's Clavis Apocalyptica*, trans. Robert Bransby Cooper (London: Rivington, 1833), 396–97, based on the second Latin edition.

In Mede's vision, the progress of the gospel is marked by the execution of Catholics and the extermination of Muslims. The vision would be catalyzed when the Jewish bride of Christ converted and repaired to Palestine, a Puritan army marching to reclaim God's land from the greedy grasp of the usurping Turk. These ideas were transported and more intensely nationalized by Puritan settlers in the New World that would become the United States.

Driving a Wedge between West and East

Enmity against Islam was a central motivation for Reformation-era English Protestantism. This civilizational, Anglo-American struggle against Islam has, through the centuries, consistently resulted in western denigrations of Christians in the East. "Western preoccupations with Islam . . . contributed to a belligerence eastward, now disencumbered of formal bonds with eastern Christians," the late Kenneth Cragg observed of fifteenth-century developments. "Eastern Christendom became to western eyes a provocation rather than an education, a subject of pity or scorn, not an index to truth." Given the perception that eastern Christians "had, at least in political terms, capitulated to Islam," Cragg concludes, "the East could not fail to become the victim of the West's impatient rejection of any *modus vivendi* with Islam."[13]

These established conceptions of the world continue to shape US foreign policy ideology. Samuel Huntington wrote in 1997, "For forty-five years the Iron Curtain was the central dividing line in Europe. That line has moved several hundred miles east. It is now the line separating the peoples of Western Christianity, on the one hand, from Muslim and Orthodox peoples on the other."[14]

13. Kenneth Cragg, *The Arab Christian: A History in the Middle East* (Louisville, KY: Westminster John Knox, 1991), 97–98.

It is tempting to view these western dismissals of Eastern Christians as mere collateral damage to the overarching goal of denigrating and defeating Islam. But the process of forming a national identity is quite intentional; collateral damage is expected. Within this conversation, it is vital to understand that the Anglo-American Protestant tradition of Judeo-centric prophecy interpretation lies at the heart of the United States' own foundational narrative and covenantal vocation.

Likewise, in the current theopolitical context surrounding the Israeli-Palestinian conflict, traditional Anglo-American constructions of knowledge about "the East" are employed in ever more strategic ways. If, in the minds of many Anglo-American Christian Zionists, Palestinian Christians cannot be understood as suffering under the yoke of Islamic oppression, they must be comprehended as having "sided" with Islam and therefore as having forfeited North American Christian accompaniment and solidarity. Thus popular western "knowledge" about the role of Christians in Palestine relies far less on the witness of Palestinian Christians themselves than on politically useful constructions of the Islamic enemy.

The Anglo-American Protestant tradition of Judeo-centric prophecy interpretation was from its inception a political theology. The tradition openly constructed friends (Jews) and enemies (Muslims and Roman Catholics) while cultivating an occidentocentric discourse that discounted Eastern Christians. These constructions are manifested in contemporary Western discourses surrounding the Israeli-Palestinian conflict that cast Jews within Christian eschatological dramas while demonizing Muslims and casting aspersions on Christians who are Palestinian or sympathetic to the Palestinian national cause. The tradition's most visible and direct impulses are manifested in Anglo-American Christian Zionism.

14. Huntington, *Clash of Civilizations and the Remaking of World Order* (New York: Touchstone, 1997), 28.

Toward an Inconclusive Definition

The American Academy of Religion seminar on Christian Zionism in Comparative Perspective has sought to provide a venue for welcoming research-based investigation into a complex and controversial topic. The chapters in this book demonstrate attempts to approach Christian Zionism through established and emerging methodologies. In each chapter, we see scholarship that is focused not simply on providing a taxonomy of an observed phenomenon. Instead, these scholars are deeply involved in the lives of human beings as they seek to create meaning in the world in which we live. As with all meaningful attempts to engage the intersection of religion and politics, these chapters have entered into the messiness and complexity of human experience.

As a meme, Christian Zionism is ultimately something that cannot be contained in a single definition. If we are to understand rather than simply opine, we must engage passionately in efforts to define more dispassionately and precisely those phenomena we can trace historically and observe closely in the present. It is my hope that the seminar and this resulting book have contributed to that goal.

Index